Foreword by
DR. WALTER MARTIN

The COMING DARKNESS

JOHN ANKERBERG *and* JOHN WELDON

HARVEST HOUSE PUBLISHERS
EUGENE, OREGON 97402

THE COMING DARKNESS

Copyright © 1993 by John Ankerberg and John Weldon
Published by Harvest House Publishers
Eugene, Oregon 97402

Library of Congress Cataloging-in-Publication Data

Ankerberg, John, 1945–
   The coming darkness / John Ankerberg, John Weldon.
     p.   cm.
   Includes bibliographical references.
   ISBN 1-56507-023-2
   1. Occultism—Religious aspects—Christianity. 2. Occultism—
Controversial literature. 3. Occultism—Psychological aspects.
I. Weldon, John. II. Title.
BR115.03A55 1993
   239'.9—dc20
                                                   93-7354
                                                   CIP

Printed in the United States of America.

Contents

Forewords: Dr. Walter R. Martin
          Dr. Kurt E. Koch

Preface

APPENDIXES

FOREWORD
by Dr. Walter R. Martin

[Before his death, Dr. Martin, noted evangelical authority on the cults and the occult, wrote this Foreword after reading an initial draft of *The Coming Darkness*.]

There is no questioning the relevancy of this book. In the oft-quoted words of C. S. Lewis: "Two equal and opposite errors of thought exist concerning devils. One is to disbelieve their existence. The other is to believe and to feel an excessive and unhealthy interest in them." We are living in a period when both errors are alarmingly evident.

Commonly, people today either believe that the devil does not exist, or that his malicious power has been exaggerated by traditional theology. They therefore conclude that they can participate in certain forms of occultism (like astrology, astral projection, or "white" magic), while maintaining a safe distance from the occult's "dangerous side."

The authors' research corroborates a position which is scriptural, if not fashionable: All forms of psychic involvement lie within the framework of satanic activity. Trifling with the occult *will* increase one's vulnerability to demonic influence, oppression, and even possession.

Occult dabblers and potential dabblers (there are many Christians in their number) need to read this book. It will also be useful to those who need a ready source for documenting the negative effects of psychic involvement.

Although I do not necessarily agree with every point this book makes, I heartily concur with its primary thesis: psychic involvement of any kind is hazardous. This fact has, perhaps, never been so convincingly demonstrated.

FOREWORD
by Dr. Kurt E. Koch

Since the end of the Second World War, it seems as if we have entered an age of humanism. We are experiencing presently a pandemonium of interest in the occult. This has been confirmed upon all continents. For example, during my 35 seminar tours in the United States, I have observed a wide-scale interest in slavery to occult practices.

On one tour through New Hampshire, I was invited by a senator to a senate meeting in the state house. The question they were pondering was not only if the schools in New Hampshire should be teaching occultism, but if it should also be put into practice. I gave these men of great responsibility many examples from American schools showing that interest in the occult had resulted in serious problems for students.

Let me give an illustration. Over 30 million Ouija boards have been sold. A psychiatrist in the state of New York reported that the Ouija board was the cause of many mental hospitals being filled.

Many American psychologists insist that Ouija boards can be used for psychological insight and that there is really nothing more to this "game" than an exploration of the subconscious. This thesis can be quickly refuted. Under proper use, the Ouija board can also reveal the future when commanded to do so. The future does not lie within our subconscious.

In the United States there are regions of massive occult interest. In my frequent visits to California I have uncovered a widespread fascination with spiritism. Occultism in America is so pervasive that my presentations in more than 100 churches, Bible schools, and seminaries brought much grief to my soul, and extensive discussions. It is no wonder that a student at Berkeley University could graduate with a Ph.D. in parapsychology or that shamans from Alaska, witch doctors from Africa, and magicians from East Asia all congratulated him for his accomplishment.

What is happening in America is happening in many other countries.

It would be impossible for me to report on them all, since I have visited over 140 nations. Everywhere I have been, I have been informed about the influence of practicing occultists. In many nations, gatherings and congresses of occultists last for months.

Even in my own Germany, the poisonous mushrooms of occult practices are shooting up from the ground in masses. Unfortunately, occultism is the devil's best business. Here I must issue a warning. Whoever is reading occult books belongs to the favorites in the dark world. Also, those who write anti-occult books or read them, must put themselves under the protection of Jesus while they launch out into "the darkness of this world."

I am very thankful the authors have made their voices known in America and that they point out the dreadful dangers of occult practice. I am convinced the authors have a commission from God to uncover the works of the devil to the people.

If the Lord so puts it on your heart, please pray for their work and their books.

PREFACE

The modern world, and especially the history of the present century, can only be understood in terms of the unusual activity of the devil and the "principalities and powers" of darkness. . . .

In a world of collapsing institutions, moral chaos, and increasing violence, never was it more important to trace the hand of the "prince of the power of the air." If we cannot discern the chief cause of our ills, how can we hope to cure them?
        —Martin Lloyd-Jones, *The Christian Warfare*

Today in our increasingly pagan culture, literally millions of ordinary men and women are intrigued by the mercurial enchantment of the genuinely psychic: that twilight zone of reality where one crosses over into the mysterious and uncharted regions of the supernatural.

If the world of the psychic, mystical, and occult is anything, it is fascinating. Whether people seek this world in Hindu and Buddhist gurus, the human potential movement, astrology, novel forms of psychology, shamanism, the holistic health circuit, psychic development, parapsychology courses, or a local medium, they are frequently captivated. Indeed, only the power of the occult to enamor and seduce can explain dramatic conversions among businessmen, medical doctors, Hollywood celebrities, scientists and, indeed, people from all walks of life. All of them are hopeful about the prospects of their newfound interests.

Because tens of millions of people have recently converted to the occult, many advocates are convinced that a new horizon has emerged on the "wasteland" of materialism. They promote a sometimes-militant spirituality and believe the last three decades have witnessed an unparalleled spiritual revolution. They foresee dramatic cultural change and the beginnings of a worldwide spiritual movement that will affect social institutions everywhere. Participants claim mankind is at the forefront of a wonderful New Age of human enlightenment.

Unfortunately, what they may have failed to realize is that the "New Age" of enlightenment is, in fact, a return to modernized versions of ancient and consequential forms of pagan spirituality which are as old as mankind itself.

The dangers are not recognized today for a variety of reasons. In America we tend to be isolated culturally and historically; we have little sense of the harmful consequences of paganism demonstrated throughout history in almost all cultures. Also, the names have changed. For example, what were once commonly accepted as dangerous witchcraft practices are now frequently seen as expressions of human potential. Finally, the categories of true and false spirituality are often confused. Even occult practices may be seen through the lens of Christian presuppositions and redefined as something godly.

For example, many people today assume that because God is loving and good, all forms of spirituality—including all forms of the miraculous—must originate in God and, therefore, are something divine. Hardly a thought is given to the possibility that spiritual evil might also exist in a personal sense, and that it, too, could produce the miraculous or that it might be far more dominant in the religious and other affairs on this planet than may first seem plausible.

Regardless, few people will deny that occultism today is everywhere. The choices are as vast as the terrain is complex and, for many who look on in disbelief, simply incredible. Examples include: psychic UFO contact, powerful near-death experiences, astral travel, bizarre mystical revelations, astrologic medicine, kundalini arousal, energy channeling, mysterious "men in black" and "walk ins," tarot cards, past-life therapies, psychic healing (or even surgery), contact with the dead, and encounters with various strange "creatures." These and a thousand other diversions dot the spiritual landscape like stars on a brilliant night. There are even a dozen "games" which seek to encourage contact with occult powers: the Ouija board, Leela, Osiris, Cartouche, Star + Gate, etc.

But even for those committed to the new spirituality, questions sometimes arise in the consciousness like the notes of an uncertain melody. What does all this really mean? Where do these powers and phenomena come from? Why are they appearing now? How do I fit in?

Of course, those who actively endorse the psychic and the occult do so for personal reasons. They have experienced the calming benefits of meditation, the security of a guru's direction, the tantalizing fascination of exploring altered states of consciousness, the guidance of a Ouija board, the thrill of a seance, the hope of knowing the future. People today are, after all, looking for answers, and the psychic world offers not only excitement but, for many, answers to the gnawing need for direction and purpose in life. How comforting to no longer fear death because you have contacted a "deceased loved one" and know he or she is existing in joy on "the other side." How encouraging to find in astrology and other forms of divination supernatural guidance for living in an increasingly uncertain world. How reassuring to sense a growing psychic power and the upwelling pride of "human potential."

But what if all of this involves something different from what participants assume it to mean? What if people are being led into labyrinths they never expected—or even wanted? What if things aren't as they seem? What then?

For example, to assume occult powers merely constitute part of human potential is, unfortunately, a faulty rationalistic assumption which prefers not to consider supernatural things like spirits. It is to evaluate psychic powers and phenomena on a surface level only, without looking deeper into what traditional religion or even occult traditions have to say.

Further, this approach ignores the consistent experience of psychics and occultists themselves who report that their powers come from the world of spirits they have contacted, whether or not those spirits were perceived in the beginning. Indeed, one reason many psychics initially assumed their powers were innate abilities of the so-called "higher self" is because the spirits had first operated through their lives invisibly. But in the end, they realized the true source of their enablement.

In other words, people who think they are only developing mental powers that are fundamentally natural need to consider that their perspective is contradicted by occult history, religious tradition, the lives of participants themselves, and even standard dictionary definitions of the term "occult," which all emphasize its supernatural nature. *The Oxford American Dictionary* defines the occult as "involving the supernatural occult powers." *Webster's Third International Dictionary Unabridged* defines the occult as "involving the action or influence of supernatural agencies." No less an authority than the *Encyclopedia Britannica* defines the occult as involving various theories, practices, and phenomena "based on esoteric knowledge, especially alleged knowledge about the world of spirits...."[1]

Dr. Ron Enroth, professor of sociology at Westmont College in Santa Barbara, California, and an authority on new religions and cults, defines the occult and its characteristics as follows:

> The term refers to "hidden" or "secret" wisdom; to that which is beyond the range of ordinary human knowledge; to mysterious or concealed phenomena; to inexplicable events. It is frequently used in reference to certain practices (occult "arts") which include divination, fortune telling, spiritism (necromancy), and magic.
>
> Those phenomena collectively known as "the occult" may be said to have the following distinct characteristics:
> (1) the disclosure and communication of information unavailable to humans through normal means (beyond the five senses);
> (2) the placing of persons in contact with supernatural powers, paranormal energies, or demonic forces;

> (3) the acquisition and mastery of power in order to manipulate or influence other people into certain actions.[2]

In this book we use the terms "psychic" and "occult" loosely and more or less interchangeably. This is not to say they are always equivalent. The term "psychic" does not necessarily imply certain types of occult involvement, such as magic ritual or Satanism, although psychic activity is a component of them. Nor is it limited to the purely psychological, as if psychic abilities reflected merely latent human capacity. For our purposes, the term "psychic" involves the supernatural (that which is *not* part of human potential). Thus, we may say that a person who is psychically involved is also occultly involved, for both are dealing with hidden forces and experiencing, to various degrees, interaction with supernatural entities and phenomena. Whether or not the supernatural is believed in, perceived, or expected, it usually surfaces in the end.

Thus, whether we turn to the Hindu and Buddhist gurus, astrology and UFO phenomena, psychic healing, parapsychology, New Age medicine, the new religions or almost any other aspect of the occult, the lowest common denominator is always the presence of spiritism. The authors have documented this in their books on these subjects.[3]

So the bottom line would seem to be this: If by definition the world of the psychic and the occult brings a person into contact with supernatural spirits, just who are the spirits? It is the thesis of this book that these spirits are not divine and that this conclusion can be reasonably proven by an objective examination of the evidence.

Although we do hold a bias against psychic involvement, we have tried to research this subject in fairness. In particular, we have attempted to assess what a wide variety of commentators on both sides of the issue have noted about the occult and its dangers.

We have done so because, at least initially, psychic involvement so often seems to be something positive—and because psychic experiences themselves can be extremely powerful persuaders that one has indeed come in contact with a divine reality.

We wish to show why we think this perception is wrong and that, in fact, the reality encountered is usually the opposite of what participants think.

Camouflage and deception have always been key aspects in human warfare. If spiritual warfare exists, then the strategy of the enemy would be the ruse of divinity. If to some extent men are participants in an unseen battle, then appearances indeed may be part of the strategy.

1

The Modern Search for Enlightenment and Transcendence: Five True Cases

The Devil is subtle, yet weaves a coarse web.
—Richard Chenevix Trench

In 1974 while doing research for our book on Transcendental Meditation (TM), we met Mike, a bright young man who was studious, eager, and idealistic—a calm reflection of the vast swirl of sixties' protests that left scars on the national psyche. He had participated in the original Keith Wallace TM experiments at the UCLA Medical School and in 1968 was initiated into TM personally by Jerry Jarvis, then national director of the student branch of TM.

Mike was both interested and impressed by the way Maharishi Mahesh Yogi had spoken of the vast benefits of meditation. He was actively involved in the TM movement and eager to experience God—the state of "absolute bliss consciousness" spoken of by his guru. The promises were as exciting as the practice was soothing. In fact, Mike expected to become a perfectly integrated human being, free from suffering, full of energy and vitality, replete with creativity and fulfillment.

Mike followed the program faithfully but, unfortunately, the end result was a six-month stint at California's Camarillo State Mental Hospital. He became the victim of a radical TM-induced personality disorder, as diagnosed by attending psychiatrists. Later, when he learned of the high suicide rate among TM teachers and other serious casualties in the ranks of the faithful, he was no longer so impressed. [1]

In fact, the problems were numerous enough that eventually an "EX-TM" group was formed in Arlington, Virginia, to document the dangers of TM from the psychiatric literature and to help those who had suffered TM-induced breakdowns or other problems.[2]

Mike wondered how a practice so simple and natural as meditation could possibly become something so destructive.

Carl was a qualified psychologist with a degree in physics and a personal interest in religion (especially Christianity) and parapsychology.[3] In fact, he became a leading parapsychologist. His personal psychic abilities amazed not only himself but those who knew him. He was enormously excited by Aldous Huxley's *Doors of Perception*; what Huxley achieved by drugs, Carl was certain he could achieve by psychic means: that, and perhaps much more. Although fascinated by Christianity, Carl was convinced that the modern churches were corrupting the "original" teachings of Christ. Hence he sought "true Christianity" through occult means. Consumed with a desire to find the real teachings of Christ, he became personally involved in reincarnation research and astral travel.

As his studies and involvement in the psychic world continued, he explored realm after realm. He was bright and enthusiastic, not to mention careful. Most of all he was certain he was on the road to vast personal discoveries. In his view, he had all the right motives, talent, and opportunities.

Eventually, a midwestern university offered Carl a professorship and allowed him to both teach and continue his parapsychological experiments, which provided numerous psychic and mystical experiences. Gradually, however, Carl admitted to himself that some deep and disturbing alteration was taking place within him.[4]

He had earlier encountered some gnawing doubts about the fundamental nature of his spiritual path, but he suppressed them because they were too uncomfortable in their implications. Any doubt as to what kind of spirit was leading him could mean a total revision of his work; it could even mean resigning his professor-ship and renouncing his parapsychological research.[5] Giving up his research would simply have been too costly, both personally and professionally. And besides, years of painstaking effort had been jeweled with benevolent motives, unique talents, and flaw-less enthusiasm. Carl was convinced he was existing within an absolutely spiritual state of being.

Yet in spite of all this, he soon became consumed by forces so evil he ended up an incoherent somnambulist requiring exorcism and 11 months of hospitalization.

His eventual renouncement of all study and research in para-psychology was deplored by fellow colleagues who, unfortu-nately, never learned the real reason for his strange disappear-ance from the parapsychological community.

Carl finally made a dramatic public confession when he was forced to conclude the following: "Solemnly and of my own free will, I wish to acknowledge that knowingly and freely I entered into possession by an evil spirit. And, although that spirit came to me under the guise of saving me, perfecting me, helping me to help others, I knew all along it was evil."[6]

Tal Brooke, a personal friend of the authors, was featured in the film *The Late Great Planet Earth* as an authority on Eastern mysticism. He is the author of *Riders of the Cosmic Circuit*, a cogent exposé of the major Hindu gurus, and *Avatar of the Night*, his bestselling spiritual autobiography, first published in India. It relates his experiences as the principal Western disciple of miracle-working guru Sathya Sai Baba.

Brooke was a young and idealistic University of Virginia graduate whose searching mind forsook everything in an attempt to find God in the massive and spiritually bewildering subconti-nent of India—that almost mortally wounded civilization to which so many Westerners flock in search of "wisdom from the East." In his own words he explained to the authors his odyssey and where it finally took him:

If a Hollywood producer were to line up all the sorts of flashy occult signs a seeker would need to get to India, I had them. In truth, I had been riding on a tidal wave of spiritual joy and hope from 1966 (when I had a massive mystical experience under LSD) until I went to India in 1969, after graduating from The University of Virginia. After the mystical experience, every time I looked into one of India's scriptures, it seemed to be speaking to me. That sense of rapport with the East seemed to urge me within: The Upanishads, Vedas, Baghavad Gita, and on and on, then the works of the modern yogis, Aurobindo, Ramakrishna (19th century), Yogananda, Ramanah Maharshi, Krishnamurti, Maharishi, Sivananda, et al. By the time I got to India, a pundit from Benares Hindu University said what they almost never allow a Westerner—"Your understanding, sir, is on par with our most educated and illumined Brahmin pundits. You must have once been here for many lifetimes." That was merely one of many confirmations.

The only thing that rippled this current of intoxicating optimism was the incredible culture shock I experienced upon arrival in Delhi. The fruits of the system I loved were appalling, staggering. India travailed as a vast suffering civilization. It was a land where people, according to its philosophy, were elevated to the position of potential gods—but the harsh realities were that never had I seen a land where people were so degraded and abused. There was an undefinable "philosophic other" hanging in the air which kept leaking through to sour my joy. Here was a civilization that could boast having the most profound system of spirituality ever devised, yet everything else about it was run down, exhausted, seedy, travailing.

For six months I met some of the leading Western gurus, including Ram Dass, Muktananda, Maharishi, Krishnamurti, and many others. That too was a disappointment. It all still felt like a spiritual Coney Island—it smelled of "con."

Then, in my most vulnerable period, in South India, when I was on the verge of giving up my great Eastern dream, I met India's premier guru, the miracle-worker Sai

Baba. And back on went the joy knob inside my soul. What further verification did I need? He was attuned to the supernatural, seemed to have known me from the beginning of time, foreordaining, he said, my visit to India. And, sign of signs, he accepted me in his inner circle. He taught the very seat of Indian philosophy I had come to love, monistic Advaita: the universe is composed of pure self-discovery. Thus the ultimate finding is that the deepest self is the central consciousness which is none other than the One, God. Gone were the threats of good, evil, sin and judgment.

Here was a candy-cane Eden without the serpent.

Then, two years later, a major trauma took place. I discovered something regarding the deep things of evil. It was so great a revelation, that I lived in a state of what I called utter "occult desolation." The circumstantial syrup that had bathed me in an ocean of milk and honey turned to wormwood, and the events of my life began to resemble a Satanic thriller along the lines of Clive Barker's *Hellraiser* or Polanski's *Rosemary's Baby*. Baba, now that I had seen behind his exterior armor, I began to realize was an Antichrist of the kind predicted in Matthew 24:24. I escaped India grateful to be alive but with a new awareness of the potential for deep evil inherent within Eastern metaphysics, an evil that had enticed me to the brink of destruction. Were it not for my turning my life over to Christ in a South Indian hotel room, I would be dead today.[7]

We first met Carole as a result of exchanging information on the famous Indian guru Swami Rama. The following information is taken from material sent to us.

Carole was very sick, and the doctors were unable to find the cause of her illness. She decided to go to a physician-nutritionist recommended by a friend. In his office she found some literature about the Himalayan Institute, of which the doctor was a staff member. The institute was founded by Indian Swami Rama, one of the most scientifically studied of the gurus, beginning with famous biofeedback researcher Dr. Elmer Green. Carole decided to attend the institute and began lessons in hatha yoga. Eventually she was initiated and received her mantra, or word of power, from Swami Rama. As he laid his hands upon her head, the typical transfer of occult energy began (termed *shaktipat diksha*). Carole was in heaven:

> Currents of electrical energy began to permeate my head and went down into my body. . . . It was as if a spell had come over me, the bliss that I felt was as if I had been touched by God. The power that had come from his hand, and simply being in his presence, drew me to him irresistibly.

The night after receiving her mantra, Carole was actually visited by a living spirit being who claimed to be the spirit of Swami Rama himself. Although no one had ever mentioned the spirit world in her church (they did not believe in such things), Carole felt that this was the means of directly communing with God. She proceeded to experience wonderful, powerful forces and energies, while thoughts were impelled into her consciousness with a magnetic-like force.

> Electrical currents were pulsating around my body and then moved into my hand, the currents were shaking my hand and strong, almost entrancing thoughts were being impressed into my mind, "Meditate, meditate. I want to speak with you." It was a miracle. I was communicating with the spirit world. I had found God. Sitting in the darkness of my living room I began to repeat my mantra. A presence seemed to fill the room. I began to see visions of being one with the universe and the magnetic thoughts were now leaving and I was hearing a voice, which identified itself as Swami Rama, saying he was communicating with me through astral travel.
> Within one week, after meditating many hours each day and still in constant communication with

this spirit, forces began to come upon me and gave me
powers to do yoga postures; I was floating through
them, the forces giving me added breath even...pos-
tures that before would be very painful to do.

However, after two weeks of daily meditation, Carole became
engulfed in a nightmare of utter dread and terror. Voices which
once claimed they were angelic turned threatening, even demonic. She was brutally assaulted, both physically and spiritually. During meditation, in the midst of being violently shaken,
she could sense that the very same energy received at initiation,
energy which was now felt to be *personal,* was attempting to remove her life-essence from her physical body—in her words, "to
literally pull the life from my shell of a body." She sensed an overwhelming and implacable hatred directed toward her, as if "mon-
strosities of another world were trying to take my very soul from
me, inflicting pain beyond endurance, ripping and tearing into
the very depths of my being."

The intermittent suffocation and torment seemed to be inter-
minable; her fears only increased as she realized there was no one
to help her. Finally the attack subsided. But unfortunately, it was
merely the first of many to come.

It seems that nothing could stop the assaults. Her agonized
pleas to the spirits were ignored; her husband was powerless. Her
father wanted her to see a psychiatrist; others also doubted her
sanity. In desperation, her mother contacted psychic friends from
a local church of the Unity School of Christianity. They laid
hands on Carole and commanded that "the divinity within"
deliver her, but to no avail.

Dr. C. Norman Shealy, M.D., Ph.D., entered the picture. He
is a noted neurosurgeon, a former professor at Harvard University, past president of the American Holistic Medical Association, and the author of *Occult Medicine Can Save Your Life.* Dr.
Shealy also works in conjunction with psychics and spiritists such
as Carolyn Myss. Dr. Shealy was unable to help and referred
Carole to Dr. Robert Leichtman, M.D., a spiritist who is co-
author of several dozen books received by revelation from the
spirits.[8]

Leichtman admitted that Carole's situation was not uncommon among followers of Eastern gurus. In fact, he told her some have died as a result of similar psychic attacks. But he, too, was unable to help. His instructions, such as visualizing herself in the white "Christ light" of protection were useless. By this time, Carole was near the end:

> I had to endure the torture, unable to free myself. To those around me I was insane. No one believed me and no one could free me. The hopelessness I felt was unbearable. No one believed me except the psychics . . . and they could do nothing.
>
> I was defenseless against these never-ending attacks . . . hundreds of presences filling my room, which itself would be filled with thick, ice cold air, my body drenched with perspiration as my whole being fought against them.
>
> After spending several weeks at my parents' we decided perhaps I could try returning home. But that night the spirits started to exert their full power.
>
> First, against my skull. It felt as if they were trying to crack it open, like the air was being cut off to my brain. Incredible pressure was exerted upon my back and chest, pulling with a wrench-like grip. It felt like they were trying to pull my shoulder from its socket, pressing on my eyes trying to blind me, pushing on my throat trying to choke me. Filled with fear and exhaustion, on the brink of death I screamed to my husband, "I'm dying; I can't take it anymore. Get me to the hospital."
>
> I was taken to the hospital where I laid like a scared dog cowering on a cart. I could hardly speak but at least the spirits were gone—temporarily. . . . The doctor on duty recommended a psychiatrist who saw me the next morning. He told me I was covering up some deep problems with this "talk of evil spirits." "There is no such thing as the devil," he said coldly.

Carole admitted herself to the hospital, but once more no one could help. The attacks finally subsided and she was released.

Upon returning home, the attacks began again. More unimaginable torment. Although she was terrified of death, death was now her desire. Wishing to take her life but too fearful of dying, in desperation she readmitted herself to the hospital. Once again, she was placed in a locked ward. She felt that here she would die—alone and in torment.

But today, Carole is alive and well. Even her psychiatrist was amazed at the miraculous transformation. She was now in perfect health, both mentally and physically.

Carole knew she was free from the spirits. But how? Carole was unable to help herself. Her best friends could not help her, nor her parents or husband. Neither the medication nor the medical profession could do anything. The psychics were the most powerless of all. Today, Carole attributes both her health and her life to a living Jesus Christ who delivered her from a desperate plight.

Reflecting today on her predicament, she is awed that such terrible destruction could be purchased at the price of a simple, supposedly harmless form of meditation.[9]

Johanna Michaelsen, another personal friend of the authors, had always believed in God; indeed, it was her desire to serve Him. As a Silva Mind Control graduate (and resultant spiritist) and as an assistant to a "psychic surgeon" in Mexico, she believed she was fulfilling her dreams. She encountered marvelous psychic experiences, "visions of inexpressible ecstasy where waves of light and peace would flow over me." In fact, she had "never experienced such joy, such light and peace, such unspeakable ecstasy." She felt, "I was on the right path at last."

And yet after years as a psychic, after 14 months assisting at "several hundred psychic operations" with medium Dona Pachita (one of the psychic surgeons discussed in Drs. Krippner and Villodo's *The Realms of Healing*), she encountered severe attacks and a "murderous demonic rage" from the very spirits she had become so close to. How could this be? These were *good* spirits—helpful, kind, and loving—*not* like the evil spirits she had also encountered on her psychic journey. These good spirits *couldn't* be evil; her own spirit guide had assured her that he was none other than Jesus Christ Himself!

Yet now her own spirit helpers had turned on her and, like the spirits that tormented Carole, seemed to want her dead. Why? What could possibly be the cause? The only conceivable reason for the spirits' dramatic change of temperament provided a startling revelation. The one difference in her life was that she had been giving serious consideration to the biblical Jesus Christ—"to accept Jesus Christ of Nazareth *as He is*, rather than as I had come to think He should be as a psychic."

But if the spirits didn't like the real Jesus, then how could they be good spirits? Worse yet, might they be demons, whose cunning was legendary? Although Johanna viewed Christians as "narrow-minded, spiritually undeveloped and undiscerning legalistic fundamentalists who simply didn't understand the vastness of the manifestations of God," she finally concluded that she herself had been the victim of a clever spiritual ruse.

The spirits really were demons.

Her story is told in *The Beautiful Side of Evil*, wherein she outlines the details of this spiritistic duplicity. In spite of the ecstatic experiences and all the apparent benevolence of her spirit helpers, she concluded these so-called "guides" were evil spirits only mimicking good spirits in an attempt to deceive her, even as the Scriptures teach (2 Corinthians 11:14). She concluded her book by warning others:

> Remember, there is a beautiful side of evil— deceptive, subtle, adorned with all manner of spiritual refinements, but no less from the depths of hell than that which is blatantly demonic.[10]

Mike, Carl, Tal, Carole, and Johanna—five bright and very hopeful men and women whose most optimistic dreams turned into palpable nightmares. Why? What kind of reality can transform the genuine sincerity of such people into the terrors they experienced?

What *kind* of psychic reality are such individuals tapping into? What manner of powers are they encountering? Is it merely human potential—the "divinity within" of the Eastern philosophy or the "latent psi" of the parapsychologist—somehow gone awry? Or is it something else? Why is it that so many people end up experiencing destructive powers, especially when they had the best of motives and initially encountered powerful and tremendously encouraging and loving experiences? How can something initially so "spiritual" and "blissful" and "beautiful" end up unmasked as something so evil—and so destructive?

In other words, why does the persistent optimism of those who promote the occult so often come crashing down on the individual level? Why the eventual destruction from *religious* practices, from seeking after *God?* Why the Bishop Pikes—those whose spiritistic odysseys lead to tragic deaths? Why the Ram Dasses—those whose personal deception by their own gurus or spirit guides lead to such destruction that they despair of knowing whom to trust or what to believe? Why have millions of people suffered as a result of what they thought were *spiritual* activities?

The reason is as disarmingly simple as it is frequently rejected: There is indeed a world of evil spirits. Their goal is to deceive people and trap them by occult practices—practices that our culture now defines as spiritual and godly. But biblically speaking, these practices are not godly. In the Bible, God declares they are sinful and idolatrous (Deuteronomy 18:9-12). They are dangerous because they attract the demonic.

The question is often raised, "Why is psychic or occultic activity as harmful as it is?" There are at least three reasons.

1. *Occult activity rejects God's will for man.* Occult practice is hazardous because it is a violation of the will of God, i.e., because God forbids it as an "abomination" to Him (e.g., Deuteronomy 18:9-12). Ignorance of God's law does not cancel the logical consequences of violating such law, just as taking poison by mistake will still cause injury. In this regard, however, occult activity is not necessarily like other disobedience.

To one degree or another, occult activity involves aligning oneself with the spiritual enemies of God (Satan and his demons), with all that implies, including their goals for men. In other words, the *degree* of confrontation with God appears to be the issue. Occult activity opposes God in a direct and active manner, whether or not one is aware of it.

For example, as we will see in Chapters 2 and 4, the occult worldview is pervasively anti-Christian.

   2. *Men are inherently ill-fitted for encounters with occult realities.* The occult is hazardous because mankind's current status as spiritually, morally, and physically fallen does not properly equip him to deal safely with the realm of the supernatural. Ultimately, his knowledge of this world is minuscule, nor does he have the means to secure protection from whatever nasty things might exist there. It's rather like playing tennis with your side of the court underwater. You can't win regardless of how well you play the game.

The history of the occult reveals that entering the spirit world is equivalent to walking unprotected on a mine field without knowledge of the number or location of the mines. If no one in his right mind would enter such a place on earth, neither should he do so anywhere else. Thus, the inherent consequences of contacting the supernatural realm tend to increase the normal consequences of ignorance, naiveté, pride, or power-seeking. For example, naiveté in repairing your car is one thing and carries its own level of risk; but naiveté in the things of Satan and a supernatural world of evil spirits is more serious and carries more risk.

In this regard, perhaps occult activity may be compared to the AIDS virus—another modern problem men are ill-prepared to deal with. Unfortunately, the occult is in many ways the equivalent of a spiritual AIDS. In both cases:

- One is exposed to something deadly.
- Infection occurs through activity that is exciting and pleasurable and often initially full of promise.
- Infected persons can be symptomless for years, unaware of the death sentence they carry inwardly.
- The disease is spreading rapidly.

- Most people refuse to believe they can be infected.
- Human ignorance concerning the exact nature of the illness is vast.

3. *Occult practices introduce people to spiritual entities who seek their destruction.* Occult involvement does not merely involve consorting with the enemies of God, but also with one's own adversaries. Any enemy, of course, may feign friendship for ulterior motives, but sooner or later it will seek to injure or destroy. In this sense, the spiritual underworld operates in ways similar to the criminal underworld. Just as the latter will use its hirelings only for its personal plans or glory and dispose of them when convenient, the spiritual underworld operates in the same manner.

In summary, the occult is hazardous because it involves first, personally confronting God and opening oneself to demonic influence and/or God's judgment; second, functioning in a hostile and alien terrain containing its own kind of booby traps; and third, encountering the devil's hatred.

However, at what *point* a particular activity becomes dangerous (in such a manner that harmful personal consequences must follow) we cannot say, for it seems to depend on a number of factors. For one person, consequences may come sooner than for another. But for everyone who remains involved in the psychic world, there will be consequences.

While we cannot say that a single deliberate exposure to a given psychic practice or event is dangerous, neither can we say it is absolutely safe. Psychiatrist Dr. Stuart Checkley warns, "I have seen patients whose involvement with relatively minor forms of the occult has caused them to suffer mental illness."[11]

Brooks Alexander, senior researcher for the Spiritual Counterfeits Project in Berkeley, California, observes:

> Many people seem to have so-called "psychic" experiences without being emotionally or spiritually injured by them. At the same time it seems clear that

the world of psychic pursuit and fascination is a demonic playground. How do we know the acceptable level of psychic involvement? We do not know. Each individual encounters the demonic danger at his own level of temptation—whatever that may be.

The fact is that no one knows how demonic beings operate in relation to psychic phenomena. Therefore it is impossible to say that "X" amount of psychic involvement will result in demonic contact. We do not know where the line is drawn between dabbling and demonism, or between curiosity and commitment, nor do we know how and when that line is crossed. It may be that the question of "how much" has less to do with it than we think. I would suggest that the neural and mental patterns set up by psychic involvement provide an *interface* with other forms of consciousness, which are extra-dimensional and demonic in nature. If that is the case, then psychic dabbling is a little like entering the cage of a man-eating tiger. You may or may not be eaten, depending in part on how hungry the tiger is. The significant point is that once you enter the cage, the initiative in the matter passes to the tiger.[12]

It should also be noted that the effects of occult activity are often not discernible (e.g., an imperceptible if increasing resistance to the gospel or the early imperceptible stages of psychological damage or even demonization). Non-Christians, of course, would not think the former was of any consequence, but it is of great concern if the gospel is true, for then one would be predisposed against the one true God with potentially eternal consequences.

Of course, if God chooses He may blunt the effects of sin and protect us from our ignorance or folly, or from the schemes and designs of the spiritual underworld. God's grace and mercy must always be taken into account, but never taken for granted. The Scripture itself warns all men, "Do not be deceived, God is not mocked; for whatever a man sows, this he will also reap" (Galatians 6:7). As Thomas Hale once warned, "We must not so much as taste of the devil's broth, lest at last he bring us to eat of his beef."

2

The Worldview and Practices of the Occult

> *People have presuppositions, and they will live more consistently on the basis of these presuppositions than even they themselves may realize.*
> —Francis Schaeffer
> *How Should We Then Live?*

> *Everything we do has a result.*
> —Goethe

> *Ideas have consequences.*
> —Francis Schaeffer

The basic philosophy and premise of the occult is described by a specific term: "monism." Monism is defined as a "philosophical theory that everything consists of or is reducible to one substance."[1] *The Encyclopedia of Philosophy* observes that monism "is a name for a group of views in metaphysics that stress the oneness or unity of reality in some sense."[2]

There are different forms of monism. The occult may be described as a mystical form of monistic belief which characteristically accepts some form of pantheism. Pantheism teaches that everything is God. For example, as one magical text teaches, "God and the universe . . . have always existed: visible and invisible, both make up the divine being."[3]

The modern influence of monism can be seen in that several major world religions are monistic. Hinduism and Buddhism are examples of world religions that reflect monistic teaching. In monistic (*advaita*) Hinduism, the one ultimate reality is defined as "Nirguna Brahman." In monistic Buddhism, the one ultimate reality is defined as an indescribable state of impersonal existence termed "Nirvana."

Christianity, on the other hand, is not monistic. Christianity teaches that an infinite-personal Triune God, who is Spirit (John 4:24), created the physical world distinct from Himself. (For an excellent study, see Francis Schaeffer's *He Is There and He Is Not Silent*.) This idea that God made the universe apart from Himself is known as "religious dualism," and it stands in contrast with occultic monistic philosophy. Thus, Christianity does not teach that reality is only one thing, but rather that reality is composed of *both* an eternal spiritual reality (a personal God) and the created universe (itself involving a material and spiritual realm of existence).

Occult monism claims, in contrast to Christian teaching, that "God" and the "creation" are ultimately the same thing—they are one in essence. Christianity maintains that because God created the world apart from Himself, God and the creation are *not* the same thing. Thus, the basic Christian doctrine which rejects monistic teaching is the biblical doctrine of *creation*.

In essence then, the occult (which is monistic) and Christianity (which is not monistic) are based on entirely different and opposing beliefs. The underlying premise of each system powerfully conditions how their proponents view God, man's relationship to God, the world, and man's place in the world. So let us further compare and contrast Christianity and the occult to understand how fully in opposition these worldviews are.

In Christianity, God is personal. The material world is a real place created by God and distinct from Him. Man is a creation of God, made in His image, having as his ultimate purpose in life a loving, personal, and eternal relationship with His Creator.

But in the world of the occult, all of this is rejected. God is ultimately impersonal and/or personal only in a provisional sense.

The material world is ultimately a secondary or illusory manifestation of God. Inwardly, all men are part of God, currently existing in ignorance of their divinity, and whose ultimate purpose is a merging of their true nature back into impersonal reality.

This is why the final goal of occult practice is to experience a condition of alleged spiritual "enlightenment" where a person supposedly understands the true nature of reality ("All is One") and his or her proper place in the world (seeking a final "reuniting" with the One).

The alleged truth of occult monism is supposedly "confirmed" through occult practices such as altered states of consciousness, magic ritual, spirit possession, drug use, meditation, or other means whereby monistic consciousness (the feeling that "All is One") is directly "experienced" and interpreted as "evidence" for the truth of one's occult philosophy.

It is the monistic premise of occultism that makes its philosophy so fundamentally anti-Christian. Dr. Gary North observes in his excellent evaluation *Unholy Spirits: Occultism and New Age Humanism*:

> Because God created the universe, there is a permanent, unbridgable gap between the ultimate being of God and the derivative being of creatures. There is a Creator-creature distinction. Though men are made in the image of God (Genesis 1:27), they do not partake of God's being. They are like God, but they are not of the same substance as God. There is no more fundamental doctrine than this one. Significantly, in every form of occultism this principle is denied, sometimes implicitly and usually explicitly. Satan's old temptation to man hinges on his denial and man's denial of the Creator-creature distinction. . . .
>
> In direct contrast to the biblical view of man and God, the occult systems, from the magical sects of the East to the gnostics of the early church period, and

> from there unto today's preachers of the cosmic evolu-
> tion and irresistible karma, one theme stands out—
> *monism*. There is no Creator-creature distinction. We
> are all gods in the making. Out of One has proceeded
> the many, and back into One are the many travel-
> ling. . . .
>
> It is such a convenient doctrine, for it denies any
> eternal separation of God and His creation and there-
> fore it denies any eternal separation of saved and lost.
> It denies any ultimate distinction between good and
> evil, past and present, structure and change. . . . [It]
> leads to rampant immorality, and . . . to a dismissal of
> earthly affairs and earthly responsibility. The re-
> sult . . . is moral nihilism.[4]

Of course, if one can indeed be a god, then to be as God and exercise one's divinity demands above all else the exercise of power—power over personal limitations, power over others (human and nonhuman), power over the creation, etc. Thus, personal "realization" of one's godhood finds "confirmation" through the development of supernatural mastery over one's environment. In other words, occult practice develops occult abilities which "confirm" personal divinity outwardly in the acts of supernatural power:

> The power that is used in magic is derived from the
> forces we have been describing and so comes from
> both within and outside ourselves. It is formed by
> linking one aspect of the magician's personality with
> the corresponding aspect of the cosmic mind. This at
> once sets up a current of power which the magician
> can draw upon for his own purposes.[5]

The above brief discussion of the differences between Christian and occult philosophy reveals why occultism in all its forms is so fundamentally hostile to Christian faith.

Below we present a brief contrast between the worldview of the occult and that of Christianity:

Occult/Psychic Worldview

Pantheism-monism—Everything is divine. There is only one divine reality (Spirit).

God is ultimately impersonal.

Man is inwardly divine, one with God in essence.

Evil is an illusion, but ultimately in harmony with God (God is amoral).

Salvation or enlightenment is achieved through self-realization (awareness of personal divinity) by various means (e.g., psychic practices).

Psychic powers normally result from psychic practices and are often used for personal power or profit.

"Eternal" cyclic incarnation or absorption into impersonal divinity (personal extinction).

Biblical Worldview

Traditional theism—God is the Creator, distinct from His creation (Spirit/matter—Genesis 1:1).

God is personal and loving (John 3:16).

Man is a creature, created in God's image, but not inwardly deity (Genesis 1:27).

Evil is a concrete fact, which operates in opposition to God's nature (God is holy—1 Peter 1:14,15; 3:12).

Salvation is based on the atonement (Christ's vicarious suffering and death for sin) and received as a free gift (by grace) through faith in God and Christ (John 3:16; 5:24; 6:47; 17:3).

Spiritual gifts are distinct from and work in contrast to psychic powers. (See our *Cult Watch*, 268-81.) They are given by God to His people for service to others (1 Corinthians 12:4-11; 14:3).

Eternal heaven or hell (personal immortality—Matthew 25:46).

What difference does all this make?

In occult monism, normal ways of thinking and perceiving are often rejected.

Because "All is One," there is no ultimate distinction between good and evil, moral and immoral, or right and wrong, because true reality is beyond these "illusory" categories. In other words, rape, theft, murder, etc., cannot finally be considered evil if evil itself has no final reality. But who can say such thinking has no consequences? Charles Manson himself once observed, "If God is One, what is bad?"[6] In the end, nothing evil is really evil.

But in the end, neither is anything ultimately good. Love, empathy, forgiveness, and truth cannot be considered "good" when "good" also has no ultimate reality. Later, we will supply specific illustrations of how occult monism can adversely affect peoples' lives and the decisions they make.

Further, there is no such thing as genuine personality, either human or divine, because true reality is impersonal. In other words, the personal God of Christianity plus all individual human personality is ultimately an illusion. Thus, as we will shortly see, in occult practice we often find an attempt to destroy the personality (as it currently exists) since it is supposedly a hindrance to true spiritual enlightenment.

Finally, in occult philosophy there is no Creator/creature distinction because inwardly man's true nature is intrinsically united to the one impersonal divine reality. Man is already God; he is simply ignorant of this fact until he becomes "enlightened" through occult practice.

It should be plain that whether we are Christians or whether we are occultists, the difference between these respective philosophies is both profound and important.

Occult philosophy, of course, has been with man from the beginning. In encapsulated form, it began when the spiritual father of the occult lied to mankind's first parents when the serpent told Eve 1) "You surely shall not die," 2) "Your eyes will be opened," and 3) "You will be like God," 4) "knowing good and evil" (Genesis 3:4,5). Respectively, these lies involve the suggestion that 1) man will live forever even if he disobeys the commands of God, 2) he can independently discover secret understanding or illumination of his true condition, 3) by self-will and disobedience to God, he can become godlike and gain forbidden power, and 4) a condition of innocence is counterproductive to his best interests because it is only the personal *experience* and final transcendence of good and evil that will make him like God.

Today the essence of occult practice involves three related but supernaturally derived phenomena: 1) the reception of secret knowledge—information normally unavailable through the five senses; 2) contacting the spirit world in various forms and at various levels; and 3) the acquisition of power to manipulate or control the creation, animate or inanimate (things, people, the spirit world). The underlying necessity of the supernatural is evident in each category; whether perceived or not, these three characteristics of the occult cannot be successfully achieved apart from supernatural assistance.

From the biblical perspective, then, the fact of the supernatural and the innate hostility of occult practices and philosophy to biblical revelation requires one conclusion.

The entire gamut of the occult realm lies under the domain of fallen angels (demons) and their leader, Satan. Their goal is part of a plan to oppose God, to deceive men, and to build a rebellious kingdom. Scripture does assert that Satan has a kingdom (Matthew 12:26). Indeed, it refers to him as the god of this world (2 Corinthians 4:4) and implies that he is the one behind the occult realm (1 Corinthians 10:20; 2 Corinthians 11:11-14). Nevertheless, in spite of the attraction of occultism, God asserts that evil and disaster will ultimately fall upon those who disregard His warnings and transgress His covenants (Deuteronomy 18:9-12; Isaiah 47:8-15). (See Appendix A.)

Before we examine occult methods in more detail, it is important to understand that, broadly considered, the world of the occult comprises a sizable number of practices and phenomena. We include here a brief listing for purposes of illustration.

Selected Practices and Phenomena

Occult Practices
seances
ritual, spells, curses
automatisms (writing, typing
     dictation, painting)

Occult Categories
magic
witchcraft/sorcery/voodoo
Satanism
spiritism

Occult Practices (cont.)

astral travel
psychometry/radionics
magic charms
psychic diagnosis/healing/
    surgery
rod and pendulum
crystal gazing
dowsing
I Ching
tarot cards
Ouija board

Occult Categories (cont.)

divination
astrology
shamanism
necromancy

Occult Related

parapsychology
mysticism
New Age holistic health
yoga
meditation
visualization
Dungeons and Dragons
    and similar fantasy
    role playing games
hypnotism

Occult Religions

(Almost all major religions and
cults are occultic to one degree
or another.)
Rosicrucians
Scientology
Theosophy
Church Universal and
    Triumphant
The Association for
    Research and Enlighten-
    ment (Edgar Cayce)
Silva Mind Control
Astara
Eckankar
Children of God
Anthroposophy
Mormonism
Kabbalism

Occult Phenomena

ectoplasmic manifestation
materializations/apparitions
telepathy
telekinesis
apports
clairvoyance/clairaudience
poltergeists (ghosts)
trance
possession
psychic transference of power
levitation
fairies, devas, nature spirits
spirit guides
polyglot mediumship
certain altered states of
    consciousness
precognition
reincarnation phenomena

As noted, one principal goal of occult practice is the acquisition of supernatural power.

Richard Cavendish is a leading authority on the history of magic and occultism. Educated at Oxford, he is the editor of two encyclopedias on the occult. He observes in *The Black Arts*, "The magician's central preoccupation is with the exercise of power, but his use of his power is also as various as his methods."[7] Significantly he begins his text discussing the occultist's attempts at self-deification (which typically accompanies the quest for power) and its theological roots:

> The driving force behind black magic is hunger for power. Its ultimate aim was stated, appropriately enough, by the serpent in the Garden of Eden. Adam and Eve were afraid that if they ate the fruit of the Tree of the Knowledge of Good and Evil they would die. But the serpent said, "Ye shall not surely die; for God doth know that in the day ye eat thereof, then your eyes shall be opened and *ye shall be as gods*, knowing good and evil." In occultism the serpent is a symbol of wisdom, and for centuries magicians have devoted themselves to the search for the forbidden fruit which would bring fulfillment of the serpent's promise. Carried to its furthest extreme, the black magician's ambition is to wield supreme power over the entire universe, to make himself a god.
>
> Black magic is rooted in the darkest levels of the mind, and this is a large part of its attraction, but it is much more than a product of the love of evil or a liking for mysterious mumbo-jumbo. It is a titanic attempt to exalt the stature of man, to put man in the place which religious thought reserves for God. In spite of its crudities and squalors this gives it a certain magnificence.[8]

Paradoxically, in his quest for personal power the occultist must somehow give way to the nonhuman power available from the supernatural realm. He must step aside and permit this supernatural reality to enter his life and his world. In one sense, he must "die" so "it" may live.

The Means to Power:
Radical Dissolution of the Personality

The methods of the occultist are pragmatic: to use whatever is effective in securing the desired end. Here the temporary destruction of normal life and perception—of time, reason, and normal consciousness—is vital. The importance of this is emphasized in almost any serious text on the occult. For example, the Hindu guru Bhagwan Shree Rajneesh teaches that the one who desires true occult enlightenment must become, at least for a time, "a perfect Zombie." He identifies this as a temporary state of catalepsy or idiocy and stresses its necessity "because it will destroy the past. . . . Your memory, your ego, your identity—all has to go."[9] Thus, "That's why a real disciple passes through a kind of insanity around a master."[10]

Another occult "master" teaches that the logical purpose of occult practice is to destroy "the separate self-sense and . . . the viewpoint of conventional cognition and perception."[11] In other words, "When the mind has been driven insane, it stops . . . and suddenly a new consciousness emerges."[12] Altered states of consciousness, leading to total detachment and "abandonment" of the personality are principal methods for enlightenment and can be induced by drugs, sex, transfer of occult power, ritual possession, meditation, intense concentration, insanity, human sacrifice, and many other means.

For example, in the agonies of shaman initiation, "The suffering has annihilated all former characteristics of the individual."[13] In the case of alleged UFO abductions, "Many who have had such initiations feel that they have ceased to exist."[14] Over and over we read that the old personality and consciousness are said to have died, "never to rise again." But if the old person has really "died" in occult practice, what now takes its place? Characteristically, it is a possessing spirit.

For example, as noted elsewhere, the research of Tal Brooke in *Riders of the Cosmic Circuit* offers a detailed examination and critique of Eastern metaphysics, including the altered states of consciousness found in the meditative disciplines of endless numbers of gurus. It reveals that altered states of consciousness are typically the means to spirit contact and possession. Consider again the late Bhagwan Shree Rajneesh, the influential Indian guru. His early experiences on the road to "enlightenment" brought him temporary insanity, possession, and almost killed him. Through intense absorption into various altered states of consciousness, the personality of the old Rajneesh literally and completely disappeared. In fact, it was permanently replaced by a new consciousness that was entirely alien. The new personality recalls, "The one who died, died totally; nothing of him has remained . . . not even a shadow. It died totally, utterly. . . . Another being, absolutely new, not connected at all with the old, started to exist." Rajneesh had become possessed by a "new consciousness," a living personality that directed his mind and body from that day forward.[15]

Consider another illustration in the text *Occult Psychology* by Kabbalistic occultist Alta J. La Dage. This book correlates Jungian psychology to Kabbalistic practice and other forms of occultism. Given Jung's occult involvement and the occult potential of many of his psychological theories, this is not surprising.[16]

At one point La Dage discusses the possibility of death or insanity along the path of enlightenment. He begins by discussing the dangers of premature entry of the consciousness to the depths of "nirvana" at the stage known as "Kether" according to the symbolic "tree of life" in Kabbalism:

> Should the human mind become open to this depth prematurely it would merely result in insanity or death. . . . There is a great danger of loss of body or mind at this critical stage. Whether or not this is "bad" can really only be answered by a person who has experienced it, and he isn't around to tell us![17]

La Dage proceeds to comment upon the massive nature of the ensuing personality change, something reminiscent of the characteristically advanced possession states among the major Hindu and Buddhist gurus:[18]

Union with Kether is the Seventh Death referred to in the *Cosmic Doctrine*. . . . The personality change is so great anyway, that even his closest friends would not recognize him were it not that physically he looks the same as before the event. . . . In such an experience we are dealing with a psychic "explosion" wherein force and form unite. Generally form (body) has to give ("you cannot put new wine in old bottles") and in some cases recorded in old Alchemical texts we find that the force of the experience incinerated the body.[19] (See p. 234.)

We are also told that an encounter with "even the slightest registry of this depth" of Kether (also called "the abyss") "causes one to lose interest in life below the abyss and it takes considerable will to make a return."[20]

Significantly, La Dage observes what other commentators have noted: Many people today experience such occult initiations "spontaneously" (as, for example, in what is termed yogic kundalini arousal).

Each abyss or crossing represents a major shift in consciousness. In ancient times (and in modern occult lodges) these events were called Initiations. Today, such initiations can happen "automatically" to people who know nothing of the Western Mystery Tradition, and they are diagnosed by medical men and are even experienced by the patient as nervous breakdowns or temporary psychosis.[21]

In La Dage's view, such ordinary psychologists have a problem here. These are the "unenlightened" therapists who are ignorant of the truth of what is occurring. As a result, they misdiagnose the phenomena of enlightenment as symptoms of mental illness. This is the reason behind his call for the integration of psychology and Western mystical-occult traditions, and his purpose in showing how Jung can be profitably utilized in this endeavor.

Significantly, however, we discover that once these states are experienced, they tend to be permanent and reinforce the need to maintain them, much like drugs. Indeed, even to return to normal life is to ask for pain and sickness:

> An ordinary psychiatrist will interpret one of these recapitulations as an ordinary run of the mill neurosis, and may try to adjust the person "back" to his previous level of functioning, when in fact the impulse of the Self is to transcend the old state. These are the casualties of our age of ignorance, the *Ira Vugari* as Crowley called it. If the person can be "adjusted" back to his *previous* level of functioning, then contrary to psychology's belief that he is "cured," the bottom will have fallen out of that person's life. . . . Furthermore, the next time he comes undone he is going to be in a far worse condition than he was the first time. If we live below or above our basic state, as I have heard my teacher say at least a hundred times, we can expect to be ill.[22]

The real problem, however, is one of dabbling in a forbidden, demonic area, one which frequently induces demonization and carries its own set of consequences. As noted philosopher and theologian Dr. John Warwick Montgomery observes of many young people today:

> They seek another kind of answer—an answer perhaps hidden in the Subjective depths of their own souls. But what key will unlock this hidden treasure? Some go the whole experiential route: sex, drugs, masochism, satanic occultism. Others seek salvation in the inward-focused Eastern religions. But the path of drugs and the occult is strewn with the wrecked lives of those who have given themselves to these false gods. And, as Arthur Koestler has so definitively shown in the account of his frustrating pilgrimage in

search of Eastern wisdom, the ambiguities of the Tantristic religions open them to the most immoral, destructive, and demonic possibilities.[23]

The Means to Power: The Use of Radical Practices

The hallmark of occultism is spirit contact in numerous forms, be it with alleged gods, nature spirits, "luminous ones," astral beings, "angels," visualized deities, sefirothic forms, etc. Usually, contact with the spirits is achieved under whatever guise the person feels most comfortable with, whether personal entity (angels, astral forms), psychological phenomena (higher self, archetypes), or impersonal concept (Akashic records, energy transference—e.g., *shaktipat diksha*) or enlightenment (*nirvakalpa samadhi*), etc. Initially, such contact becomes the means to power and as in shamanism, mediumism, etc., dependence on the spirits is a natural result.

Occult Ritual

All occult rituals center around the theme of summoning supernatural power to effect a cause. As one witch told us, "During rituals we raise power and send power to do whatever we wish done, whether it is good or evil." In occult magic, proper ritual is needed in order to secure the magical intention successfully and safely. Lifelong occultist David Conway explains:

> Rituals are conducted in two stages: first, the worshipper attunes himself to the sacred mystery being performed and then, usually as the climax, the presence of a particular deity is invoked. . . . The adept's slightest gesture can thus extend through all the worlds of being into the depths of the Godhead, and any words he whispers will echo throughout the length and breadth of the universe. . . . The climax to all magical ritual occurs when the adept draws into himself the astral force he has evoked so as to project

it towards a chosen object. To do this he must surrender his complete being to the astral force which is waiting to possess it, and this he does by cultivating a state of mind or, rather, madness, akin to the divine frenzy of the Bacchantes. There are various ways of doing this, and the adept must choose the one that suits him personally. . . . It demands, above all, a very close rapport with certain astral entities known as Group Forms. These are immensely powerful beings who on occasion can assume human shape, when they will cooperate with the other participants in a ceremony that combines the spiritually elevated with the wildest dreams of wantonness.[24]

In magic ritual, every object is carefully chosen for its symbolic reality and/or effect upon the mind of the occultist. Proper objects are necessary for particular goals and proper sounds with required vibrations are expected to successfully influence the astral planes.[25] Absolute precision is vital unless one wishes to court disaster:

All the world is like an enormous container of nitroglycerine. It must be handled with ritually exact care when it is being manipulated, and at all other times the magician must be devious, fluid, totally unpredictable, in order to escape the manipulations of others. This is the animists' world, where living, malevolent beings strike out and trap the ritually negligent. Perfection is a matter of precise ritual. The magician must content himself with subduing only minute portions of his world on a piecemeal basis. . . . In order to subdue portions of the world, the magician must link himself to mysterious powers that threaten his very existence. . . . The problem with power is always the same: the user is simultaneously subjected to it. . . . Similarly, if a magician uses the power of an ally or demon to produce certain effects, he inevitably places himself under the power of the ally. At the very least, he is subjected to a rigorous series of rituals that must be used when calling forth occult power. To command power—any power—is to acknowledge the sovereignty of the source of that power, whether God, demons, natural law, random variation, or whatever. Men will serve that which they believe to be sovereign.[26]

Thus, as Conway warns, "But even the cleverest and most knowledgeable magician realizes that the demons of the pit are waiting for the one false step that will deliver him to them."[27]

Drugs and Sex

Drugs and sex (typically perverted sex) are rampant in the occult. Conway observes in *Magic: An Occult Primer*:

Apart from all the material means to induce the required states of consciousness, some occultists also advocate the use of sex and drugs. . . . Although sex does play a part in magic, it is not indispensable. Like drugs and mantric recitation it is one of several ways of achieving that complete involvement which is the climax of all ritual. . . . Sex also releases its own form of power which can then be used in magic to reinforce or propel the elemental power [e.g., spirit or demon] evoked by ritual.[28]

In *The Dust of Death* British scholar Os Guinness also supports the correlations between drugs and spirit possession. In essence, drugs place the mind in an altered state which can open the door to the world of the occult:

For those of our generation who stumble on the spirit world accidentally, the two most common paths are LSD and misapplied meditation techniques. . . . Many who take acid regularly or who practice yoga or

Zen meditation have found they have opened their minds to blackness and spiritism, seeing themselves as mediums and describing themselves as possessed.[29]

Along with a number of other commentators he observes that ritualistic "Satanism is often related to heroin. A tragically high proportion of those involved in the Satan groups are also junkies."[30] Psychiatrist R. Kenneth McAll reveals that "it is common for addicts, especially for those addicted to heroin and alcohol, to become involved in black magic and visa versa."[31]

Conway also discusses the use of magical power in order to attain one's goals. This is characteristically accompanied by temporary loss of sanity and spirit possession. His discussion typifies the essence of the common, if more radical, forms of occult practice (whether East or West), and so we cite this revealing if startling passage at length:

> By now the adept has visualized the required forms and, it is hoped, contacted their astral equivalents. In addition, the force behind these forms will have been admitted into the circle. At this point we come to the most important part of the ritual. Everything that has gone before was merely a preparation for the impending moment when, to revive our earlier comparison with electricity, we shall flick the switch that lets in the cosmic power.
>
> This is something no book can teach; the assembled correspondences, the visualization and all the other ritual details can do no more than help the adept find the switch, and as that switch is situated inside himself, he alone can turn it on. To do so he must temporarily lose his reason, for it is reason which bars the doors of the conscious mind where the astral world lies waiting. The way to open these doors is to assume a state of unreason similar to the divine frenzy of the Bacchantes. Like their delirium the aim of such unreason will be to receive the deity that is being invoked. . . .
>
> There is no doubt that alcohol—and drugs too for that matter—are the surest means of breaking down mental

barriers, but, as we have said, they do tend to weaken the will while they are about it. This is why drugs, though often used in group ritual, are not something to be tried in magical work where inadequate supervision is available.

Some magicians cultivate the sweet madness by reciting one word over and over again. The adept begins by heaping incense on the charcoal and then, kneeling before the altar, he starts his verbal repetition or mantra. . . . While engaged in this, the adept imagines that the god-form or the most congenial of the planetary or sefirothic forms is materializing behind his back. He visualizes this in as much detail as possible. Slowly, as the altar candles flicker, he will sense with a sureness which precludes all doubt that the visualized form is in fact towering inside the circle behind him. On no account must he turn his head to look at whatever is there; nay, temptation to do so must be sternly resisted: the form may be unbearably hideous or else possess a beauty that may literally be fatal.

In the meantime the adept should endeavor to continue his mantra, although by now his heart will no doubt be beating furiously. Whatever else happens he must not move, even when he senses that the form is so close as to be almost touching him. Above all he must not panic, but should comfort himself with the thought that he is safe enough provided he stays where he is. At last—and he will certainly know when—the god-form will take control of him. To begin with, the adept will feel an exquisite giddiness somewhere at the base of his skull and quickly convulsing the whole of his body. As this happens, and while the power is surging into him, he forces himself to visualize the thing he wants his magic to accomplish, and wills its success. He must put all he has into this and, like our friends the Bacchantes, must whip himself into a veritable frenzy. It is at this point that the force evoked will be expelled to realize the ritual intention.

As he feels the force overflowing inside him the adept, while still visualizing the realized magical intention, bids it go forth to fulfil his wishes. . . .

For some magicians the dislocation of reason coincides with the moment of sacrifice. Others perform this sacrifice before proceeding to the climax of the rite, arguing that the vital energy discharged by the victim's blood assists the possessing entity to appear inside the circle.

Traditionally the victim's throat is cut and the warm blood allowed to gush into a chalice of the appropriate planetary metal. Those for whom the oblation coincides with the climax to the rite generally visualize the god-form behind them in the usual way, but possession then occurs as the magician drinks from the chalice or, if he is squeamish, plunges his hands into the blood it contains. At the same time the intention is visualized and willed in the normal manner.

Sacrificial acts are cruel, messy and, above all, unnecessary. More common, fortunately, is the use of sex to attain the desired climax. The outburst of power is effected at the same time as orgasm is reached, with possession occurring a few seconds before.[32]

As should be obvious from the above reading, occult philosophy and practice involve another world entirely. Literally millions of people today are risking everything to seek this world and its alluring powers. Yet a mere generation ago, the occult hardly even existed in America. The question is, how did we get here from there? In our next chapter we will see.

3

Reasons for the Modern Occult Revival

Occultism has now settled comfortably into American culture. Even many Christians are involved in psychic or occult practices, directly or indirectly. However, occult revivals in this nation are nothing new. The mid-nineteenth and early twentieth centuries boasted significant occult activity. If we consider this phenomenon historically, we may understand the potential of occultism to shape our future. For example, in 1851 there were an estimated 1200 mediums in Cincinnati, Ohio, alone—as well as hundreds of mediums in other major cities.[1] By 1855, America boasted several thousand mediums and some two million followers, which led to an estimated eight to eleven million supporters by 1871.[2]

These early "channelers" and their followers undergirded an entire century of American parapsychological research—the scientific study of the occult.[3] This research, in part, finally helped to pave the way for our modern occult explosion.[4]

For example, observe the consternation of G. H. Pember in *Earth's Earliest Ages.* If we had not identified the date of publication as 1876, the reader could easily have assumed it originated with a modern author, so accurate is it in describing events of our own era:

> Nay, almost every characteristic of antiquity seems to be reappearing. Open intercourse with demons is being renewed on a vast scale in the very heart of Christendom, and even among the hitherto somewhat

Sadducean Protestants: numerous circles are carrying on magical practices: attempts are being made to restore the influence of those ancient Mysteries which are said to have been always kept up by a few initiates: the old mesmeric healings are again performed: stargazers and planet rulers have greatly increased, while many amateur students are zealously assisting to reestablish the power of astrology over the human race: the use of the divining rod, and countless other practices of primal and medieval times, are once more becoming common. And, impossible as it would have seemed a few years ago, all these "superstitions" are floating back to us upon the tide of "modern thought." They come no longer veiled in mystery, nor claiming to be miraculous or Divine; but in accordance with the spirit of the age, present themselves as the fruit of science, as an evidence of the progression of knowledge in regard to the laws of the visible and invisible worlds.[5]

In our own period, a worldwide occult revival is mushrooming in obvious and less obvious guises—such as the human potential movement and certain psychotherapies in transpersonal and some forms of humanistic psychology.[6] Even the military and some major corporations are turning to or promoting pseudoscience and the occult.[7]

In 1979 *Time* magazine estimated some 40,000 witches were active in the United States. Today, the figure may have quadrupled, with an equal number of Satanists; regardless, over 300 universities, colleges, and educational institutions (over 75 are accredited or state-approved) now offer programs or even degrees on New Age topics; some 100 American universities also offer courses in witchcraft, and in Britain alone today there are an estimated 50,000 to 75,000 spiritists plus 40,000 to 100,000 witches and Satanists.[8] Forty years ago all this was unheard-of.

Our current occult revival can be explained, in part, by the following factors:[9]

1. *The failure of rationalism, secular humanism, and material-ism as comprehensive worldviews.* While such ideologies have provided a welcome insulation against the occult, they have also indirectly promoted it by default. Millions of people have found such philosophies cannot meet their deeper personal needs, pro-vide an outlet for spiritual expression, or offer a legitimate basis for genuine meaning in life. This explains why those who have no religious affiliation, far from being committed rationalists, are frequently the first to explore the supernatural.

According to the Bible, man is created in the image of God (Genesis 1:26,27), and has an innate need for fellowship with God. This explains why the history of mankind is the history of almost endless religious involvement—a search after divine real-ity. Unfortunately, men and women often turn to counterfeit religious expression in an attempt to satisfy these yearnings.

Thus, thinking the world of the psychic realm is something divine, many have turned to the paranormal, mystical, and occult in search of what they would not or could not find elsewhere.

2. *A spiritual vacuum has resulted from the abandonment of orthodox Christianity, providing a cultural reorientation to greater acceptance of an occult/mystical worldview.* Perhaps the most important cause of our occult revival is our nation's turn from Christian faith. It is a simple fact that wherever Christianity is biblically practiced, occultism is rejected. Several decades ago there was at least a general consensus that the Bible was a divine revelation, that a personal God existed, that prayer was impor-tant—regardless of the number of people who actually lived such a philosophy in their daily lives. Even non-Christians benefited from a culture influenced by a Christian worldview. Such a cultural consensus provided a buffer against not only occult practice but also the barren implications and nihilism of non-theism.

However, our culture today has rejected even the minimal tenets of Christianity, and occultism, agnosticism, humanism, and religious and cultural relativism have come to power; as a result, in some ways our society is imploding from within. A substantial cultural shift is currently underway:

Recent developments not only in science but in the arts, politics, psychology, and religion indicate a broad shift in Western culture to increased acceptance of a common set of presuppositions that parallel the occult/mystical world view, which is in stark contrast to the biblical world view of historic Christianity.[10]

The influence of an Eastern-occult/New Age-mystical world-view can be seen in education, literature and the arts, business, theology, medicine, psychology, government, science, popular movies, etc.—in virtually every segment of our culture. Witness as examples the modern influence of transpersonal (occult) education,[11] the revival of spiritistic literature which now sells in the millions of copies,[12] astrology and human potential seminars in the business world,[13] the influence of parapsychology and cultism in Christian theology,[14] the growing influence of New Age medicine,[15] how Western psychologists are being powerfully influenced by Eastern traditions;[16] how our own government now sponsors psychic research and, for lack of a better term, the various renditions of the new "physics mysticism" seen in Fritjof Capra's *The Tao of Physics* and other texts.[17]

Well-known businessmen and movie stars routinely seek the advice of psychics and mediums; prestigious universities offer courses in the occult and conduct research into parapsychology; some hospitals even utilize the assistance of psychic healers, whom they may not identify as such to their patients lest they frighten them.

George Lucas, the cinema genius behind the Star Wars saga and the Indiana Jones movies, is only one Hollywood mogul who believes that cinema "should deal more with the occult."[18] Television now offers daily 900 ads or "infomercials" promoting psychic advice on half a dozen forms of divination (tarot, I Ching, astrology, etc.). These ads have reached and persuaded millions of people. Booklets are sold at supermarket checkout stands which are designed to enable the average person to "become psychic" and which encourage the development of psychic healing, spirit contact via the Ouija board, automatic writing, pendulum use, etc.[19]

Researcher Brooks Alexander discusses how such metaphysical ideas have been successfully assimilated into our culture:

> Eastern teachings have risen to prominence and prosperity in the West with remarkable speed. . . . As Eastern and occult ideas are propagated to Occidentals on a mass scale, they are filtered through the pervasive secularism of our culture. In this way, they are demystified without changing their essential content. The basic components of an Eastern/occult world view are recast in forms of expression that are naturalistic, scientific, and humanistic in orientation. Occult philosophy is being secularized and psychologized with increasing refinement. In such forms, its fundamental concepts are easily adopted and easily applied by contemporary intellectuals.
>
> Thus these mystical doctrines have influenced areas of society far removed from the sometimes bizarre world of the counterculture. Their underlying themes run through contemporary science, economics, politics, art, psychology, and religion.[20]

3. *The explosive growth of the new religions.* The influx of Eastern gurus, and the emergence of hundreds of alternate religions and New Age seminars (e.g., Silva Mind Control, est/The Forum, Lifespring, MSIA, Actualizations, Mind Psibiotics, etc.) have provided another socially legitimate outlet for psychic participation. Indeed, literally scores of the most popular religious sects in this country—religions that influence tens of millions— either accept or promote occult activity.[21]

Most Eastern religions are excellent breeding grounds for occult experimentation and development. Yoga practice, for example, characteristically develops psychic powers. In studying more than 20 modern gurus, we found that almost all promoted the occult and, further, described themselves (including their spiritual practices and behavior) in terminology that fits well with a hypothesis of their own spirit possession.[22]

Finally, many of the new religions are fundamentally spiritistic in origin or practice. Our own findings after studying almost one hundred of the "new" religions are consistent with those of other researchers. For example, Brooks Alexander and Mark Albrecht of the Spiritual Counterfeits Project (SCP) in Berkeley, California, state:

> Our research into [scores of] cults both large and small has revealed that the lowest common denominator is often that of direct spirit influence.[23]

Dr. Robert S. Ellwood, Jr., professor of religion at the University of Southern California, discusses over 40 of the new religions in *Religious and Spiritual Groups in Modern America*. He observes that they all have "striking parallels" to shamanism, a primitive form of spiritism. "The cult phenomena could almost be called a modern resurgence of shamanism," he says.[24] In that the new religions are fundamentally spiritistic, their promotion of the occult is not surprising.

4. *Liberal Theology*. Many people attend church hoping to find genuine spiritual reality and teaching. But thousands of churches in this country are theologically liberal. As such, they reject the divine inspiration of the Bible, deny salvation through Christ, and ridicule the existence of the miraculous. Thus indirectly, liberal theology is also one of the principal factors for promoting the occult.

When people find spiritual reality ridiculed in church, it is not surprising they might turn to other sources for spiritual nourishment, whether in the cults or the occult. Unfortunately, since liberal theology rejects the authority of the Bible, such people have no guidelines for evaluating or testing the validity of the spiritual experiences they encounter.

5. *A new parapsychological/New Age view of human potential and the reclassification of occult powers*. To classify occult practice as something entirely normal and/or as the proper means to contact God is to legitimize it in the minds of millions of people. Thus, various disciplines today are forging a new occult view of

man which assumes that psychic development is inherently natural to the human condition and a process that leads to personal knowledge of God.

For example, a mystical approach to the "new physics," transpersonal psychology, parapsychology, the study of higher consciousness, holistic health practices, and the New Age Movement all directly or indirectly promote the legitimacy of personal psychic development as an innate unfolding of psychological potential. The humanistic and transpersonal approach to psychology is a problem here since psychology as a discipline has little practical concept of evil to begin with. As noted psychiatrist M. Scott Peck points out in *The People of the Lie*, "The concept of evil has been central to religious thought for millennia. Yet it is virtually absent from our science of psychology—which one might think would be vitally concerned with the matter."[25] Thus, when segments of modern psychology begin to adopt occult philosophy and practice in purely psychological terms, it not only "naturalizes" occult powers, it *a priori* assumes their benevolence.

While parapsychology has placed a scientific credibility on developing psychic abilities, the New Age Movement in general has helped legitimize them as divine forms of spiritual expression. In fact, for dozens of religions, new and old, these new powers of the mind are seen as a means to divine health, wealth, power, and happiness.

Unfortunately, attitudes which legitimize psychic practices as "scientific," exhibiting "human potential," or "divine" mask the sinister reality of the occult as something neutral, benevolent, and/or benignly spiritual.

Most gurus, psychics, spiritists, mediums, and occultists stress their powers come "from God." In a similar manner, the various "Christian" parapsychological societies reinterpret psychic abilities as the gifts of the Holy Spirit, and the New Age Movement reclassifies mediumism itself as a "channeling" of higher aspects of the divine mind.

Again, to claim your powers originate in God gives them divine authority and legitimacy. In times past, psychic powers were at least acknowledged as originating from the spirit world. But while the motives or character of mercurial "spirits" can easily be questioned, that which involves the activity of God cannot be doubted.

6. *The reality of the supernatural.* Finally, what explains our modern explosion of occult activity is the stark reality of the supernatural world. It does exist. Indeed, there are now literally millions of personal testimonies of people contacting this world directly.

But unfortunately, the pervasiveness of the occult in our society is underestimated by many rationalistic secularists who view it as "nonsense" or "a passing fad." Even those who claim to be open-minded tend to debunk it. Thus, they fail to understand why converts to the occult continue to include all segments of society, including the intelligentsia: There really is something there.

A relevant example is Colin Wilson, an initial skeptic, whose seminal *The Outsider* and other works have had wide impact. Wilson went on to pen *The Occult: A History* (1973), *Mysteries* (1978), *Dark Dimensions: Celebration of the Occult* (1977), and other books on the occult which, worthy treatments to be sure, nevertheless have helped to legitimize it socially.

But with broader social legitimization, its absorption or redefinition by the secular culture makes its influence more subtle. As Robert Burrows argues, "Since the sixties, occult mysticism has widened its base. As it is filtered through the secularism of Western culture, it is increasingly difficult to detect. Mysticism in its secularized forms has gained the greatest ground, making its influence felt in every major facet of contemporary life."[26]

7. *Freedom from conventional morality.* Modern America has largely rejected moral absolutes. Indeed, national polls reveal that 70 percent of adults do not think there is such a thing as a moral absolute. If so, it would seem that around a hundred million people are now predisposed against absolute concepts of right and wrong. This might explain why many of them turn to the occult. Occult teachings offer a *spiritual* justification for

freedom from morality. Thus, occult participation represents a rejection of God's benevolent desires for man as expressed in His law, and man's own inclination to seek his own form of spirituality—a form which typically exalts moral independence. This allows man to live however he pleases (1 Samuel 15:23; Isaiah 5:12-30; 30:8-11; Jeremiah 5:30,31; 2 Timothy 4:3,4). As the notorious occultist Aleister Crowley emphasized, "The whole of the law is 'Do what thou wilt.' " Several teenage "Satanists" have told us, "I've read *The Satanic Bible* and it says I can do anything I want. That's why I like Satanism." Neopagan feminist Margo Adler observes that witchcraft and neopaganism are "incredibly anarchistic movements" with hardly any dogmas, hence their popularity.[27] In her book on the revival of neopaganism (*Drawing Down the Moon: Witches, Druids, Goddess-Worshippers, and Other Pagans in America Today*), she observes: "Many people said that they had become pagans because they could be themselves and act as they chose, without what they felt were medieval notions of sin and guilt."[28]

But "medieval notions" of sin and guilt reflect universal human experience. Occult philosophy will indeed free one from moral constraints—but at what cost?

4

Evidence for the Devil

*What appears to me incredible is not the Devil, not
the Angels, but rather the candor and the credulity of
the skeptic, and the unpardonable sophism of which
they show themselves to be the victims: "The Devil is a
gent with red horns and a long tail; now I can't believe
in a gent with red horns and a long tail; therefore I don't
believe in the Devil." And so the Devil has them precisely where he wants them. Those who stick to old
wives' tales are those who refuse to believe in the Devil
because of the image they form of him, which is drawn
from old wives' tales.*

—Denis de Rougemont
*The Devil's Share, An
Essay on the Diabolic in
Modern Society*

The spirits have come out in the open today: Through possessed "channels" they have spoken in public seminars, via
books, cassettes, and videos, and even on national television.
They have initiated an assault in ways that a generation ago would
have seemed unthinkable. Polls such as those conducted by
Gallup, Roper, and the University of Chicago's National Opinion
Research Council reveal that literally tens of millions of Americans claim to have had some kind of contact with spiritism. Thus,
the occult can no longer be conveniently put to one side as
belonging exclusively to Eastern/Oriental countries.[1] It is now

out in the open, part of the recognized culture of the West. And it is the thesis of this book that all this is the devil's business.

Unfortunately, many people ridicule even the idea of a literal devil or demons as primitive superstition. They believe that in our modern scientific age we can finally do away with such medieval nonsense and its corresponding "witch-hunts."

But is this attitude realistic? Is it unscientific to believe in a personal devil, or is there a preponderance of evidence that suggests his existence? The famed evangelist Billy Graham once remarked,

> Why do I believe in the devil? *For three reasons.*
> 1. Because the Bible plainly says he exists.
> 2. Because I see his work everywhere.
> 3. Because great scholars have recognized his existence.[2]

It is a more logical assumption that Satan really does exist than that he does not. As Dr. J. I. Packer, professor of historical and systematic theology at Regent College in Vancouver, British Columbia, argues:

> The natural response to denials of Satan's existence is to ask, who then runs his business?—for temptations which look and feel like expressions of cunning destructive malice remain facts of daily life. So does hell in the sense defined by the novelist John Updike—"a profound and desolating absence" (of God, and good, and community and communication); and "the realisation that life is flawed" (Updike goes on) "admits the possibility of a Fall, of a cause behind the Fall, of Satan." Belief in Satan is not illogical, for it fits the facts. Inept to the point of idiocy, however, is disbelief in Satan, in a world like ours; which makes Satan's success in producing such disbelief all the more impressive, as well as all the sadder.[3]

It is also quite logical that evil would seek to camouflage itself for strategic purposes, just as the Mafia launders its money in legitimate businesses. Camouflage has been a key ingredient of military tacticians for millennia—it would hardly be surprising to find it in the spirit world. Such camouflage could assume any number of guises from promoting itself as myth to the opposite extreme of promoting itself as ultimate reality or God. Indeed, the majority of people in our culture *do* believe either that Satan does not exist or that the realm of the psychic world is indeed divine. Of course, the only way out of this situation is to unmask the real myth: the lies the devil spreads about himself. As Brooks Alexander well argues:

> The nature of illusion is the ruse of misdirection. It is the misplacement of our attention through the manipulation of *false images,* both personal and collective. The devil's disappearance provides a clear example of collective misdirection—a form of social deception. Once that image is accepted, *whatever response we make to it* will be as false as the image that provokes it, and therefore play into the devil's hands. Its direction will be amiss by definition. . . .
>
> It is not the existence of Satan that should alarm us, but the fact that our contemporaries are so ill equipped to deal with reality on *any* level, let alone to recognize the *fundamental* danger. De Rougemont's articulation of this point is elegant and concise:

> > One of the reasons why confusion is spreading in the world is that we are afraid to face its real causes. We believe in a thousand evils, fear a thousand dangers, but have ceased to believe in Evil and to fear the true Dangers. To show the reality of the Devil in this world is . . . to cure ourselves. We are never in greater danger than in moments when we deceive ourselves as to the real nature of a threat, and when we summon our energies for defense against the void while the enemy approaches from behind.

It would be irresponsible for us to exclude [the devil] from consideration simply because we dislike the connotations we have given him. Even if we acknowledge the concept without comprehending it, at least it puts us on notice that "spiritual" things may be more subtle and complex than they appear. Healthy caution is an antidote for fear, not its cause.[4]

Eight Arguments for the Devil

Thus, we can suggest eight lines of reasoning to infer the possibility of a real devil and/or the reality of spiritual evil.

- the consensus of history and religion
- the testimony of practicing occultists
- the testimony of former spiritists
- the phenomenon of spirit possession
- the authority of the Bible
- the testimony of Jesus Christ
- the hostility to historic biblical Christianity displayed in virtually all spiritistic literature
- the destructive power of the occult and the testimony of brilliant thinkers

We examine these in turn.

The Consensus of History and Religion

Belief in Satan and/or a world of evil spirits has been with man throughout his history. It has been an accepted truth for a majority of people in most times and cultures, ancient and modern (e.g., Assyrian, Babylonian, Celtic, Egyptian, Greek, Hebrew, Indian, African, Muslim, Roman, Tibetan, Persian, Chinese, Buddhist, Hindu, Christian, Jain, Japanese, Slavic, etc.).[5] In light of this vast testimony within the canons of history, culture, and religion, the relatively recent assertion of the devil's lack of existence is less tenable. Modern scientific rationalism has actually explained very little of the height and depth of the universe.

The Testimony of Practicing Occultists

Magicians, psychics, gurus, mediums, and Satanists are well aware of the reality of spiritual evil, however they choose to define it. Many of these practitioners do believe in literal evil spirits and have had personal encounters with them. Such encounters leave little doubt as to their malevolent nature.[6] Occult magician Conway warns, "Their appetite for destruction and discord appears to be insatiable" and "We shall call them evil for the good reason that given the chance they would do us immeasurable harm."[7]

Spiritist Sri Chinmoy also discusses the deceptive nature of spirits, that even allegedly "good" spirits will turn on a person and then "they try to cut your throat" if the individual attempts to declare independence from them.[8] He further observes, "The hostile forces [can] take the form of a particular spiritual Master and ask the disciples to commit suicide. 'If you commit suicide, I will be able to give you liberation sooner' it would say. . . . These hostile forces are very clever."[9]

The Testimony of Former Spiritists

The testimony of many former spiritists and occultists is that the spirits they once completely trusted were really demons who were seeking to deceive them. Their once-friendly spirit guides turned on them and/or attempted to destroy them. These frightening accounts are reported by Raphael Gasson in *The Challenging Counterfeit*, Victor Ernest in *I Talked With Spirits*, and Ben Alexander in *Out From Darkness*, all former long-standing spiritistic mediums. Douglas James Mahr was the author of *Ramtha: Voyage to the New World*; Mahr had a significant personal history with "Ramtha." Yet today he is convinced that Ramtha's true identity is not that of a venerable "mystical embodiment of 35,000 years of life experience," but rather that of a lying, demonic spirit.[10] Doreen Irvine was a leading European witch who relates her horrifying story in *Freed From Witchcraft*. As noted, Johanna Michaelsen was former psychic and assistant to a noted Mexican psychic surgeon. Michaelsen discusses her experiences in *The Beautiful Side of Evil*.

All of these people agree that the spirit guides they once considered divine or enlightened entities were actually demons.

The Phenomenon of Spirit Possession

This malevolent phenomenon has occurred in nearly every culture and religion, ancient or modern. One former witch declares, "Demon possession is real, very real and is increasing at an alarming rate in this present day and age."[11] Indeed, the very act of a spirit invading and controlling a person implies, even demands, hostility and malevolence (see Mark 5:2-7). In *People of the Lie*, well-known psychiatrist M. Scott Peck observes:

> It seems clear from the literature on possession that a majority of cases have had involvement with the occult—a frequency far greater than might be expected in the general population.[12]

Dr. Peck also records an incident he witnessed personally at an exorcism:

> When the demonic finally spoke clearly in one case, an expression appeared on the patient's face that could be described only as Satanic. It was an incredibly contemptuous grin of utter hostile malevolence. I have spent many hours before a mirror trying to imitate it without the slightest success. I have seen that expression only one other time in my life—for a few fleeting seconds on the face of the other [mentioned] patient, late in the evaluation period. Yet when the demonic finally revealed itself in the exorcism of this other patient, it was with a still more ghastly expression. The patient suddenly resembled a writhing snake of great strength, viciously attempting to bite the team members. More frightening than

the writhing body, however, was the face. The eyes were hooded with lazy reptilian torpor—except when the reptile darted out in attack, at which moment the eyes would open wide with blazing hatred. Despite these frequent darting moments, what upset me the most was the extraordinary sense of a fifty-million-year-old heaviness I received from this serpentine being. It caused me to despair of the success of the exorcism. Almost all the team members at both exorcisms were convinced they were at these times in the presence of something absolutely alien and inhuman. The end of each exorcism proper was signaled by the departure of this Presence from the patient and the room.[13]

The phenomenon of possession is well-documented in both Christian and non-Christian literature.[14] Dr. John Warwick Montgomery asserts:

The problem involved in determining whether demon possession occurs and whether witchcraft works is absurdly simple. The documentation is overwhelming. Even if ninety-nine percent of all witchcraft cases are thrown out (and that would be very difficult to do) the remainder would easily establish the reality of the phenomenon.[15]

In a major text on altered states of consciousness, *Religion, Altered States of Consciousness and Social Change*, Dr. Erika Bourguignon (ed.) observes that of 488 societies surveyed, fully 74 percent believed in possession by spirits:

It will be noted that such beliefs occur in 74% of our sample societies, with a maximum of 88% in the Insular Pacific and a minimum of 52% in North America. The beliefs are thus characteristic of the great majority of our societies.[16]

In *The Devil's Bride: Exorcism Past and Present*, psychic researcher Martin Ebon observes that "The uniform character of possession, through various cultures and at various times, is striking."[17]

Therefore, we must ask ourselves where, in fact, such a dominant belief came from if not from the fact of spirit possession itself? Are rationalistic explanations credible? We don't think so. Rather, we think its very uniformity suggests (in Ebon's words) the "universal presence of devils, demons or possessing spirits."[18]

Note the following illustration from John S. Mbiti, *African Religions and Philosophy*. Here we see not only the universal fact of spirit possession in Africa but also the resulting bondage to the alleged spirits of the dead:

> Spirit possession occurs in one form or another in practically every African society. Yet, spirit possession is not always to be feared, and there are times when it is not only desirable but people induce it through special dancing and drumming until the person concerned experiences spirit possession during which he may even collapse. When the person is thus possessed, the spirit may speak through him, so that he now plays the role of a medium, and the messages he relays are received with expectation by those to whom they are addressed. But on the whole, spirit possessions, especially unsolicited ones, result in bad effects. They may cause severe torment on the possessed person; the spirit may drive him away from his home so that he lives in the forests; it may cause him to jump into the fire and get himself burnt, to torture his body with sharp instruments, or even to do harm to other people. During the height of spirit possession, the individual in effect loses his own personality and acts in the context of the "personality" of the spirit possessing him. The possessed person becomes restless, may fail to sleep properly, and if the possession lasts a long period it results in damage to health.

Women are more prone to spirit possession than men.[19]

If belief in spirit possession is a dominant belief of the vast majority of cultures throughout human history, is it not a bit presumptuous to deny the fact, especially if such a denial is based on personal preference or presupposition, not real evidence?

The Authority of the Bible

Biblical authority is predicated upon its claim to be the Word of God. If the Bible is the Word of God, what it says about the existence of a personal devil must be true; therefore, in light of the overabundance of data supporting its divine inspiration,[20] we may assume the Bible's statements about Satan are authoritative.

As Denis De Rougemont observes in his *The Devil's Share: An Essay on the Diabolic in Modern Society*, "If one believes in the truth of the Bible, it is impossible to doubt the reality of the Devil for a single moment."[21]

The Bible does teach that the spirits who operate in the world of the occult are not what they claim to be (enlightened spirits sent from God) but demonic spirits bent on the deception and destruction of human beings.

What are some of the Scriptures relating to spiritism and the occult that warn men against occult involvement? The following illustrations prove that God considers occult involvement a serious matter, and that it is better avoided wherever it is found.

God warned ancient Israel not to adopt the occult practices of the pagan nation surrounding it:

> When you enter the land which the LORD your God gives you, you shall not learn to imitate the detestable things of those nations. There shall not be found among you anyone who makes his son or his daughter pass through the fire [human sacrifice], one who uses divination, one who practices witchcraft, or one who interprets omens, or a sorcerer, or one who casts a spell, or a medium, or a spiritist, or one who calls up

the dead. For whoever does these things is detestable
to the LORD; and because of these detestable things the
LORD your God will drive them out before you (Deuteronomy 18:9-12).

God also judged the ancient kings of Israel when they dis-
obeyed Him and practiced occultism. The reference below is to
King Manasseh of Judah:

And he did evil in the sight of the LORD according to
the abominations of the nations whom the LORD dis-
possessed before the sons of Israel. For he rebuilt the
high places which Hezekiah his father had broken
down; he also erected altars for the Baals [evil gods of
human sacrifice] and made Asherim, and worshiped
all the host of heaven and served them [astrology].
. . . And he made his sons pass through the fire in the
valley of Ben-hinnom [human sacrifice]; and he practiced witchcraft, used divination, practiced sorcery,
and dealt with mediums and spiritists. He did much
evil in the sight of the LORD, provoking him to anger
(2 Chronicles 33:2,3,6).

As this passage suggests, in ancient Israel occult practices
were associated with idolatry (worship of false gods and spirits)
and inevitably led to human sacrifice—as is increasingly occurring in the Western world today. This gruesome practice is
discussed in such books as Nigel Davies' *Human Sacrifice in
History and Today* (1981). Thus, the Israelites

mingled with the nations, and learned their practices,
and served their idols, which became a snare to them.
They even sacrificed their sons and their daughters to
the demons, and shed innocent blood, the blood of
their sons and their daughters, whom they sacrificed
to the idols of Canaan; and the land was polluted with
the blood. Thus they became unclean in their practices, and played the harlot in their deeds. Therefore

the anger of the LORD was kindled against His people,
and He abhorred His inheritance (Psalm 106:35-40).

The Bible further identifies the spiritistic powers behind idolatry as demonic:

They made him jealous with their foreign gods and
angered him with their detestable idols. They sacrificed to demons, which are not God—gods they had
not known, gods that recently appeared, gods your
fathers did not fear. You deserted the Rock, who
fathered you; you forgot the God who gave you birth
(Deuteronomy 32:16-18 NIV).

But the sacrifices of pagans are offered to demons,
not to God, and I do not want you to be participants
with demons (1 Corinthians 10:20 NIV).

At the time of Isaiah, the people had become practitioners of
various sorceries which God condemned:

They [judgments] will come upon you in full measure, in spite of your many sorceries and all your
potent spells. You have trusted in your wickedness
and have said, "No one sees me." Your wisdom and
knowledge mislead you when you say to yourself, "I
am, and there is none besides me." Disaster will come
upon you, and you will not know how to conjure it
away (Isaiah 47:9-11 NIV).

In the New Testament, the practitioners of the occult are seen
as those who lead people astray from the faith:

There they met a Jewish sorcerer and false prophet
named Bar-Jesus, who was an attendant of the proconsul, Sergius Paulus. The proconsul, an intelligent
man, sent for Barnabas and Saul because he wanted to
hear the word of God. But Elymas the sorcerer (for

that is what his name means) opposed them and tried to turn the proconsul from the faith. Then Saul, who was also called Paul, filled with the Holy Spirit, looked straight at Elymas and said, "You are a child of the devil and an enemy of everything that is right! You are full of all kinds of deceit and trickery. Will you never stop perverting the right ways of the Lord?" (Acts 13:6-10 NIV).

Many also of those who had believed kept coming, confessing and disclosing their practices. And many of those who practiced magic brought their books together and began burning them in the sight of all; and they counted up the price of them and found it fifty thousand pieces of silver. So the word of the Lord was growing mightily and prevailing (Acts 19:18-20).

The New Testament also reveals that when the spirit is cast out from someone with occult powers, the powers are lost, revealing that psychic powers are not human (i.e., natural and innate) but given by demons. The apostle Luke reports on one spiritist who was apparently seeking to validate her own practices by linking them with the apostle Paul's ministry.

Once when we were going to the place of prayer, we were met by a slave girl who had a spirit by which she predicted the future. She earned a great deal of money for her owners by fortune-telling. This girl followed Paul and the rest of us, shouting, "These men are servants of the Most High God who are telling you the way [hodon; lit. "a way"] to be saved." She kept this up for many days. Finally Paul became so troubled that he turned around and said to the spirit, "In the name of Jesus Christ I command you to come out of her!" At that moment the spirit left her. When the owners of the slave girl realized that their hope of making money was gone, they seized Paul and Silas and dragged them into the marketplace to face the authorities (Acts 16:16-19 NIV).

Finally, we present below a selected list of additional Scriptures relating to the existence of spiritual warfare.

The Spirit clearly says that in later times some will abandon the faith and follow deceiving spirits and things taught by demons (1 Timothy 4:1 NIV).

Finally, be strong in the Lord, and in the strength of His might. Put on the full armor of God, that you may be able to stand firm against the schemes of the devil. For our struggle is not against flesh and blood, but against the rulers, against the powers, against the world forces of this darkness, against the spiritual forces of wickedness in the heavenly places (Ephesians 6:10-12).

I [Jesus] am sending you [Paul] to them [to the Gentiles] to open their eyes and turn them from darkness to light, and from the power of Satan to God, so that they may receive forgiveness of sins (Acts 26: 17,18 NIV).

The god of this age has blinded the minds of unbelievers, so that they cannot see the light of the gospel of the glory of Christ, who is the image of God (2 Corinthians 4:4 NIV).

The coming of the lawless one will be in accordance with the work of Satan displayed in all kinds of counterfeit miracles, signs and wonders, and in every sort of evil that deceives those who are perishing. They perish because they refused to love the truth and so be saved (2 Thessalonians 2:9,10 NIV).

For such men are false apostles, deceitful workmen, masquerading as apostles of Christ. And no wonder, for Satan himself masquerades as an angel of light. It is not surprising, then, if his servants masquerade as servants of righteousness. Their end will be what their actions deserve (2 Corinthians 11:13-15 NIV).

But for the cowardly and unbelieving and abominable and murderers and immoral persons and sorcerers and idolaters and all liars, their part will be in the lake that burns with fire and brimstone, which is the second death (Revelation 21:8).

The Testimony of Jesus Christ

No one else in human history can speak with more authority than Jesus Christ. No one else in all history ever directly claimed to be God (John 5:18; 10:30; 14:9) and proved the truth of His claim by literally rising from the dead (Matthew 20:18,19; John 20:24-28; Acts 1:3). In our book *Do the Resurrection Accounts Conflict? And What Proof Is There That Jesus Rose From the Dead?* (available from the Ankerberg Theological Research Institute, P. O. Box 8977, Chattanooga, Tennessee 37411), we have detailed the persuasive, logical, historical, and legal evidence for the fact of Christ rising from the dead.

But if He rose from the dead, something unique in all human history, then He is both Lord and God, and what He says is true, including His statements about the devil, demons, and spiritual warfare.

The New Testament is replete with references to the reality of a personal devil as an apostate angel who fell from heaven.[22] Most of these references are spoken by Christ Himself (John 8:44; Luke 10:18; Jude 6). The devil is called the tempter (1 Thessalonians 3:5), wicked and evil (Matthew 6:13; 13:19), the prince of devils (Matthew 12:24), the god of this world (2 Corinthians 4:4), the prince of this world (John 12:31; 14:30; 16:11), dragon and serpent (Revelation 12:9; 20:2) and a liar and murderer from the beginning (John 8:44).

He has a kingdom (Matthew 12:26) which is hostile to Christ's kingdom (Matthew 16:18,19; Acts 26:18), and he rules a realm of demons (Matthew 9:34). His key abilities are power and cunning.

He is called a "strong man" (Matthew 12:29) and has great power (2 Thessalonians 2:9). His subtlety (Genesis 3:1) is seen in his treacherous snares (2 Timothy 2:26), wiles (Ephesians 6:11), devices (2 Corinthians 2:11), and transforming ability (2 Corinthians 11:14). He is so powerful that he deceives the "whole world," which is said to be "under the control of the evil one" (1 John 5:19 NIV; Revelation 12:9; 13:14). He thus works in the children of disobedience (Ephesians 2:2), worked among the apostles (Matthew 16:23; Luke 22:31; John 13:2), opposes the people of God (1 Chronicles 21:1; Zechariah 3:1,2; Acts 5:3; 1 Thessalonians 2:18; 2 Corinthians 2:11) and even tried to gain the actual worship of God Himself in the person of Christ—an act suggestive of his extreme mental imbalance (Mark 1:13; Matthew 4:1-10).

Satan unendingly sows seeds of error and doubt in the church (Matthew 13:38,39), blinds the minds of unbelievers (Mark 4:15; Acts 26:18; 2 Corinthians 4:4), is capable of possessing men (John 13:27), has the power of death (Hebrews 2:14), and prowls about like a roaring lion seeking those he may devour (1 Peter 5:8).

Christ appeared to destroy the work of the devil (1 John 3:8) who will soon be defeated (Romans 16:20) to spend eternity in hell (Matthew 25:41; Revelation 20).

In conclusion, the biblical testimony concerning the existence of Satan is beyond doubt.

The Hostility to Historic Biblical Christianity Displayed in Virtually All Spiritistic Literature

The fact that *all* spiritistically inspired literature opposes biblical teaching confirms the biblical view of spiritual warfare expressed above. Otherwise, why should godly spirits oppose biblical teachings at all? Their own teachings prove that what the Bible says of them is true (i.e., that they are not who they claim).[23]

In our book *Cult Watch* we stated in brief that the evidence demonstrates that these "loving" spirits with their endless disguises—from "angels" to "aliens" to "nature spirits"—fit the category of the demonic. It can be shown that these spirits—despite their frequent use of religious words and claims to spirituality—promote sin and immorality, and endorse occultism. Some even promote criminal activity and such perverse rituals as necrophilia (sex with corpses). They also pervert and distort biblical truth, reject Christ and hate the God of the Bible, and purposely deceive those who listen—sometimes with sadistic intent. If the above can be demonstrated (as it can), what other conclusions may we arrive at other than that these creatures are deceiving spirits? Why should we listen to them?

Consider the teachings of the spirit entity "Emmanuel" as found in the text by Pat Rodegast entitled *Emmanuel's Book*. Morally, Emmanuel teaches the permissibility and desirability of divorce ("incompatible" marriages); the possibility of "open marriage" (adultery); the permissibility of abortion ("a useful act" when done "with willingness to learn" for "nothing in your human world is absolutely wrong"); and homosexuality and bisexuality as normal behavior, even in full recognition of the AIDS plague.[24]

Emmanuel also demeans political leaders as ignorant and sick and teaches that the six million Jews who perished in the Holocaust really chose to be murdered in order to grow spiritually. Thus, Emmanuel says that Hitler and Stalin should not be condemned too severely for they also are part of God.[25]

One book by a psychologist/channeler having wide experience with channeling says that a common theme of almost all modern channeling is that because men are literally creators of their own experience, "There are no victims." *All* personal experiences with evil are simply things we choose to create to "learn certain experiential lessons."[26] But are these teachings logical? Are they the kinds of moral codes man should live by? Are they good, ethical teachings in any sense? Can they be considered socially constructive? Are these ideas what we would expect from morally pure, divine, or highly evolved spiritual beings?

Or, on the other hand, are they what we would expect from evil spiritual beings? The fact is that such teachings are not the exception; they are merely representative of hundreds of other spirits' teachings as reflected in occult literature today (see Appendix B, "The Teachings of the Spirits").

The Destructive Power of the Occult and the Testimony of Brilliant Thinkers

The personal damage to people's lives revealed throughout the history of the occult is powerful evidence that occult practice links one to a world of evil spirits. Since we document this in the remainder of our book, we only mention it here. Nevertheless, this may explain why some of the most energetic minds of the modern era have accepted the reality of demons: They do leave evidence of both their existence and their nature.

The astute Cambridge professor C. S. Lewis said in regard to the existence of demons:

> It seems to me to explain a good many facts. It agrees with the plain sense of Scripture, the tradition of Christendom, and the beliefs of most men at most times. And it conflicts with nothing that any of the sciences has shown to be true.[27]

Trial lawyer, philosopher, and theologian J. W. Montgomery holds eight earned degrees, including two doctorates, and is the author of over a hundred books and articles. He owns one of the largest personal occult libraries in the country and is convinced "there is overwhelming extra-biblical data and empirical confirmation" documenting scriptural claims for the existence of a personal devil and demons.[28]

If even veteran psychic researchers admit the following concerning our ignorance of the psychic realm, certainly there is no reason to reject the idea of demons outright:

> In truth, even the most knowledgeable among us must admit that when dealing with psychic aspects, we command no more than varying degrees of ignorance.[29]

Is the skeptics' position really tenable? J. W. Montgomery argues that, in controversial areas especially, special care must be taken to objectively assess the facts of the matter, whether or not it is personally comforting:

> We must "suspend disbelief," check out the evidence with the care demanded for events in general, attempt to formulate explanatory constructs that best "fit the facts" and at the same time be willing always to accept facts even if our best attempts to explain them prove inadequate.[30]

Let's offer a final illustration of why we feel we cannot ignore the possibility of a real devil and demons. It is a fact that all men everywhere believe that at any given moment, an invisible world of living creatures hovers about us (such as viruses and insects); indeed they even play an important role in the outcome of affairs on our planet, such as crop harvests and disease levels. Nevertheless, we rarely see them.

There are literally billions of creatures about us that we never see—in the air, water, and soil. Yet we know they exist, either by careful observation or the evidence of their visits.

It is a little strange that in a world where billions of creatures are not seen and yet believed in, that men refuse to accept the existence of God, angels, and demons merely because they have not yet seen them—when, in fact, their "tracks" are virtually everywhere. Perhaps some people cannot see them because they rule out their existence to begin with; hence, their "tracks" are explained by recourse to other theories. But for those persons who observe both nature and religion carefully, the "tracks" of the invisibles are only too obvious.

Dave Hunt uses the analogy of the subatomic particle called the neutrino as an illustration of the closed-mindedness the skeptic has toward the spiritual world.[31] The neutrino is a particle that has no physical properties (no mass), no electrical charge, and is unaffected by gravitational or electromagnetic fields. A neutrino traveling toward the earth would pass right through it as if it simply did not exist. In fact, only one in ten billion neutrinos passing through matter the equivalent of the earth's diameter would react with a neutron or proton!

Now, let us assume there are intelligent "neutrino" beings. They would, of course, not be able to detect our universe; to them it would simply not exist. A neutrino entity could, at the very most, suspect our existence from certain secondary effects. But he would undoubtedly be ridiculed by his fellow colleagues and could never prove his suspicions since his neutrino instruments would simply be incapable of detecting our universe.

If such beings existed, we who live upon the earth might find it unendingly amusing that these entities would refuse to admit our existence merely because they could neither see us or detect us directly. Their philosophical and logical "proofs" of our nonexistence would make good party fare. And if it were possible that we could in some manner interact with their world (while they could not affect ours), no doubt humans would have a very merry time with any curious neutrino beings willing to investigate our effects or "prove" our existence. To those neutrinos willing to dedicate their lives to our research, it would undoubtedly be most profound, with many disturbing implications.

The parallels here to the materialist's unwillingness to believe in a spirit world and the parapsychologist's eagerness to try and prove one exists is obvious. Both are caught, as it were, in a "neutrino trap": The former's closed-mindedness prevents his realization of another dimension; the latter's curiosity and credulity permits unending manipulation. And note carefully how *little* a neutrino being could ever really discover about our world. All his time would be spent with the enticing and fascinating secondary effects which, at best, would constitute the tip of the iceberg. After all his painstaking investigation, after all the theoretical constructs he could muster, he would remain infinitely ignorant about the real makeup of our world. He would know nothing of our physical constitution or abilities, our morality or civilization, our social structure and laws, our penchant for cruelty or wars.

The psychic's dilemma is also obvious: He is the equivalent of a neutrino being poking and prodding a foreign environment, with absolutely no genuine knowledge of its inhabitant's makeup and morality, or its world's laws or dangers.

A neutrino being was never meant to exist on an earth world, and neither is an earth being capable of exploring a neutrino world without courting whatever unknown hazards might be present.

But to say evil spirits cannot exist, or that there is no evidence for them, is simply untenable by the canons of biblical, cultural, and empirical data.

In conclusion, a person would be hard-pressed to maintain that demons simply do not exist after considering not only the divine authority of the Bible and the testimony of Christ (who, as God, is an infallible authority), but also the consensus of history and religion, the testimony of active and former occultists, the phenomenon of spirit possession, the hostility to biblical revelation displayed in spiritistic literature, and the personal wreckage in the history of occultism.

In the end, one either trusts the spirits and ignores the facts, or trusts the facts and ignores the spirits.

5

Satanism and Witchcraft: The Occult and the West

Some members smoke a little pot.... Other members use cocaine because they believe it heightens their senses and gets them piqued to accept the spirits. Next we call upon Satan.... We ask the Prince of Darkness or sometimes lesser demons to come into our sanctuary. Once we feel the power around us—we know that Satan is here.... We may decide that on this certain night we're only going to do destructive magick. The group will save up its demands for that night that concern hurting someone else. We would never hurt anyone within the group. But we couldn't give a s____ about someone outside.

—Satanic high priest Nolan
Waters, in Kahaner, *Cults
That Kill*

I. *Do you have human sacrifices?*
S. *Yes, mostly babies.*
I. *Where are the sacrifices held?*
S. *At houses in the woods. . . .*
There are three rings of guards. The first would stop somebody, tell him he's on private property. The second would try to run you off. He might take a shot at you, but

it would be just to scare you. The third would kill you.
—Satanist describing eye-
witnessed killings, in
Kahaner, *Cults That Kill*

*I'm convinced that our own nation is rapidly under-
going demonization.*
—Mark I. Bubeck,
The Satanic Revival

In 1989 15 bodies were uncovered in a mass grave in Mata-
moros, Mexico, just a few miles from the Texas border. The
victims, including one American, were murdered as part of the
practices of Santeria ("worship of the saints"), which is a mixture
of African tribal religion and Catholicism that has "white" and
"black" forms. In this case, the particular form is called Palo
Mayombe and had been syncretized with a mongrel variation of
Satanism. Black magic, voodoo, and drug-smuggling were all
involved. In Cuba, Santeria is called Palo Mayombe or Abaqua.
In Haiti it is called Voodoo; in Brazil, Umbanda and Macumba.
In its various forms, this religion has experienced significant
growth in some cities of America, including Washington, D.C.,
Miami, Denver, and Tucson, and is responsible for drug trafficking, human sacrifices, and other felonies.[1] But it is only one
illustration of the increasing paganization of America.

In 1974 Arlis Perry, a young Stanford University student and
committed evangelical Christian, was, while in California, kidnapped and horribly tortured and killed in a satanic ritual. She
had, apparently, been attempting to witness to members of the
group. As it turns out, "Son of Sam" murderer David Berkowitz
was also apparently a member of this group—part of a linked
nationwide satanic network which had ties to Charles Manson as
well.[2] In fact, Berkowitz "emphasized the hideous torture Arlis
endured—indicating knowledge that went far beyond any newspaper account."[3] Berkowitz had smuggled a book out of jail. On
pages 114 and 115 of Peter Haining's *The Anatomy of Witchcraft*,
he had written the following message on the top of the pages:

"Stanford University" and, to the left, "Arlis Perry, hunted, stalked and slain, followed to California."[4]

From Haining's book, the following text was underlined, "The shade of Aleister Crowley looms large in the area, but his excesses pale into significance compared to today's devil worshippers" and "there can be no doubt that Manson exerted complete authority over his followers and when he preached to them that evil was good and that nothing he as their Christ/devil asked them to do could be wrong, they accepted it without question." The quote continued, "Their lives were his for whatever purpose he chose . . . devoting themselves to drugs, music and magic."[5]

On another page ran the following notation of satanic murders:

> Several years ago, at Port-Louis, a certain M. Picot made a pact with the Devil, assassinated a child and ate its heart still warm.
>
> Last year, in the same town in January, a sorcerer called Diane tried to win the services of the Infernal Powers by slitting the throat of a seven-year-old boy and sucking his blood straight from the wound.[6]

The text continued from the earlier quotation:

> The bizarre and gruesome trial which followed . . . proved one of the most extraordinary in American legal history. . . . Counsel for the Prosecution asked the young woman if it was true that she regarded Manson as Satan and that she was one of his witches:
>
> "Yes, sir, I am."
>
> "And you consider that witches have supernatural powers?"
>
> "Yes."
>
> "Would you tell us what you thought your powers as a witch were?"
>
> "I could do anything I wanted. I was made to believe I was a witch, right from the beginning. Charlie (Manson) said we were going to build this new culture and learn to control others by witchcraft."

One of the men also expressed similar beliefs and devotion to Manson's cause in the witness box:

"It's hard to explain. It's like nobody else counted but us and we would learn how to have all our desires fulfilled by using the same kind of magic that the witches used in ancient times. He told us that there wasn't any right or wrong.... 'There is no good, there is no bad. There is no crime, there is no sin.' ...Everywhere he went he got this suicidal loyalty from everyone. He was big on Black Magic. It was pretty powerful stuff. He was continually hypnotizing us, not the way they do in night clubs but more like mental thought transference."[7]

Today, a dozen books collectively present evidence that Satanism has now gained an impressive hold in America and, because it seeks to destroy the foundation of American social and moral values, constitutes a genuine threat to society. Among these books are Jerry Johnson's *The Edge of Evil: The Rise of Satanism in North America* (Word, 1989); Mark I. Bubeck, *The Satanic Revival* (Here's Life, 1991); Ted Schwarz and Duane Empey, *Satanism* (Zondervan, 1989); Arthur Lyons, *Satan Wants You: The Cult of Devil Worship in America* (Mysterious, 1988); and Bob Larson's *Satanism* (Nelson, 1989).

For example, Dr. Carl Raschke received his Ph.D. from Harvard and is an authority on the history and philosophy of occult religion. He is currently professor of religious studies at the University of Denver and director of its Institute for Humanities. He is the author of a book whose title tells it all: *Painted Black: From Drug Killers to Heavy Metal—The Alarming True Story of How Satanism Is Terrorizing Our Communities*.

Maury Terry is an award-winning investigative journalist whose years of research resulted in *The Ultimate Evil: An Investigation of American's Most Dangerous Satanic Cult*, which linked Manson and "Son of Sam" killer Berkowitz to a satanic networking. Arthur Lyons states in *The Second Coming: Satanism in America*, "Satanic cults are presently flourishing in possibly

every major city in the United States and Europe. . . . The
United States probably harbors the fastest growing and most
highly-organized body of Satanists in the world."[8]

In *Cults That Kill: Probing the Underworld of Occult Crime*,
award-winning investigative journalist Larry Kahaner chronicles
interviews with police officials and occultists throughout the
country showing that occult crimes, including drug peddling,
child abduction/rape/pornography/sacrifice, and worse are now
practiced in places across America.[9]

For example, detective Pat Metoyer of the Los Angeles Police
Department observes,

> We think we discovered a correlation between Eas-
> ter week and occult-related crime. From Palm Sunday
> to Easter Sunday is the week for killing babies. We
> watch for kidnapings and that sort of thing. The pa-
> tients we're dealing with have told us that babies are
> killed during those days. One person said she has seen
> six babies killed during that time period. . . . These
> groups don't always kidnap babies. Some have doctors
> within the group who will perform the birth and not
> fill out a birth certificate. Then when they sacrifice
> the baby they're not really killing anyone who existed.
> . . . Before we say something like this, it has been
> verified with a minimum of five separate people who
> don't know each other, who have never spoken to each
> other. Minimum five people.[10]

Most people are simply not ready to believe these kinds of
things are really happening, which, of course, works to the Satanist's advantage. Frankly, we were not quite ready for it either.

We have knowledge of confidential police reports of murders
committed by Satanists that are so vile we cannot describe them
publicly—merely reading about them makes one feel debased
and sick.

The fact that there are currently hundreds of thousands of
witches, Satanists, animists, and other pagans in the country is

reason enough for genuine concern. But that such acts can and are being committed should not be surprising.

What is surprising is that some people refuse to admit to the fact of a neopagan revival of considerable proportions[11] and that groups which engage in ritual murder do so on the basis of an amoral philosophy and religious necessity. Whether it be rewards from the devil or spirits or gods; the reducing of the victim's alleged karma; the supposed psychic rush and infusion of occult power from the act of human sacrifice, or other "benefits," the point is that the activity is condoned by an amoral worldview and justified on the basis of religious (pagan) principles.

The attainment of power is common to witchcraft, Satanism, and magic, and here we again see the necessity for the abolition of time, history, and normal consciousness. Possession and sacrifice are key ingredients. For example, the witches' magic circle is a place

> where time disappears, where history is obliter-
> ated. . . . Some covens use music, chanting, and
> dancing to raise psychic energy within the circle.
> . . . The most common form of "working" is known
> as "raising a cone of power." . . . Many of the revival-
> ist covens have rituals in which the Goddess, sym-
> bolized by the moon, is "drawn down" into a priest-
> ess of the coven who, at times, goes into trance and is
> "possessed by" or "incarnates" the Goddess force.
> Similarly, there are rituals where the God force is
> drawn down into the priest who takes the role of the
> god in the circle. In these rituals Witches *become* the
> gods. [12]

Witch Justine Glass observes in *Witchcraft: The Sixth Sense*:

> The object of ritual, including the Black Mass, is to
> raise power (paraphysical power) to implement and
> strengthen the mental force of its practitioners. Some
> form of measurable energy is given off by intensely-

experienced emotion, the exact character of which is not known—but then neither is the exact character of electricity; and there is no doubt that the emotions generated by the Black Mass constitute a considerable energy potential.[13]

In *The Black Arts*, Richard Cavendish discusses one rationale for human sacrifice: the dramatic increase of occult energy:

In the later grimoires the sacrifice tends to be more closely associated with the ceremony itself and in modern rituals the victim is sometimes slaughtered at the height of the ceremony. This is done to increase the supply of force in the circle. In occult theory a living creature is a storehouse of energy, and when it is killed most of this energy is suddenly liberated. The killing is done inside the circle to keep the animal's energy in and concentrate it. The animal should be young, healthy and virgin, so that its supply of force has been dissipated as little as possible. The amount of energy let loose when the victim is killed is very great, out of all proportion to the animal's size or strength, and the magician must not allow it to get out of hand. If he is unsure of himself or lets his concentration slacken, he may be overwhelmed by the force he has unleashed.

It is an ancient magical principle that blood is the vehicle in which an animal's life-energy is carried. The spirit or force which is summoned in the ceremony is normally invisible. It can appear visibly to the magician by fastening on a source of energy on the physical plane of existence. It may do this by taking possession of one of the human beings involved in the ritual. Alternatively, it can seize on the fumes of fresh blood, or on the smoke from the brazier, but blood is more effective.

The most important reason for the sacrifice, however, is the psychological charge which the magician obtains from it. The frenzy which he induces in himself by ceremonious preparations, by concentration, by incantations, by burning fumes, is heightened by the savage act of slaughter and the pumping gush of red blood.[14]

He proceeds to refer to human sacrifice:

> It would obviously be more effective to sacrifice a human being because of the far greater psychological "kick" involved. Eliphas Levi said that when the grimoires talk about killing a kid they really mean a human child. Although this is highly unlikely, there is a tradition that the most effective sacrifice to demons is the murder of a human being. . . .
>
> In practice, human victims normally being in short supply, the magician's bloody sacrifice is the killing of an animal or the wounding of the magician himself or one of his assistants, whose skin is gashed till the blood runs. If this is combined with the release of sexual energy in orgasm, the effect is to heighten the magician's frenzy and the supply of force in the circle still further.[15]

Satanists have various reasons for human sacrifice. With specific body parts, they can allegedly garner increased power. The head may be believed to contain the spirit and may even be slept with for a period of weeks until the power of the spirit is absorbed by the Satanist. The heart may contain the soul and may actually be eaten for its power, etc.

A candle made from the fat of an unbaptized baby is allegedly a prized possession among some Satanists.[16]

Witches are also involved in human sacrifice, though to a much lesser degree; several cases are mentioned in Kahaner's *Cults That Kill*.[17] But witchcraft easily becomes a recruiting ground for Satanism as the need for more power grows. And as the need for power grows, occult crime increases. (See pp. 199-201, 298.)

Indeed, for the last 30 years, stories about devil worship, witchcraft, satanic ritual, and criminal activity have become increasingly common across the world. In Australia, the *Melbourne Observer* tells the tragic story of Lorrian Faithfull who died in bizarre circumstances in her St. Kilda flat. It was some 15 days after she died of a suspected overdose of drugs that her rotting body was found, no longer beautiful, a bloated and blackened thing.

Only ten days before her death, she had spoken to reporter Brian Blackwell and revealed how deeply troubled she was— afraid of members of the satanic cult to which she once belonged. There were paintings and books about the devil all over her apartment, and little bells draped around the walls were supposed to keep the evil spirits away. The air had been thick with incense, and she constantly drew on her marijuana joint as she told about her life as a so-called daughter of the devil.

She admitted that she had taken part in a number of satanic orgies, and that those taking part sought Satan's help to bring harm to other people. According to Lorrian, it had worked in a number of cases. However, the time came when she felt she could not continue with these practices. According to the newspaper report, the crisis came when she saw a privately made Italian film showing an actual human sacrifice. She left the cult, but could never shake off the past, and night and day she was tormented. Though she had rejected the macabre world of the satanic underground, she still felt its power and did not seek deliverance in the only way that could be effective spiritually.

In the end this tortured and bewildered girl tried, for the tenth time, to commit suicide by an overdose of drugs. She finally succeeded.[18]

In his book *Kingdom of Darkness*, F. W. Thomas tells the story of a photojournalist and magazine photographer who set out to investigate black magic in London—an attempt to secure material for a newspaper story. This man, Serge Kordeiv, and his wife eventually found themselves in a room where ceremonies were conducted in the name of Satan. They were told to kneel and then to swear perpetual homage to Satan, and they signed an oath written in contract form, with their own blood.

> Satan's high priest then formally welcomed this couple into the coven by abruptly placing his hands on their genitals. [Here we have a Satanic mockery of the Christian rite of the laying on of hands to impart spiritual blessing.] The strange thing about this part of the ceremony, report the Kordeivs, was the sudden inexplicable, "surge of energy" that went all through them when the obscene hands grabbed their private parts.
>
> After going through the Satanic initiation ritual, Serge Kordeiv found his whole life was dramatically changed. Everything he touched turned to money. Never had he and his wife enjoyed such financial prosperity. But after attending several more meetings, Serge and his wife decided to quit the group.[19]

Thomas proceeds to tell of some of the activities that caused them to realize how evil were the activities with which they had become associated. In one Black Mass, a wax dummy representing a prominent businessman was "killed" by a knife being plunged into it, whereupon red liquid gushed over a nude girl who was stretched out on the altar. The members of the coven had to drink the blood from a bird that was killed, the blood having been first drained into a chalice. At the next meeting of the group, Kordeiv was shocked at being shown a newspaper report of the sudden death of the businessman they had murdered in effigy—he had collapsed and died of a heart attack on that same night.

The Kordeivs decided to withdraw at a later time when they were supposed to go through a satanic confirmation ceremony involving sex acts. They broke off, and in the days and weeks that followed, they went through a series of terrifying incidents and experiences. As is often the case, where before they had known great financial success, now the opposite was true. In various other ways, they were made to realize that they had displeased the powers of darkness. The report continues:

Such was the experience of an unwise couple whose curiosity for black magic dragged them through untold anguish and despair. One cannot just pick up the dark bolts of magical fire and drop them at will without getting burned. There is always a price to pay for use of these forbidden powers, in this world as well as in the world to come.[20]

In the mid-1980s *Rolling Stone* reported on the satanic murder of 17-year-old Gary Lauwers.[21] Whether or not the satanic cult, "Knights of the Black Circle," was a serious group or a loosely knit association of teenage drug users playing on the fringes of Satanism, one of its founding members was serious about the devil. Richard Kasso, who later hanged himself in jail, would use drugs to attempt to contact the devil. In graveyard rituals he would chant "Satan, Satan, Satan," and he allegedly "wanted to be the devil's second hand." At the time of Lauwers' death, Kasso forced him to his knees and made him say "I love Satan." He then took out a knife and repeatedly stabbed the youth until he died.

The above story was the leadoff for a special report on the May 16, 1985, ABC Newsmagazine show "20/20," titled "The Devil Worshippers." It referred to "perverse, hideous acts that defy belief" including "suicides, murders, and the ritualistic slaughter of children and animals." It noted that cases of satanic activity are found in every state but that "even more frightening is the number of reported murders and suicides with satanic clues." It reported on three different categories of Satanism: 1) self-styled Satanists, like the Kasso group above, who dabble in Satanism; 2) religious Satanists who publicly worship the devil; and 3) satanic cults constituting highly secretive groups who commit criminal acts, including murder. The segment interviewed a number of authorities and cited other examples of horrible acts done in the name of the devil.

We note a few comments by some of the authorities interviewed.

Dr. Lawrence Pazder, psychiatrist and author of *Michele Remembers* (1980), a book on ritual child abuse in Satanism:

Children are involved in graveyards, in cremato-
rias, in funeral parlors, because one of the primary
focuses of these people is death. Everything is attempted to be destroyed and killed in that child and in
society, everything of goodness. And death is a major
preoccupation. . . . These people cover their tracks
very well. . . . They're not going to do some simple
murder and leave a body in a stream for you to pick up
the pieces of.[22]

Police Chief Dale Griffis:

When you get into one of these groups, there's only
a couple of ways you can get out. One is death. The
other is mental institutions. Or third, you can't get
out.[23]

Tom Jariel, "20/20" investigator:

Nationwide, police are hearing strikingly similar
horror stories, and not one has ever been proved.
. . . Police are very reluctant to investigate these
crimes as satanic crimes. . . . They prefer to try
to categorize them as drug-related crimes, sex-re-
lated crimes or robbery or something that they're
more familiar with.[24]

Anton LaVey, founder, Church of Satan:

This is a very selfish religion. We believe in greed,
we believe in selfishness, we believe in all of the
lustful thoughts that motivate man, because this is
man's natural feeling.[25]

The Napa *Register* tells of a man who was convicted for the sex
slaying of a teenage girl: "The purpose of calling [the girl] to the
house was to sacrifice her to Satan," the defendant testified.

He slashed her throat, violated her sexually, and hid her body
under his house. He was also found guilty of beheading a hitch-
hiker, of molesting him sexually, and then leaving his body near a

freeway. Three prosecution psychiatrists testified that the guilty man was sane, and a jury of seven women and five men deliberated for only one hour after a two-week trial before finding him guilty of first-degree murder on both counts.[26]

The San Francisco *Chronicle* states that "a group of 'Satan cultists' tortured and beat a 17-year-old to death, believing he was an undercover narcotics agent." He was not, but he had been lured to an apartment where members of a Satan cult had been living commune-style; and he underwent a bizarre weekend of torture before he died. The report states that he was tied to a bed and beaten, then moved into a basement altar room that was decorated with a long black table on which candles had been placed in blackened bottles. In this room satanic tridents and chains were hanging on the wall, the wall itself being painted with splotches of red that were meant to signify blood. It seems the 17-year-old youth was tied to the table, flogged with chains, and slashed with pieces of glass. When his body was eventually found in a wooded area, his head had been crushed, apparently by a club.[27]

Such accounts can now be multiplied hundreds or thousands of times. Worldwide, since the 1960s, literally millions of people have been involved in satanic and/or witchcraft ritual. Witchcraft and Satanism are spreading like a cancer today, in ways that only a generation ago would have been considered impossible. The newspaper reports in many countries are remarkably similar in their acceptance of the fact that this dreaded phenomenon in our midst is a serious problem.

Even today in America there are thousands of adults who claim to remember satanic abuse as a child, including such things as rape, cannibalism, and human sacrifice done in honor to Satan.

Most people tend to scoff at such reports either from an inbred skepticism or because little or no evidence exists to corroborate the claims of these individuals.

We cannot say how many of these stories are true, but we think it is wrong to dismiss them all. If occultism has a long history of such activities, and if no one denies that there are tens of thousands of members of Satanist and related groups in America, we think some of these accounts are more likely to be explained by something real than merely by people's imaginations.

We think that we ignore the revival of paganism at our own risk. Let us give an example. Like some science-fiction horror story where the AIDS virus assumes human form and hunts down victim after victim, serial killers now stalk the land—estimates range from several hundred to several thousand. We think the chances are good that many (not all) serial killers initially began their slaughter inspired by Satanism or other forms of the occult.

Collectively, serial killers may be responsible for thousands of murders. (A few have at least confessed to murders in the hundreds.) We are familiar with some of the names: Ted Bundy and Charles Boardman each murdered over 40 people; John Wayne Gacy murdered 33 young men and boys. Richard Ramirez (the night stalker) allegedly murdered two dozen people. David Berkowitz ("Son of Sam") murdered at least six individuals, with seven wounded; Peter Sutcliffe (the "Yorkshire Ripper") murdered 13 women. Henry Lee Lucas murdered who knows how many. There are also the older cases: Richard Benjamin Speck murdered eight nurses; Charles Manson's family murdered at least seven people, but according to some authorities probably over 30.

These persons kill large numbers of people wantonly, without remorse; they often murder in a vicious manner. Further, there are sometimes indications of possible or actual occult or satanic involvement in the lives of these people: Ramirez, Lucas, Berkowitz, Sutcliffe, Manson, etc:

> Convicted mass murderers Richard Berkowitz (Son of Sam) in New York and Henry Lee Lucas in Texas have both confessed to being part of Satanic cults involving blood sacrifice. In Montana, Stanley Dean Baker dismembered a man he had stabbed 27 times, took out his heart and ate it. He had one of the

man's fingers in his pocket at the time of his arrest. . . . In Massachusetts, a Satanic cult killed a 20-year-old woman, cut off her fingers, slit her throat, and severed her head and kicked it around. The leader, Carl Drew, then had sex with the decapitated body.[28]

Further, the connection between gruesome murders and spirit possession has long been noted. Psychic researcher and authority on spiritism in the 1920s, Carl A. Wickland, M.D., observed that "in many cases of revolting murder, investigation will show that the crimes were committed by innocent persons [sic] under the control of disembodied spirits who had taken complete possession of the murderer."[29] Although we disagree such persons are "innocent," or with Wickland's mediumistic view of such spirits (deceased men who were evil), the spiritistic hypothesis is credible biblically (Psalm 106:35-40; John 8:44), historically, and culturally. In *Murder for Magic: Witchcraft in Africa*, Alastair Scolri notes, "This type of killing [ritual murder] can be found in a great many African tribes and districts."[30] He refers to "the rise in ritual murder, the utter brutality of the crimes [and] the hideous beliefs that lead to them."[31]

Why do we think some serial killers may be satanically inspired?

In 1987 award-winning reporter Maury Terry published *The Ultimate Evil: An Investigation of America's Most Dangerous Satanic Cult*.[32] In that text he links mass murderers Charles Manson and David Berkowitz to a gruesome satanic networking that crisscrosses America and is murdering untold numbers of persons:

> There is compelling evidence of the existence of a nationwide network of satanic cults, some aligned more closely than others. Some are purveying narcotics; others have branched into child pornography and violent sadomasochistic crime, including murder. I am concerned that the toll of innocent victims will

steadily mount unless law enforcement officials recognize the threat and face it.
   Unlike some of those authorities, I've been there. I
know how serious the situation is.[33]

   With the drug/pornography/snuff film/occult links to the Atlanta child murders in mind as well (see Appendix C), one can
only ask, How many serial killers were bred and born within the
blood-soaked loins of that segment of occultism that has traveled
throughout history within almost all cultures, murdering and
sacrificing collectively *millions* of innocent people?

   Now America is receiving a taste of that paganism which she is
increasingly turning to. And as far as the satanic cult leaders
whom Terry exposes, "There is not a shred of evidence to suggest
they have stopped recruiting young people, stopped twisting
impressionable minds or stopped planning the periodic slaying of
victims."[34]

   But concerning the level of ignorance that exists within society
in general and the church in particular as to these activities, we
are reminded of a statement by scientist Ralph Lapp, concerned
over the implications of the scientific and technological revolu-
tions:

   No one, not even the most brilliant scientist alive
   today, really knows where science is taking us today.
   We are aboard a train which is gathering speed,
   racing down a track on which there are an unknown
   number of destinations. No single scientist is in the
   engine cab and there may be demons at the switch.
   Most of society is in the caboose looking backward.[35]

   And that seems to be the position of society, law enforcement
agencies, and the church concerning Satanism: in the caboose
looking backward. Larry Kahaner's *Cults That Kill* reveals that
police authorities often give their officers strict orders not to
discuss occult crimes. Many captains simply refuse to believe
such crimes even exist. It is too bizarre, it is bad public relations

for municipalities, lawyers will use the concept of satanic influence to plead diminished capacity, Satanism is protected by the First Amendment, etc., are some of the reasons for avoiding the reality.

We simply do not want to believe in evil at so horrendous a level, and so nothing is done and the evil proliferates.

Maury Terry shows that (as was true for the Atlanta murders) the Berkowitz murders were done on witchcraft holidays[36] and he cites certain types of murders connected with corpses, body wounds, and sexual activity that are sickening beyond belief. He observes that police departments are still skeptical, "virtually powerless," and woefully unprepared to deal with the problem, and yet that most of the Satanists "are young and successful people from professional walks of life."[37] He also makes it clear that no one is safe. In mentioning one of the groups he reveals some startling facts:

New information which made its way to me in mid-July of 1986 was specific: not only was the Chingon cult still active; it had now established strong financial ties with a private college in the Los Angeles area. *The cult's wealthy leaders were said to be funding the institution, and satanic activity was in fact flourishing on the campus.*

At the same time, police in the Los Angeles area and two former L.A. Satanists sent word that an East Coast cult branch allied with the Chingons—the Black Cross—was operating as an elite "hit squad" for various U.S. satanic groups involved in drug and pornography enterprises. Obviously, the narcotics and child-porn details further confirmed earlier New York prison allegations. And as for the Black Cross itself, it appeared to be closely linked to the [Son of] Sam cult in New York and existed for one purpose: murder.

Its function, the California contacts said, was the elimination of defecting cult members or other enemies, including innocent people who inadvertently learned about a given group's illegal activities. Murder, anywhere in the country, was now but a phone call away for the cults tied in to the Chingon network.[38]

When Satanist high priest Anton LaVey heralded our modern era as "the Age of Satan"[39] he was apparently not far from the truth. Today books on Satanism have sold in the millions. LaVey's first book, *The Satanic Bible*, has sold over 750,000 copies;[40] and apparently, it frequently turns up in police investigations of occult crime.[41]

Since *The Satanic Bible* was published in 1969, Satan worship has increased dramatically. Many park rangers encounter satanic sites so frequently they may no longer report them.[42] Satanism is producing problems in many American communities. Several major cities on the West Coast have aired special segments dealing with Satanism. For example, Channel 7 Eyewitness News in Los Angeles, California, ran a week-long special devoted to the topic in February 1986. It documented the increase of Satanism, the secrecy, the desecration of churches, ritual animal sacrifices, etc. Satanic graffiti included "Hail, Satan" and "Kill all the Christians." Satanists were interviewed who stated their beliefs. One man (who had carved 666 on his arm) stated: "This says I believe in Satan, worship Satan, believe that he is master, that he is lord."

Another Satanist replied that the reason for his involvement was "strength and power and everything else that goes along with it: drugs, women, money, violence." Both were members of a gang called "the Stoners" and were interviewed from the California Youth Authority in Chino where they were wards of the state. A connection was noted between devil worship and heavy metal rock music; indeed, there are apparently hundreds of heavy metal/"Stoner" gangs with various degrees of involvement in Satanism.

A number of murders related to Satanism were also cited. One former Satanist admitted on camera to murdering his father and to the attempted murder of his mother when he was 17. His story began early in the fourth grade with an interest in the occult which developed into an interest in Satan. Richard Frederickson, the Orange County assistant district attorney, noted a gruesome local fact. Where one or more parents were murdered by their children, "Of those 6-8 cases there is probably 5 that have had some sort of overtones of Satanism."

Incredibly, in spite of the obvious evils of Satanism, there are actually respected scholars today who laud its alleged "social benefits"![43]

Cases of probable or actual Satanist-related murders/suicides are found in *Maclean's*, March 30, 1987; March 26, 1990; June 22, 1992; *Redbook*, April 1989; *Rolling Stone*, June 11, 1992; *The Cleveland Plain Dealer*, February 3, 1985; *The San Diego Tribune*, January 23, 1986; *Christianity Today*, April 18, 1986; the *Dallas Morning News*, February 25, 1982; *The Detroit News*, January 13, 1988; *Jefferson City (MO) Post Tribune*, September 20, 1989; *Orange County (CA) Register*, March 8, 1990; *San Francisco Chronicle*, March 15, 1988; *Milwaukee (WI) Journal*, June 4, 1989; *The Star-Ledger* (Fairfield, CT), March 21, 1986; and many other sources. The Cable News Network reported on August 25, 1985, that a family found to be involved in making snuff films had allegedly murdered children in the process. They were suspected of involvement in Satanism and ritual murder and had been arrested on child molesting charges three years earlier.

It is a lack of evidence in satanic crime which is the greatest problem law enforcement agencies face (see Appendix C). Without hard evidence, police are powerless. Yet, the highly secretive nature of serious Satanism means that all evidence of a crime is carefully disposed of. Thus, when the police or TV news reporters usually conclude, "We found no evidence of a satanic crime," the public tends to think no crime was ever committed. But anyone who has studied Satanism knows that crimes are being committed, for criminal activity is inherently compatible with Satanism—and much other paganism.

High school teacher Joy Childress is one wounded survivor of Satanism who tries to warn others:

I was in the Satanic cult from birth until I was twenty-one years old. My whole family was in the cult. It was generational as my grandfather on my mother's side also participated. My experience deals with ritualistic rape, ritualistic sacrificing of children and dogs, mainly German shepherds, ritualistic eating of flesh, feces, vomit and urine, and ritualistic drinking of animal or human blood. . . . It was a family cult—made up entirely of families. At one time, the high priest was an ordained Baptist minister of a prominent church in Denver, Colorado. . . . Some of the ceremonies would be performed to gain Satan's power through the terror of the child. The child would be starved, tortured, and raped in order to gain that power. Some of the ceremonies were strictly for sacrificial killings for Satan. The child would be killed with a knife through the heart while a cult member was raping the child. The point of all this was to have the sexual climax at the point of death of the child. . . . The bodies were always burned. Some of the bones were kept as implements for the ceremonies. . . . These things do upset me very much when I talk about them, but people need to know and understand that these things really did happen and are still happening.[44]

Detective Sandi Gallant of the Intelligence Division of the San Francisco Police Department is among the most respected of police officers who investigate occult crime. She observes, "With organized groups, it is very deliberate that we were not finding any evidence of criminal activity. They're much too careful and hide their tracks very well."[45]

Lack of evidence and public denials by Satanists may fool some people, but it will never change the nature of serious Satanism itself, which is inherently anti-moral and dedicated to the promulgation of evil. Having said this, we must observe that Satanism and satanic practices may vary by group.

Varieties of Satanism

What is Satanism? Satanism is the belief in and/or invocation and worship of Satan as a supernatural being. Some Satanists view Satan as an impersonal force or energy, or even a religious symbol representing the material world and carnal nature of mankind.[46]

Properly, Satanism must be distinguished from witchcraft and other forms of the occult. Witches and other occultists are not typically Satanists (a few are) and usually resent the association. Of course, all categories of occultists engage in biblically forbidden practices and, scripturally, the devil is associated with these, but such persons neither worship nor necessarily believe in Satan, nor do they necessarily deliberately pervert Christianity ritually and morally in the manner of Satanism.

Satanism is not a monolithic entity, hence a given sect cannot by definition be lumped with all other groups. Groups are eclectic and draw upon various occult, magical, and pagan sources. Other groups are autonomous and garner their activities and beliefs from different Satanist traditions or tributaries. As a whole, Satanism is not uniform in its organizational structure, practices, or beliefs.

Thus, there are different types of satanic groups, from traditional to nontraditional, and many different types of practitioners, from zealot to dabbler. Both groups and individuals may vary in their degree of secrecy, degree of hostility to Christianity, eclecticism, religious worldview (e.g., philosophy of magic, view of God and Satan, the afterlife, etc.), and their degree of deviancy and criminality.

But whatever we may note of the differences among Satanists, strong commonalities remain: 1) every individual Satanist has chosen to identify himself with a being, practice, or symbol that virtually all society correctly views as malevolent, deviant, and evil; 2) every Satanist sooner or later personally engages in evil —and often unimaginable perversion; and 3) every Satanist rejects the Christian God and courts the devil whether or not he/she accepts these categories as biblically defined.

Whatever Satanism's sociological or religious classification then, Satanism per se is *inherently* evil. This must never be forgotten. Hawkins observes of one grouping of Satanists:

> . . . their seething hatred and utter contempt for God and Christians. . . . They feel it would be better to fully indulge themselves in this life, and if nothing else, be alive and burning with hatred for all eternity than to merely exist in heaven. In short, they feel it is more satisfying to live ungodly and follow the most ungodly of all—Satan—than to live with and for God.[47]

Hawkins also observes some of the inherently religious, pagan motivations behind human sacrifice:

> Besides these there are two other possible reasons for sacrifices. The first is connected with the notions of the supernormal latent psychic abilities and forces or laws of nature. The sacrifice is slaughtered at the height of the ritual to augment the Satanist's own psychic energy (a psychological charge), thus increasing the Satanist's chances for success in obtaining the purpose of the ritual. The idea is that the energy or life-force of the sacrifice when killed is released into the surrounding atmosphere and can be harnessed by the Satanist. . . . Second, pertaining to the supernatural (demonic) view, the slaughtering of the victim is literally a sacrifice to the demons, who in return will grant or cause to be brought about whatever is desired. The greater the request, the "greater" the sacrifice must be. . . . The younger and healthier the animal, and more so with humans, the worthier the sacrifice. Also, since this type of Satanist operates on the principle of completely perverting and reversing Christianity, he believes that he will increase his power by performing more and more heinous acts.

The most precious and innocent thing for a Christian
is a little child: Conversely, the sacrificing of a child
would be the most efficacious (supreme sacrifice) for
a Satanist. It is plainly one of the greatest perversions
of Christian principles possible, and for this reason it
is considered the more magically potent.[48]

In "Satanism and the Devolution of the 'New Religions,' " Dr.
Carl Raschke mentions a taped interview with a seminary student involved in occultism who describes a secret society he
claims is responsible for the kidnapping and sacrifice of children,
and he also notes the fact that there are U.S. military personnel
who are members of secretive Satanist groups. (Incidentally, the
military is required by law to recognize Satanism and witchcraft
as legitimate religions. A U.S. government handbook for Satanist chaplains in the armed forces is now available.)[49] Raschke
also ties together some of the interrelationships between Satanism, the new religions, and modern decadent American culture.[50] (Lest we think "decadent" too strong a term, we should
be mindful of the statistics on abortion, pornography, crime,
homosexuality, suicide, drug abuse, alcoholism, sexually transmitted disease, and related issues.)

Raschke points out that the decadence and criminality which
may be found in the new religions, in Satanism, and in American
culture itself have certain social and spiritual ties that bind them
together and reveal they are part of a similar spiritual genus.

He observes that the "upsurge of Satanist practices . . . must
be interpreted not as some kind of odd wrinkle in the present day
texture of religious change, but as a culminating phase of the
"New Age" movement, for which the so-called new religions of
the past two decades have provided a fertile environment in which
to flourish.[51] He also points out the satanic elements found in
some heavy metal rock groups (aspects of which these authors
have personally confirmed), and secular culture in general may
help to spread an underground Satanism among the youth. Thus:

The Satanist mindset is not "religion" in the regular sense of the word, but a mystification of the most

corrupt secular passions and values.... When the
invidious amorality of secular culture traps certain
individuals in its own unreality, which is ritually rein-
forced by the electronic media, it is very likely that a
similarly bizarre and demonic kind of religious thea-
ter will come into play. Satanism is but the spiritual
Frankenstein created by a social order that has attempted to sustain itself without God.[52]

Of course, drug use also plays a key role in Satanism, and tens
of millions of Americans use illegal drugs. In fact, the drug and
cult culture of the 1960s helped pave the way for modern Satanism. Significantly, drug use is not only common in Satanism,
witchcraft, and pagan religion; drug trafficking is also found
among certain of the new religions.

Drug use was religiously "romanticized" in the popular culture through various books such as Carlos Castanadas' *Don Juan*
series and observed in many anthropological investigations of
tribal life as one key means to contact the spirit world.

Drug use is thus evident in all three categories: Satanism,
decadent culture, and the new religions. Concerning the latter,
Raschke observes that the "overwhelming majority of cult
inductees in the early seventies had been substance abusers" and
goes on to refer to several former cult members' testimonies as to
their sect's involvement in heavy drug trafficking.[53] Our own
research into scores of the new religions confirm this, as do
reports in the popular press. Drugs, of course, provide not only
"instant transcendence" and openness to the spirit world through
altered states, but they also make members more compliant and
dependent on the cult (not to mention providing a sizable cash
flow to undergird cult operations).

Thus, the various connections between the original counter-
culture of the sixties with its widespread drug abuse and the new
religious movements which are typically occultic indicate the
linkage to Satanism. Raschke observes:

The most alarming aspect of the alliance between
cultism and the world of drugs has to do with the now

widely reported cocaine epidemic. Cocaine has been the preferred drug for ceremonial purposes in black witchcraft circles since Aleister Crowley first commended it (Grinspoon & Bakalar, 1976). Its manic and ego-bolstering properties increase the feeling of "power," which is so critical for magical rituals. Additionally, in the Satanist perspective the historical association of cocaine use with the priestly religions of pre-Columbian civilizations lends the drug an archaic mystique. There are numerous stories circulating about the revival of "authentic" human sacrifices among contemporary Satanists, which perhaps indicates another link with the pre-Columbians who did likewise. These practices, together with the tales about them, may very well be an integral element of the sadism and terrorism furthered within Satanist networks. . . . If cocaine trafficking is as clearly bound up with Nazi/Satanist occultism as the evidence is beginning to show, then the widespread occurrence of the former must of logical necessity indicate the influence of the latter (Geyer, 1985).[54]

Again, that such evil should be perpetuated by Satanists is not surprising; killing others is part of their reason for living. Also not surprising is the deviant nature of many individual Satanists or their connection to deviant culture. For example, Professor E. J. Moody of the Queen's University of Belfast, Ireland, was a member of the "First Church of the Trapezoid, the Church of Satan" in San Francisco for two-and-a-half years as a "participant observer." In his article "Magical Therapy: An Anthropological Investigation of Contemporary Satanism," he noted the connection:[55]

A single factor seemed to typify all of them; all were deviant or abnormal in some aspect of their social behavior. . . . The roots of abnormality among the pre-Satanists interviewed reported childhoods marred by strife: they spoke of broken homes, drunken parents, aggressive and hostile siblings, and so on.[56]

Raschke also points out the following:

> In one of the few genuine "anthropological" investigations of Satanism, written over a decade ago, Arthur Lyons noted that the typical recruit for that form of demented religiosity was the sociopath or hardened criminal (1970). Thus, from a purely analytical standpoint, Satanism represents a kind of hallowing of the deviant, a glorification of what is noxious and felonious. Indeed as Stephen Kaplan, a national radio celebrity who specializes in the investigation of "blood cults," told me during a telephone interview several years ago, the peculiar "ethic" of Satanism is to harm, injure, kill—to do evil deliberately. In the Satanist mentality the method for achieving special distinction is an ever flagrant transgression, not only of social conventions, but of time-honored codes of morality and justice. That is the royal road to power. "Do whatst thou wilt," thereby freeing the conscience from all constraints, was the imperative pronounced earlier this century of Aleister Crowley, the tutelary genius and inspiration for so many of today's dabblers in black magic.[57]

Certainly then, there have been preexisting social tendencies for the emergence of Satanism, and by its very nature the practice tends to reinforce socially and religiously deviant personalities. So who should be surprised that Satanists commit crimes?

One three-month investigation, involving personal interviews and eyewitness testimony, claims that in 1984-85 in Los Angeles alone there were 27 neighborhoods with reported satanic activity, including at least six murders with Satanic ties.[58] It also claims the Satanists have deliberately organized foster homes and day-care centers to help further their purposes.[59]

The Satanists' strategy against children is also noted, quoting Lawrence Pazder, M.D.:

> One of the primary aims is to destroy the belief system within a child, to make a child turn against what they believe in, in terms of who they are, of who God is, and to desecrate all manner of flesh, all manner of church institution, all manner of sign and symbol that a child could in any way be attached to. Many of the children who have been ritually abused won't go near a church or have anything to do with the clergy because their abusers have molested them in churches while dressed as priests or other clergy members. Other perpetrators have dressed as policemen.[60]

One psychologist stated:

> The children have been abused in a way that is meant to make them sadistic. It is meant to make them murderers. It is meant to make them pedophiles. It is meant to make them sadistic, hateful, hurtful individuals.[61]

But we should not forget that, in spite of their activities, many Satanists are indistinguishable from our next-door neighbors. They are successful professionals who appear (at least outwardly) to be emotionally well-adjusted. Unfortunately, because Satanism and Satanist practices are by definition abnormal and deviant, any person who becomes a Satanist will sooner or later become corrupted far beyond what the normal course of his life would have produced.

What does all this mean? Perhaps it means our nation is in trouble. It means that parents, without overreacting, need to be vigilant over the activities of their children. It means all of us need to pray more, for Satanism is not the real problem. It is only the tip of the iceberg—one more symptom of spreading spiritual death in our culture.

6

Satanism and Witchcraft: The Occult and the East

In this chapter we will discuss the relationship between witch-craft and Satanism on the one hand and Eastern religion (espe-cially Tantrism) on the other. We have included this chapter because of the great influence of Eastern religion in the West and the fact that few people seem to be aware of such connections. For millions of Westerners, Eastern religions are viewed rather benevolently as examples of "wisdom of the East." Unfor-tunately, Eastern religion also carries a dark undercurrent with which even devotees are often unfamiliar.

In her *Drawing Down the Moon: Witches, Druids, Goddess-Worshippers and Other Pagans in America Today*, Margo Adler interviewed numerous prominent witches who discussed the expe-rience and philosophy of witchcraft. The parallels to East-ern religion and occultism were obvious. These witches make correlations to yoga, shamanism, developing altered states of consciousness, the realization of inner divinity, and alleged con-nection to the "infinite." Witches themselves speak of witchcraft as being "the Yoga of the West" and that "a Witch is a type of European shaman":

> Adrian Kelly told me, "What really defines a Witch is a type of *experience* people go through. These experiences depend on altered states of con-sciousness. The Craft is really the Yoga of the West." Morning Glory Zell said that a Witch is a type of

European shaman, and being a Witch involves being a priestess or priest, a psychopomp, a healer, a guide. . . .

Most Witches stressed that the goal of the Craft was helping people to reclaim their lost spiritual heritage, their affinity with the earth, with "the gods," with the infinite.[1]

It is well documented that numerous perversions (including human sacrifice) occur in witchcraft and Satanism, and yet these also have a rich tradition in Eastern religion (e.g., Hinduism), as well as pagan occult religion in general.[2] In his *Occultism, Witchcraft and Cultural Fashions*, the noted cultural anthropologist Mircea Eliade of the University of Chicago refers to the interconnections between European witchcraft and Hindu Tantric yoga. He points out that "even a rapid perusal of the Hindu and Tibetan documents" reveals the connection:

As a matter of fact, all the features associated with European witches are—with the exception of Satan and the sabbath—claimed also by Indo-Tibetan yogis and magicians. They too are supposed to fly through the air, render themselves invisible, kill at a distance, master demons and ghosts, and so on. Moreover, some of these eccentric Indian sectarians boast that they break all the religious taboos and social rules: that they practice human sacrifice, cannibalism, and all manner of orgies, including incestuous intercourse, and that they eat excrement, nauseating animals, and devour human corpses. In other words, they proudly claim all the crimes and horrible ceremonies cited *ad nauseam* in the western European witch trials.[3]

"The Witches of Orissa" is another article by Satindra Roy published in a Bombay anthropology journal. It makes the following observations about a particular sect of Indian witchcraft. Roy begins by noting the connections between the witch cult and Tantra's Shakti (power) worship.

The witches of Orissa still show a great reverence
for the cult of Tantras. . . . Their deep reverence for
the cult of the Tantras and their intimate connection
with the Tantric shrine at Kamrup leave no shadow of
doubt that witchcraft, whatever it is, has its connection with Shakti worship. . . . The powers for evil
develop themselves by worshipping the terrible aspect of Shakti, and some worshippers after passing
through the lower stages . . . use their evil influence
on all and sundry with whom they come into contact. . . .

It may be noted here that Orissa was at one time,
almost wholly converted to Tantric Buddhism, which
slowly made room for Vaishnavism, which is now the
popular religion of Orissa. . . . The Tantrics also used
to develop great powers of evil, which they could
apply against their antagonists if enraged or pro-
voked.[4]

He proceeds to show that the witches apparently derived their
powers for evil from magical incantations learned from Hindu
gurus. Significantly, we find they may endure the characteristic
death struggle of occultists:

It is believed that the witches derive their powers
for evil from certain incantations which they learn
from their gurus. . . . It is believed that the witches at
the time of their death suffer intolerable pain if they
cannot transmit these incantations to a willing convert. Witches during their lifetime also show very
great solicitude for the propagation of the secret cult
and make converts whenever possible. . . .

There are some witches whose evil-eye is so strong
that it would kill a playful child within a few minutes if
it is cast upon him.[5]

An anti-moral pragmatism is a strong feature of Satanism and
witchcraft on the one hand and much Eastern religion on the

other. For example, in a standard text entitled *Yoga: Immortality and Freedom*, the late yoga authority and University of Chicago professor Mircea Eliade observes the amoral orientation of much yoga.

> The tantric texts frequently repeat the saying, "By the same acts that cause some men to burn in hell for thousands of years, the yogin gains his eternal salvation." ... This, as we know, is the foundation stone of the Yoga expounded by Krishna in the *Bhagavad Gita* (XVIII,17). "He who has no feeling of egoism, and whose mind is not tainted, even though he kills (all) these people, kills not, is not fettered (by the action)." And the *Brhadaranyaka Upanishad* (V, 14, 8) had already said: "One who knows this, although he commits very much evil, consumes it all and becomes clean and pure, ageless and immortal."[6]

Further, the goals of the sexual union in Tantra and witchcraft on the one hand and in magic/Satanism on the other are also similar.[7] For example, in Tantra and witchcraft we find the predominance of the feminine energy theme.[8] In both categories we find occasional cannibalism, ritual cruelty, a preoccupation with death, ritual sacrifice, ritual insanity, anarchy, and horrible degradations in general.[9]

In *Our Savage God: The Perverse Use of Eastern Thought* (1974), Spalding professor of comparative religion at Oxford, R. C. Zaehner, discusses the monistic goals of Hinduism and Buddhism and how certain persons have applied such philosophy to their own ends.[10]

For example, the notorious Satanist Aleister Crowley was influenced by Eastern concepts and experienced an enlightenment undergirded by his belief in the philosophical monism of the East:

> Crowley has been condemned as the arch-Satanist, but this is perhaps to do him less than justice, for he

belonged to an age-old tradition which saw the Eternal as the ultimate unity in which all the opposites were reconciled, including good and evil. He had lived in the East and was familiar with the scriptures of both the Hindus and Buddhists for whom these ideas were commonplace, but whereas the early Buddhists at least considered that training in good life was a necessary prerequisite for the realization of the Eternal, there were occult sects among both religions who disputed this and practiced what they preached. [11]

Zaehner also discusses Crowley's achievement of Buddhist "enlightenment," the results of which were accordingly "revised" by his spirit guide "Aiwass" who, having helped him go beyond the categories of good and evil, now taught him not renunciation but, with the Tantrics, indulgence:

It may be assumed that in which John Symonds calls his "Buddhist phase," when, in what is now Vietnam, he attained to one of the higher Buddhist trances ("Neroda-Sammapatti," more correctly spelt *nirodha-samapatti*), which corresponds to what we would call the annihilation of the ego, he was tempted to turn his back on the world which, for the Buddhists, is not only full of sorrow and anxiety but actually is sorrow and anxiety, thereby attaining to the unutterable peace of Nirvana. This, however, was not the way of his "Holy Guardian Angel," Aiwass, who taught him that absolute bliss could only be attained by enjoying the good things of this world to the full—riches, power, and above all sex, the earthly counterpart of the transcendent union of the opposites. [12]

As a result, Crowley began the utilization of sexual rites for ostensibly "spiritual" ends. His "Ordo Templi Orientalis" (Order of the Oriental Temple or O.T.O.) became a branch of

Western Tantra; indeed Crowley seems to have been the principal agent responsible for introducing the perversion of Eastern sexual magic to the West.

> He developed elaborate rites of sexual "magick." . . . OTO . . . had connections with the left-hand Tantra in India, the adepts of which practiced sexual magic, their purpose being to attain to the Absolute through the union of the opposites, that is, the male and female principles allegedly inherent in the one true God. [13]

Yet strangely, Crowley's first experience of this "union of opposites" was an act of sodomy. "Be that as it may, the fact remains that it was largely Crowley who was responsible for introducing Indian sexual magic into the West." [14]

Zaehner proceeds to discuss how Manson also carried Crowley's philosophy to its logical conclusion: "If God is one, what is bad?" [15]

> Manson carried Crowley's premises to their logical conclusions: if God and the Devil, good and evil, life and death, can really be transcended in an eternal Now, then sadism and sexual profligacy are not enough: you must transcend life and death itself either by killing or being killed. Charles Manson did not shrink from this ultimate "truth." [16]

Manson, of course, was only convicted of nine murders—brutal and sadistic as they were. He most certainly committed many more. In *Helter Skelter*, prosecutor Vincent Bugliosi cites a figure of 35 that even Manson boasted of[17]—and some suspect this number is probably too low.

> "It was fun," said Tex Watson after the so-called Tate murders in which five human beings were stabbed and gunned to death, including the actress Sharon

Tate, heavy with child and pleading for the new life within her. What a hope! They left her to the last so that she could see the butchery of her friends and then sliced her up in her turn. "It was fun." Or, in the words of Susan Atkins, the most savage as well as the most devoted of Charlie's Family: "It felt so good, the first time I stabbed her." "Charlie was happy."[18]

Nevertheless, a major justification for such vicious murders was provided by Eastern philosophy and texts, a philosophy which is, unfortunately, increasingly permeating Western society:

> Charles Manson had claimed to be Jesus Christ, but he was also much influenced by Indian ideas which filtered through to him through such sects as OTO, "The Process," and "The Fountain of the World." From these ultimately Indian sources he derived the theory of reincarnation and *karma*.[19]
>
> So spake the ancient Hindu text; and it spoke rightly, for in eternity there can be no action, but in time each man seems to have his own particular part to play: everyone has his own *karma,* as Charlie knew, and, for better or for worse, "death was Charlie's trip."
>
> This is a great mystery—and the eternal paradox with which the Eastern religions perpetually wrestle. If the ultimate truth, or the "perennial philosophy" as Aldous Huxley called it, is that "All is One" and "One is All," and that in this One all the opposites, including good and evil, are eternally reconciled, then have we any right to blame Charles Manson? For seen from the point of view of the eternal Now, he *did* nothing at all.[20]

By achieving an Eastern form of "enlightenment," Manson apparently believed he had become free from all constraints.

Charles Manson had achieved what the Zen Buddhists call enlightenment, the supreme lightning flash of which shatters the time barrier, and through which one is reborn in eternity, where time does not exist and death is an almost laughable impossibility. All things are fused into one. . . .

Lucidly he drew the obvious conclusion which our modern Zen Buddhists do all they can to hush up. Where he had been all things were One and there was "no diversity at all": he had passed beyond good and evil. At last he was *free!*[21]

Along with a number of modern Eastern gurus (e.g., Rajneesh—see Tal Brooke, *Riders on the Cosmic Circuit*), the end point for Manson was a preoccupation with death:

The experience provided by Zen is sometimes called cosmic consciousness. This is the second level of consciousness from which Charles Manson acted. . . .

Once you have reached the stage of the eternal Now, all is One, as Parmenides taught in ancient Greece. "After all," Manson said, "we are all one." Killing someone therefore is just like breaking off a piece of cookie.[22]

Manson was merely driving Eastern principles to their logical conclusions:

The end and goal of both Hinduism and Buddhism is to pass into a form of existence in which time and space and all the opposites that bedevil human existence are totally transcended and in which one is literally "dead" to the world but alive in a timeless eternity. This ritual death Charlie had already experienced, and, as a result of the experience, he had taught his disciples that they must kill themselves in this way in order to kill others and be free from remorse.[23]

One of the earliest scriptural texts that seems to justify Manson's philosophy of killing and being killed is found in the *Katha* Upanishad (2:19): "Should the killer think: "I kill," or the killed: "I have been killed," both these have no [right] knowledge: he does not kill nor is he killed." So too Charlie Manson draws his conclusions: "There is no good, there is no evil. . . . You can't kill kill" and "If you're willing to be killed, you should be willing to kill." In terms of Indian religion this makes sense as we shall see: if all things are ultimately One, as Heraclitus in our own tradition said, then the individual as individual does not really exist. So, according to his disciples, Charlie had transcended all desire: *qua* Charlie, then, he was dead. "It wasn't Charlie any more. It was the Soul. They were all Charlie and Charlie was they."[24]

Thus, Manson was not really crazy; he was acting "rationally" in accordance with the metaphysically insightful "wisdom" of the East.

Charles Manson was absolutely sane: he had been *there*, where there is neither good or evil. . . .
"This is not I: this is not mine: this is not the self: this has nothing to do with self." This refrain runs throughout the whole Buddhist tradition in all its multifarious forms. Your ego does not exist in any shape or form that you could possibly identify with yourself. This is indeed the essence of the gospel according to Charles Manson too.[25]

The fact that Manson had also perverted the book of Revelation to his own ends underscores an important point. Zaehner subtitled his book "the perverse use of Eastern thought." But what is clear both from his text and monistic Eastern religious philosophy in general is that the perverse use of Eastern thought is also "the logical use of Eastern thought"—no matter how many of the romantically inclined may assert otherwise. The justification of any and all evil is indeed a logical, permitted conclusion flowing from a monistic, amoral premise—whether Hindu, Buddhist, or occult.

But such is a logical conclusion which cannot be extrapolated from biblical Scripture because of 1) the holy and good nature of its God, 2) the inherent value and dignity of man who is created in God's image, and 3) the logical connection that exists between the prohibitory commands against murder ("Thou shalt not kill") and the holy, loving nature of the God who issued the commands.

On the other hand, in Hinduism and Buddhism or in the occult, the lesser gods are often evil and God or ultimate reality itself is impersonal and amoral—hence unconcerned with human actions of any type.

As Eliade observes in *The Sacred and the Profane*, "What demands emphasis is the fact that religious [pagan] man sought to imitate, and believed that he was imitating, his gods even when he allowed himself to be led into acts that verged on madness, depravity and crime."[26]

Thus, literally every perverse act—orgies, murder, human sacrifice, rape, sex with demons, copulating with and then eating human corpses, and other things vile—became justified by pagan religion. Indeed, such religion has always justified its own evils. What is so disconcerting today is the extent to which the West is turning to paganism and perhaps preparing the soil for ancient practices to be resumed.

Dr. Nigel Davies is an archaeologist and anthropologist who has written *The Aztecs*, *The Toltecs*, and an important subsequent text called *Human Sacrifice in History and Today* (1981), which dispels certain scholarly biases. Davies documents that human sacrifice is not a historical anomaly. Rather, it is an "Aztec Specialty," a natural component of pagan religion, and far more common than most persons think. Indeed, it is

> part of the common heritage of mankind, present in
> practically all societies in every era—among higher

civilizations just as much as among primitive peoples —and with surprisingly universal similarities.... Human sacrifice continues today.[27]

One thing is clear. It was the twisted logic and demonism of pagan religion which justified murder for a variety of religious motives.

> In essence human sacrifice was an act of piety. Both sacrificer and victim knew that the act was required, to save the people from calamity and the cosmos from collapse. Their object was, therefore, more to preserve than to destroy life.[28]

and,

> Ancient gods... expected flesh and blood, obtained through the medium of a ritual, without which the gift had neither worth nor meaning. Ritual and religion are inseparable from human sacrifice; indeed, we may define the term as killing with a spiritual or religious motivation, usually, but not exclusively, accompanied by ritual.[29]

The reasons for the murders were numerous, because the "gods" needed appeasement to stay the endless problems of humanity. Thus, men were murdered for the satisfaction of their own deities or to secure their supposed help.

> In the course of many millennia, legions of men have been offered up to the gods.... In return the gods were expected to ward off famines, stay the course of plagues, guard buildings, care for the departed, enrich harvests and win battles. These were the favors man needed from his gods. The latter usually responded in the end; it was merely a question of waiting or, if necessary, of making bigger offerings;

given time, the rains came again, the floods subsided, or the pestilence ran its course.[30]

Sacrifices were even necessary in order to "sanctify" new buildings or other structures, already presumed to be the domain of a potentially offended spirit:

> Another very common form of human sacrifice was the rite of interring adults or children in the foundations of new buildings under city gates and bridges. . . . A new building is also a form of intrusion on the domain of the local spirit, whose anger may be aroused and who therefore has to be appeased. . . . Foundation sacrifice was as widespread in Europe as in Asia. . . . The Druids also practiced this rite.[31]

Crop fertility and human procreation also demanded the murder of the innocent:

> In their most basic forms, fertility rites required the sprinkling of human blood or the burial of pieces of human flesh in the fields before sowing; the practice survived into the nineteenth century among certain tribes of India, who reared and fattened victims specially for the purpose. Sacrifices to river gods belong to the same category since the waters that they brought were needed to make plants grow. . . . Barrenness was often held to be an act of God, who deliberately kept back children who would otherwise have been born. The best remedy was to send him other infants to take the place of those he had withheld; slave children usually served the purpose. In some places, in India, for example, the practice was carried to such lengths that if a wife had one son and wanted more, the first-born was slain on the supposition that the gods would then provide a series of

children to take his place. In certain Australian aboriginal tribes, the mother would kill and eat her first child as a means of obtaining more.[32]

Men were even killed to supply the gods with "attendants" in the next world[33]—according to on-site researchers, the Atlanta child murders had a similar theme.[34]

But there are also other motives for sacrifice that are found in some Tantric and occult sects operative today. The goal is to achieve a mystical union with the gods for a variety of purposes.[35]

In conclusion, considered historically, human sacrifice was absent only where a high view of man himself prohibited the taking of life:

> The gods continued to exact the highest gift, that of a fellow-being, as the price of meeting man's pressing needs. They were only forced to settle for less when human beings ceased—in a handful of societies—to be regarded as mere chattels or a means of exchange like any other.[36]

What is difficult to accept is the apparent conclusion of Davies' text. After surveying millennia of ritualized slaughter, he gives a rather novel suggestion. In light of the modern-day penchant for killing other people merely for "mundane" reasons (e.g., anger, jealousy, or money)—he says it might be preferable to return to the ritualized slaughter of the past. This would help exchange one form of slaughter for another, as it were. This would allegedly reduce the number of victims or help "balance" a society so imbalanced that murder and violence are commonplace.

That such a recommendation is even suggested is perhaps a symptom of our times. But it ignores a host of accompanying issues whose collective consequences would be far worse than our current problems with violent crime—not the least of which is pagan religion in general. Of course, we already legalize gambling and abortion to suit our whims. Why not legalize religious murder? Why not, indeed? Why not instead propose a return to

Christian values rather than pagan ones? Why sympathize with paganism? Yet this is the author's approach. After all, can we not at least *understand* the "necessity" for religious murder in the past, given the people's beliefs, however horrified we may be over what are in effect modern religious pagan sacrifices of a slightly different nature?

> Both Manson and Jones had a diabolical hold over their flock, and at times used sex as a weapon to maintain this hold. Under Manson's hypnotic spell Sandy Good was able to declare, "I have finally reached the point where I can kill my parents." Equally Jones mesmerized his people to the degree that they were ready to kill themselves and their children. . . .
>
> So if today a single demonic will can drive hundreds to self-slaughter, it becomes less surprising that in ancient times people were ready if not eager to be slain on the god's altar, when the whole fabric of society and the whole weight of religious tradition demanded this of them.[37]

Thus, lamenting our daily exposure to violence on TV and in real life, and our "ambivalent" attitude toward death, Davies suggests that a return to the past is perhaps worth considering:

> Faced with the mass brutality of our century, real as well as simulated, one may ask whether in its place, man might not do better to revert to the ritualized killings of the past. . . . If violence is endemic, sacrificial violence is at least a more restrained form.[38]

So many people have been sacrificed in so many ways in so many places throughout the world! Will a pagan America offer its own children in sacrifice in the next century? If it adopts pagan religion, it certainly could. We are already seeing the groundwork being laid. For example, in *The Sacrament of Abortion* neo-pagan Ginette Paris, author of *Pagan Meditations* and

Pagan Grace, argues that abortion shouuld be accepted and interpreted as a sacrificial *religious* act, as a sacrament to the pagan goddess Artemis. By sacrificing unborn children to the goddess, we prevent them from living unwanted lives here, Paris alleges. The unborn baby is sacrificed to Artemis, the goddess of childbirth, because unless the gift given to her is pure (in this case, symbolizing a wanted child), she supposedly will refuse to aid in giving birth and life. Therefore, abortion is the proper religious sacrament and sacrifice to Artemis, according to Paris.

Yet the theme of human sacrifice is so universal, one is almost tempted to suggest the devil has instituted his own form of religious sacrifice merely to mock God. Has the devil perverted the idea of a singular divine sacrifice and twisted it into an endless religious evil—a necessary "sacrament" for allegedly securing human welfare and salvation? Is an impotent, ritualistic, demonic murder mocking a loving, divine self-sacrifice—as do the deliberate perversions of the "divine" acts common to Satanism?

But most people today simply turn their heads. A report in the calendar section of the *Los Angeles Times* ("The Bloody Reality of the Maya") is a good illustration of the tendency to believe what we wish. The report by William Wilson discusses translations in a Mayan art exhibit, "The Blood of Kings," organized by the Kimbell Museum of Fort Worth, Texas. Wilson indicates the scholarly will to disbelieve in demonic "blood-soaked" rituals covered up the fact that some Mayan practices even made the Aztec ritual excision of human hearts "seem downright humane." Yet typically, the Maya were convinced that their brutalities were necessary to the preservation of their society.[39] Wilson concludes: "Mayan ways were visible in chilling graphic detail long before the translations. Why didn't Mayan experts of the past see these people clearly? The answer is always the same. They didn't want to."

And with the will to disbelieve we also reject the warnings around us. Manson, Berkowitz, and other mass killers have said they are by no means alone in their "holy" quest.

Sometimes, late at night, one can know the truth of their words. Through the darkness, a foreboding wail can be heard. Faintly at first, then more insistent and nearer, the reverberations ring through urban canyons, roll across the shadowed byways of Scarsdale and Bel Air, and are carried on the night wind to the remote reaches of rural countrysides.

It is a mournful, curdling cry.

It is the sound of America screaming.[40]

7

What Occult Practitioners Say

*Who are the casualties in warfare? The disobedient,
the unarmed, the weak, the undisciplined, and those
with illusions about the war being somewhere else. So
too are the casualties in spiritual warfare.*
—Michael Green, *I Believe
in Satan's Downfall*

A widespread myth in our society is that psychic practices are
something good. Perhaps they are controversial or questioned as
to their legitimacy, but they are certainly not considered harmful.
In the following chapters we will prove this perspective is inde-
fensible and offer specific documentation from a variety of
sources and categories.

We will begin by examining the concerns of occult practitioners themselves. In this chapter we will document that even
those occultly involved are aware of the pitfalls of psychic practice. Unfortunately, such persons often order their thinking along
the lines of a "careful versus careless" approach to the occult,
and it is primarily the latter which they warn about. This view is
itself problematic because it is not how one *approaches* occult
practice that determines safety. All occult practice should be
avoided on the basis of God's warnings and the fact that psychic
exploration easily links one to a demonic realm that is, put simply,
beyond human capacity to master. For example, in his astute
study of human evil, *People of the Lie*, M. Scott Peck points out
that, among humans, evil people are far more prevalent than

most suspect and that "these who are evil are masters of disguise; they are not apt to wittingly disclose their true colors—either to others or to themselves."[1] If this is true among men, how much more must it be true among those spirits who are even yet more cunning and more evil?

For example, no rational person goes swimming in shark-infested waters. The only people who do either don't believe in sharks, don't know sharks are present, or are just plain fool-hardy. Of course, there are those who might enter the water because they have been assured the fins they see are the fins of playful dolphins. But in a moment of terror they will discover too late that a horrible mistake was made.

Nevertheless, those who practice the occult today believe in the safety of their activities for a variety of reasons.

Psychics are convinced their psychic gifts are from God (hence "godly"), or that they constitute benevolent higher powers of the mind available to anyone. What could be wrong with seeking God? What could be dangerous about developing *human* poten-tial?

Occultists who engage in more serious rituals, but are care-fully trained by adepts, believe they have the personal wisdom to conduct their practices safely. One Satanist told us that because he was united to the powers of darkness he had no *reason* to fear them.

Parapsychologists believe they retain the safeguards of science in their research into occult phenomena.

Followers of Eastern paths accept the promises of their guru that he will protect them from possible harm.

But in every case, these people are pursuing a path of potential danger.

Unfortunately, even when confronted with the hazards, most of those involved seem to feel that the dangers don't apply to them personally and that somehow they are beyond the level of suscep-tibility. Such people may trust the "assurances" of their spirit guides, or feel that they have advanced to "higher levels of consciousness" and are "in control," or that they are simply neutral scientific investigators, who won't be affected by some silly superstition of occult dangers or "curses."

But who has ever explored the psychic realm and claimed they have understood its true nature? If our ignorance of the physical universe is still galactic, how much more of the unseen universe? Is not humankind's perpetual inability to ever know what really goes on in that world, and the dangers that might exist, sufficient reason at least for caution?

Why would a loving God warn against occult activity to begin with if such activity were harmless—or helpful (Deuteronomy 18:9-12)?

When the American spiritualist movement began with the Fox sisters in 1848, the first messages from the spirits were typically warm and loving: "Dear Friends . . . you must proclaim these wonderful truths to the world. This is the dawning of a new era. God is with you and good spirits will protect you in this vital endeavor."[2] But after a lifetime of proselytization for spiritism—and a life of misery, including being led into alcoholism and immorality—Margaret Fox herself confessed the following publicly in 1888: "I am here tonight, as one of the founders of spiritualism, to denounce it as absolute falsehood . . . the most wicked blasphemy the world has ever known."[3]

Former witch Audrey Harper initially thought witchcraft a good thing. But it took 17 years of psychiatric care to undo the damage it did to her.[4]

If real dangers exist in the physical world, can we logically expect the spiritual world to be full of goodness? If a race of more powerful beings inhabits that world, if their hatred for man is proven (Appendix F), if experimentation can mean deception with eternal consequences, who in their right mind would risk everything? Isn't it possible that the fact of man's historic belief in demons and devils tells us something about learning a lesson the hard way? Is it not just *possible* that malevolent entities, far greater in power (2 Peter 2:11), would seek to deceive men in such a way as to ensure their spiritual death? Are there not thousands of personal testimonies to these very facts: that deceptive and evil spirits exist, and that their purpose is man's spiritual and other destruction? Then one can but wonder how psychic practitioners think themselves immune from all dangers.

In considering the warnings given by occultists, we must reemphasize they simply don't go far enough because, biblically speaking, they are dealing in a realm "which they do not understand" (Jude 8,10). Indeed, usually they are openly promotional. They believe in "safe" and "mature" mediumism, in the "responsible" development of psychic abilities, in the "scientific" investigation of the occult—in the prevalent error that with the right wisdom or information man in his own power apart from God is able to distinguish spiritual good from spiritual evil.

For example, one prominent psychic researcher stated his belief that greater personal development of mediumism and knowledge of its ways is the best safeguard against its dangers.

> Mediumship is necessary! Without it there would be no means of knowledge, no instruments through which to study the psychic plane; but mediumship, in exact proportion to the magnetic powers it confers, becomes a greater and ever greater source of danger, the further its development is carried, unless the control of those powers can be handled with a firm hand and understood in all its aspects. Knowledge is the best safeguard, and knowledge will be best obtained by those who can study all the conditions of psychic development.[5]

Expertise is certainly necessary for something like handling explosives, but occult knowledge per se would seem to be useless when confronting lying spirits whose primary goal is deception and entrapment. This was the conclusion of no less an authority than the famous eighteenth-century medium Emanuel Swedenborg:

> When spirits begin to speak with a man, he ought to beware that he believes nothing whatever from them; for they say almost anything. Things are fabricated by them, and they lie. . . . They would tell so

many lies and indeed with solemn affirmation that a man would be astonished. . . . If a man listens and believes they press on, and deceive, and seduce in [many] ways. . . . Let men beware therefore [and not believe them].[6]

Psychical researcher J. D. Pearce-Higgins, vice chairman of the Churches Fellowship for Psychical and Spiritual Studies (Great Britain) writes of the hazards of Ouija board use and automatic writing in his "Dangers of Automatism." He points out that people who endorse such methods have little understanding of the disastrous possibilities:

> I am a little surprised to find that some para-pyschologists tend to take a rather optimistic view of the possible dangers. But those who write in this way have had little experience of the disastrous psychological effects that can be produced; it is precisely unstable individuals who resort to this form of experiment. Inevitably, the personalities of young people who try this method are still in a formative and therefore unstable period. Such disturbances are difficult to cure, and there seems little reference to them in the literature of psychiatry.[7]

While advocating allegedly safe mediumism, he still warns:

> These apparently simple methods of attempting contact with the dead are extremely dangerous. All the experienced mediums I know say the same— don't do it!—and they know, because they so often have people brought to them who are obsessed or possessed by some mischievous or damaging spirit who has got control of them and won't let go. They find they are compelled to go on with automatic writing—at all hours of day and night, they may begin to hear hallucinatory voices telling them to do

stupid and filthy things; they are no longer master in the house of their own minds and souls. It is often a difficult matter to cure them, and there aren't many mediums who can do it.[8]

He concludes with a somewhat unique warning for a parapsychologist, at least in the realm of automatism:

So it would seem that it is not merely the unstable who should avoid this sort of practice but we can guarantee no protection to ordinary balanced people, and the only safe procedure is to stop all automatism, once and for all.[9]

Charles Tart is the editor of *Transpersonal Psychologies* which discusses numerous occult psychologies, including those from the traditions of yoga, Taoism, alchemy, Kabbalism, Buddhism, Sufism, and Christian mysticism. In the section titled "Patterns of Western Magic," occultist William Gray discusses some of the hazards along the Western magical path:

There are many dangers on all [e.g., occult] Paths of Life, and the Western Magical Way is no exception. The worst danger is definitely *imbalance* in every imaginable direction. . . . It is a fact that frequently after initiation ceremonies there are sudden "flare-ups" of outrageous behavior in the subject; analogous to inoculation reactions. Also symptoms of paranoia may develop. . . . A chief hazard especially of the Magical Path is breakdown of mental and physical health if safeguards are ignored. Diseases are nonetheless real because of psychosomatic origins. Most of these troubles arise through misuse of Magic applied to mind or body, and are traceable to wrong intentions, disregard of calculable risks, carelessness, or just lack of common sense. Genuine accidents can occur as with everything else, but the majority of ills through Magic are invited ones. For example, those who poison themselves with chemical drug compounds and exhaust their physical energies while contorting their consciousness into painfully unnatural knots can scarcely complain when the account for all this has to be paid. Their mistreatment of Magic deserves small sympathy. Magic makes its own retribution on misusers.

It is also true with Magic that there are dangers arising from misinterpretation of intelligence gained from Inner sources, or acceptance of influences from antihuman entities. . . . The upshot of this results very often in troubles coming from sheer gullibility, deceived Inner senses, and plain credulity due to inaccurate Self-estimates. Human beings enjoy flattery and Pseudo-Self aggrandisement. They like supposing they have been singled out for special spiritual messages, and are delighted to discover an awakened ability to make contact with other than human types of consciousness. This makes them liable to any kind of confidence trick or subtle manipulation they may meet with from immediate Inner quarters which are not necessarily in favor of human progress.[10]

Another warning comes from veteran psychic researcher Martin Ebon in an article in *Psychic* magazine. He also admits that in the psychic world "there is much darkness and greed" and likens participation to a game of Russian roulette: "A game in which the element of danger is ever present and must be acknowledged."[11] He lists representative case histories of the hazards, e.g.: 1) suicide (justified by the desire to experience the "wonders of the other world"); 2) the destruction of families through adulterous liaisons or divorce among those who accept a belief in reincarnation (these were justified because psychic revelations indicated the new partner was one's "soul mate" in a previous lifetime and hence the perfect "karmic partner" for this life), 3) major financial loss through the deception of fraudulent mediums, (justified by vital instructions from the "other side"); 4) serious mental illness from various causes; and 5) bogus exorcists who financially prey on the gullible for "deliverance."

Indeed, it is just such themes as these which are common among occult practitioners: death, immorality, financial loss or ruin, emotional illness, and fraud. Ebon proceeds to point out that for every case that comes to light, "dozens remain submerged, unrecognized, suppressed or ignored."[12]

Matters become more complex when we consider the assessment of Raymond Van Over of New York University, former editor of the *International Journal of Parapsychology*:

> My personal observations (which span over twenty years in studying the occult and meeting people with varying degrees of interest in it) bear out the conviction that unstable personalities dominate the occult population.[13]

He concludes that the occult world:

> . . . is a world where few stabilizing or discriminating personalities function as a counter example. It provides fertile ground upon which neurotic and dangerously unstable personalities can flourish unquestioned.[14]

Other authorities agree that occultism tends to attract the less-than-psychologically-healthful:

> So many stupid, wicked, irresponsible, and other inadequate people are attracted to Magic for the wrong reasons that it is scarcely surprising that their mismanagement of it is apt to make a very bad impression upon un-Magically minded people.[15]

But are occult tragedies adequately explained by a recourse to "unstable personalities," or is this wishful thinking? While it is certainly true the occult draws unstable individuals, we suggest it is more often true that occult activity is the breeding ground producing such personalities in the first place. Those who view occult practices as high forms of spirituality will naturally view the human wreckage they see as resulting from some other cause, such as from previously unstable personalities who were simply unable to successfully integrate occult experiences properly. But to argue that the problem is not with psychic activity per se, but with the ignorance or defective personality of the practitioner, is ultimately to ignore the reality of what occult practice involves: spiritual warfare with demons and the corresponding possibility of God's judgment.

In addition, we must ask another question. How many of these unstable personalities resulted from prior causes related to occultism? What of a family history of occult involvement that resulted in a person's mental instability *before* he or she began occult practice? For example, Dr. Koch lists scores of examples where children of occult practitioners have suffered emotionally even though they were not directly involved in such practices themselves. "It is actually quite usual for such a marriage [of occultists] to produce children who are severely oppressed."[16]

Again, no one denies that some occultists have pre-existing emotional problems and were attracted to the occult by the hope of personal power and security. But in light of scriptural warnings, it is wrong to say that psychic activity is safe for stable people and harmful only for the unstable.

Consider another example of how occultists think they can engage in their practices safely. Paul Beard was president of the College for Psychic Studies in London. In "How to Guard Against 'Possession'" he asserts that spirit contact is permissible and even desirable, as long as you contact the right spirits. But he also notes the presence of certain spirits who attempt to "break down the personality [they are] obsessing in order to reduce it to neurosis or even possible suicide."[17] This pattern of spirit obsession "is virtually universal and has been observed by the victims of such influences, as well as by psychic researchers and spiritualists in many parts of the world."[18]

How can we identify these harmful spirits in order to avoid them? Presumably, we can do so by knowing the kinds of arguments they are likely to give:

> Quite a number of people who are well aware in theory of the dangers of automatic writing nevertheless allow themselves to become obsessed, because they are insufficiently alert to see through and resist the types of argument which the influence [the spirit] will use in order to retain contact with them.[19]

But what if the spirits are more clever than we are? What if they know enough about us to use arguments they know will be effective? What if they first establish trust and then have what seem to be perfectly valid explanations for problems that arise?

Further, how can we tell when a spirit is lying to us? Who can determine the motives of a spirit they know nothing about? If the spirit's real intent is to hide its true nature and purpose, what protection is there against it?

For example, as a skeptic experimenting with a Ouija board, Alan Vaughan descended into what he termed "a pit of horror" where the "gates of hell opened." He experienced "the most abject terror" and suffered what he called "the awful consequences" of spirit possession. Yet after it was all over, he went on to teach classes in psychic development![20]

On the one hand, he freely confessed, "I had been possessed by a spirit." But did he ever suspect that additional goals were intended by the entity? Vaughan remarks, "If the possession by Nada [the spirit] and my consequent self-exorcism had been terrifying, they had the net good result of propelling me full time into parapsychology."[21] But how does Vaughan know this wasn't the hidden purpose of the spirit all along?

In other words, Vaughan concluded that his real problem was simply one of, as he terms it, a "profound ignorance" of the wise use of psychic activity. This ignorance could be remedied by the wisdom of a parapsychological discipline that would prevent the kinds of tragedies he personally experienced. His own "deliverance" proves this.

On the other hand, one might think that the spirit would be happy to leave during the "self-exorcism" if possession were not its real concern. What if its real purpose was to produce a respected defender of parapsychology—one who would lead many other people into the influence of the spirit world through "safe" and "responsible" psychic development? This was indeed the end result: By temporarily possessing someone open to the occult, the spirit had strategically maneuvered Vaughan into the realm of parapsychology and a belief in the "proper" use of psychic knowledge. Vaughan became a respected psychical researcher who influenced thousands through his editorial and other work with *Psychic* magazine.

Again, those persons who practice occult magic often warn of its dangers. Practicing magician David Conway states, "Magic offers us the most effective way of contacting the supernatural reality we have been discussing."[22] But as we saw earlier, the occult rituals he refers to involve the generation of a severely altered state of consciousness—literally, a temporary madness—which culminates in spirit possession and envisages potentially lethal hazards.

In addition, Conway shows how the various magical methods of cursing others can lead to great mental damage.[23] Elsewhere he discusses demons. Even the adept can easily be deceived by demons' "consummate skill." Coming from someone who has spent a lifetime in occult practice, his insights are highly relevant:

> Everyone who reads occult literature or has any experience of magic will soon be brought up against forms which seem every bit as personal as the adept himself. . . . We shall call them evil for the good reason that given the chance they would do us immeasurable harm. The shapes generally assumed by demons are far from horrendous—at least to begin with, when their owners may still be trying to give a good impression: Little children, gentle old folk and beautiful young people of either sex are some of their favourite human disguises. Though not themselves

human, they will frequently display as much resourcefulness as the most cunning human being. They will flatter, charm, threaten and cajole the adept with consummate skill in an attempt to gain the upper hand, and the unwary magician can all too easily succumb to their clever ploys . . . their chief aim which is to destroy anyone, in this case the magician, who dares approach their domain. . . .

From this there arises the ever present need for caution before you scale the heights of magic. Even in the foothills there lurk dire perils, which is why the rites so far described should not be undertaken lightly. When someone sets out deliberately to contact the astral world, be that world inside or outside his mind, he at once faces many dangers which only knowledge can help to overcome. But even the cleverest and most knowledgeable magician realizes that the demons of the pit are waiting for the one false step that will deliver him to them.[24]

Conway proceeds to observe that if your ritual intention is a negative (i.e., evil) one, in that case: "These creatures will, without too much persuasion, do their utmost to help you realize it since their appetite for destruction and discord appears to be insatiable."[25]

All this is supposedly "white" as opposed to "black" magic. But the attempt to give such occult activity religious trappings and a benign "white" or "pure" image only underscores the subtlety of the devil, who uses every possible guise to suit his purposes.[26] Even sincere "white" witches and other "good" occultists sometimes confess they fail to live up to their image; in the end, they discover they will also use their powers for evil.

Yet, one might suspect that this temptation would be yielded to more readily than claimed, given the following facts: 1) magic is an evil activity to begin with, 2) man has a fallen, self-seeking nature, and 3) the ever-present temptation exists to use power for solely pragmatic ends, not to mention the deliberate influence of demons on the "white" practitioner also. As a former black witch observes:

> I will mention here that although white witches claim never to harm anyone, I can say that I've known white witches who did so. Practices called voodoo by black witches were followed by white witches, who use "fithfath," a doll made of clay in the image of the person they wish to harm.[27]

Dr. Koch concludes, "The cost of indulging in magic is extremely high. Every example drawn from counselling work of Christians reveals the terrifying effects."[28]

But even what most people consider relatively harmless or "milder" forms of the occult, such as divination, are not harmless. W. B. Crow, writing in *A History of Magic, Witchcraft and Occultism*, alleges of any type of divination, that it is "nearly always dangerous."[29] Finally, the famous medium Stanton Moses confessed of his own profession, "It would not be honest of me to disguise the fact that he who meddles with this subject does so at his own peril."[30]

In conclusion, occult practitioners are well aware of the hazards of the occult. Unfortunately, they offer a humanistic perspective. The psychic realm is seen as merely another frontier for man to explore and conquer for his own glory. Admittedly, they say, occult practice has its hazards, but which frontier doesn't? Given insight, patience, and wisdom, man can benefit greatly from this exploration.

But this new perspective neglects the warnings given by God. In a questionable area already littered with human tragedy and spiritual destruction, woven with endless unknowns, and at best ordered by conflicting human speculation, certainly the one sure voice that should be heeded is that of God Himself.

8

What Psychic Counselors Say

With the casualties from occult practice mounting, a few organizations are beginning to take notice. The Freedom Counseling Center in Burlingame, California, began a nationwide hotline connecting willing therapists to assist people having difficulties brought on by their psychic experiences.[1] The Psychic Integration Institute of Navato, California, and the Institute of Noetic Sciences in Menlo Park, California, both make referrals.[2] The John F. Kennedy University, a leading U.S. parapsychology center offering accredited master's degrees in that discipline as well as a psychic training program, includes an emergency telephone service for people in need of help.[3] On a more expanded level, in 1980 Christina Grof established a worldwide "Spiritual Emergence Network" (SEN) of crisis intervention counseling for people having spiritual crises resulting from their psychic practices.[4] Involving over 1100 counselors and 40 regional coordinators, its goal is to support those undergoing what SEN terms "spiritual emergence" and to validate crises experiences as higher forms of spirituality.

A number of books supporting SEN philosophy have now been produced to help people accept and reinterpret their occult emergencies as forms of "spiritual development" because allegedly "these states have tremendous evolutionary and healing potential."[5]

In other words, what frequently turns out descriptively to be the phenomenon of demonization and its accompanying physical/emotional manifestations[6] is now seen as forms of ultimately

139

benevolent or divine "spiritual emergence." For example, Stan and Christina Grof categorize the varieties of "spiritual emergence" as including 1) the shamanic crisis, 2) kundalini arousal, 3) psychic opening, 4) past-life experiences, 5) channeling and other direct contact with spirits, 6) near-death experiences, 7) UFO close encounters, and 8) possession states.[7]

Consider the kinds of experiences we are talking about. Shaman initiation involves "attacks by demons who expose them [humans] to incredible tortures and ordeals."[8] Kundalini awakening produces powerful, controlling currents of energy, overwhelming emotions, violent shaking and spasms, and strange uncontrollable behaviors such as making animal sounds and movements.[9] UFO abductions comprise "unimaginable tortures."[10] States of possession include "serious psychopathology, such as antisocial or even criminal behavior, suicidal depression, murderous aggression or self-destructive behavior, promiscuous and deviant sexual impulses or excessive use of alcohol and drugs."[11]

We are asked to believe that all these crisis phenomena are supposedly potential manifestations of "spiritual emergence" which, handled properly, can lead to true spiritual wholeness and personal knowledge of God.

Unfortunately, this is a kind of Tantric/Zen approach to counseling which sees encounters with the demonic as legitimate avenues to the experience of God.[12] Unfortunately again, this kind of approach seems to dominate the field.

In *A Source Book for Helping People in Spiritual Emergency*, psychic counselor and New Age practitioner Dr. Emma Bragdon explains: "Spiritual emergency is a new diagnostic category which refers to profound disorientation and instability that sometimes accompanies intense spiritual experience. It appears as an acute psychotic episode lasting between minutes and weeks, and eventually having a positive transformative outcome."[13]

She also proceeds to describe the outcome as a "spiritual emergence" that involves classic occult phenomena, including astral travel, kundalini arousal, psychic healing, channeling and other direct spirit contact as well as monistic consciousness wherein a person "becomes God."[14]

In essence, people who are clearly demonized from a biblical standpoint and who even willingly describe themselves as possessed by spirits are the very ones described as encountering a benevolent "spiritual emergence." Demonization itself can thus become the means to spiritual growth since this, too, is a "gateway" phenomenon to "a profound spiritual experience."[15]

Regardless, those who function as counselors for psychic practitioners are well aware of the hazards that exist. Psychologist and psychic Eleanor Criswell observes the large range of problems that are encountered:

> The experiences dealt with in a psychic counseling setting have an exceptionally broad range: Individuals have reported such problems as being psychically controlled by others from a distance, poltergeist activities, problems with psychic children, bi-location experiences, encounters with entities associated with automatic writing and Ouija boards, beginning mediumistic experiences, hyper-sensitivity, feeling witchlike, having a low level of self-esteem, feeling haunted, a feeling of being psychokinetic, visual illusions, "seeing too much, hearing too much," feeling possessed, caught up with so called past life impressions, etc. . . . Perhaps one of the most common psychic problems that we have encountered is the lack of validation received by individuals regarding their experiences. . . . Frequently such individuals have been hospitalized in mental institutions and have sometimes undergone electro-convulsive therapy and other somatic treatments in order to stop the psychic process.[16]

In the final analysis it is usually psychically oriented therapists who do the actual counseling. As such, they tend to encourage psychic involvement rather than repudiate it. For example, when counseling a person who is experiencing difficulties from auto-matic writing, the counselor may urge him to temporarily aban-don the activity, but also to join a mediumistic "development circle" so that his/her "latent and natural" abilities may be more "responsibly" and "carefully" cultivated. The counselor imag-ines he has done the troubled individual a good turn.

> The psychic counseling process usually follows a consistent pattern: there seems to be a movement from confusion and fear to understanding and in-creased self-acceptance. . . . Having come to terms with their psychic natures, clients sometimes decide to use their abilities directly by developing their medi-umistic tendencies through further study or by using them indirectly in their main work, such as being a highly empathic psychotherapist.[17]

In "Emotional Reactions to Psychic Experiences," clinical psychologist Freda Morris provides another example. A woman who was harmed by her first exposure to psychic experiences came to Dr. Morris for counseling. Characteristically, the woman was suffering for attempting to escape these experiences. As those involved will testify, anyone can open the door to the psychic world, but closing it is another matter entirely. The spirits have a vested interest at stake. They can make a person's life a living hell unless that individual gives in to their agenda.[18] (See pp. 230-33.)

Nevertheless, Dr. Morris provided positive reinforcement through hypnotic sessions and encouraged her client to give a lecture on psychic phenomena to a large group of high school students. As a result a new convert emerged:

> She began to read psychic literature avidly and was delighted that scientists would seriously consider these phenomena. She asked the author to help her gain more control of her trance states through the use of hypnosis. In the hypnotically induced trance state

she was able to have psychic experiences without becoming overwhelmed as she had in the past. Within a few weeks she had secured a job as executive assistant for a psychical research society in Los Angeles and was enjoying herself immensely. She became happy and out-going and is doing an excellent job in the Society. [Thus] In the case of Patricia, severely maladaptive emotional turmoil followed efforts to suppress psychic experiences and a happy outcome followed development of an active interest in psychical research.[19]

In a similar vein, most other counselors, such as Stuart K. Harary of the Freedom Counseling Center, stress "that individuals suffering from anxiety or depression over their psychic experiences should be advised about the normalcy and universality of psychic experiences and urge that this message be repeated until the client has come to accept it."[20]

The existence of these counseling attempts, if nothing else, indicates many people are asking for help—whether or not they are getting it. As the late D. Scott Rogo, author of almost 20 books on parapsychology and related topics, revealed in *Parapsychology Review*:

Probably everyone working in the field of parapsychology has had to counsel callers or visitors to their laboratories who so often complain about the psychic experiences they are having and are finding disturbing. . . . Such cases suggest that the parapsychological community should begin thinking about providing the general public with mental health services.[21]

But regrettably, the individual counseled by psychics or their sympathizers is only furthering his problem in the guise of "more responsible" psychic development. Typically, the person is unaware that to develop one's "psychic ability" is to open oneself to spiritual forces of darkness,[22] rather than to contact divine realms or to develop an alleged "natural human psi." (See Acts 16:16-19.)

As ex-witch/Satanist Irvine confesses:

> I had known that power often enough, but I believed it was not a natural, but rather supernatural power working through me. I was not born with it. The power was not my own but Satan's.[23]

While the psychic counselor believes he has displayed a superior knowledge of what is helpful or harmful in the psychic arena, he has really helped ensure further occult bondage and a hardening to genuine spiritual truth.

Compounding the problem, today even scholars and physicians are advocating that occultists themselves become adjuncts to the mental health profession. Roger Lauer, M.D., suggests that mediums can be useful in counseling sessions and that "psychic-psychiatric alliances may be quite useful. . . . Attempts should be made to develop and assess them. . . . Mental health personnel should . . . consider professional collaboration with psychics."[24] But if we really begin to turn the mentally ill over to experienced occultists for counseling, we may only hazard a guess at the outcome.

And how far are we to take this? In an article entitled "Magical Therapy—An Anthropological Investigation of Contemporary Satanism," the author suggests that for some people even *Satanism* might be of benefit as a form of personal and societal improvement.[25]

By the preceding examples, we can see that the psychic community is aware that dabbling in this area can be detrimental to people's health. But one consequence of an increased awareness of psychic casualties is an increased exposure to the psychic interpretation of the solution. Thus, Rogo observes, both mental health professionals and Christian clergy need to be re-educated to accept the "normalcy" of psychic development.

> The most imperfect solution to this mental health crisis is, of course, massive public education. If the

general public were made aware of the normality of psychic experiences, how they can be used for personal growth, and how common they seem to be, negative reactions to these manifestations (as outlined above) could be prophylactically alleviated. . . . One long-term plan would call for the massive dissemination of information about psychic phenomena to members of the "helping" professions. . . . We also need more education within the religious establishment. We should therefore be seeking to educate ministerial students as well as priests, ministers and rabbis, about the nature of psychic phenomena.[26]

This is precisely the kind of approach that should be rejected by anyone seeking to help the occultly oppressed. (See Chapter 17 and Appendix H.)

9

What Eastern Gurus Say

In an earlier chapter we examined some of the associations between Eastern religion and Satanism/witchcraft. In this chapter we will bring our concerns closer to home by examining the beliefs of some popular American gurus. Among Eastern gurus as a whole, occult practices are widely accepted. Typically, they include not only various forms of spiritism but also astrology, magic, sorcery, necromancy, development of psychic abilities, shamanistic practices, the transferal of occult power in initiation (*shaktipat diksha*), etc.

As veteran researcher Brooks Alexander observes of Rajneesh, Muktananda, and Sai Baba:

> All of these gurus espouse a similar philosophy, and they all turn it into practice in a similar way. It is a pattern that we find not only in tantra (Indo-Tibetan occultism), but in European satanism, antinomian gnosticism, and ancient pagan sorcery as well.[1]

Bhagwan Shree Rajneesh, for example, states that witchcraft constitutes "one of the greatest possibilities of human growth."[2]

Part of the disciples' required obedience to the guru is to follow the guru's *sadhana*, or spiritual path. By definition, this places a person on the path of occultism. In fact, psychic powers and spiritism are to be expected.[3] For example, spirit contact frequently occurs with what are believed to be various Hindu deities, "nature" spirits, or the guru himself after death (or even while alive via his alleged "spiritual form," as we saw in Chapter 1 with Swami Rama). Thus, Muktananda tells his students they will encounter various Hindu gods and other spirits as well as the alleged dead.[4]

Paramahansa Yogananda's spiritual autobiography, *Autobiography of a Yogi*, is replete with occult experiences: astral projection, psychometry, astrology, psychic healing, spiritistic materializations and apportations, amulets, etc.[5] For example, Yogananda teaches, "True spiritualism [mediumism] is a wonderful science.... It is possible by meditation and spiritual [occult] development to contact departed loved ones."[6]

The text *Sri Aurobindo and the Mother on Occultism* claims that true occultism is "dynamic spirituality . . . an indispensable instrument along the spiritual path."[7] Aurobindo and the "Mother" emphasize that "to talk about occult things is of little value; one must experience them."[8]

Our research into some two dozen of the major gurus revealed that many of them were, in fact, possessed (defined as God possession or spirit possession, but not demon possession) and that their spiritual paths were often designed to *lead* to spirit possession, defined as a form of higher spirituality or enlightenment.

Thus, because Eastern gurus constitute a class of occultists, they, too, are familiar with the territory and warn of the hazards of occult practices. For example, medium Sri Chinmoy, a spiritual "adviser" at the United Nations, states:

> Many, many black magicians and people who deal
> with spirits have been strangled or killed. I know
> because I have been near quite a few of these cases.[9]

He refers to deceptive spirits who will impersonate a person's guru in visions and urge disciples to commit suicide. He also mentions several people who died from yogic breathing exercises.[10]

Meher Baba warned about the possibility of death or insanity from the Eastern path and, in fact, like other shamans, believed insanity was evidence of higher spirituality; he also accepted the possibility of suicide as a form of liberation, if it was done with the "proper" motive.[11]

Regardless, like psychic counselors in general, the gurus usually teach that given proper instruction and technique, occultism is safe. This is a bit ironic because most gurus have characteristically experienced a terrible insanity/possession on their own road to so-called "enlightenment." Meher Baba himself was seriously insane for a time; so were popular gurus Ramakrishna, Muktananda, Prabhupada, Rudrananda, Nityananda, Da Free John, and many others.[12]

Note for example the following description of events relating to Muktananda's own spiritual enlightenment, a path he endorses for his disciples. During so-called kundalini arousal, such experiences may last for months or even years, in which case a protracted insanity and/or demonization must be endured. We quote at length so the reader may have a better understanding of the frightening reality that is frequently involved on the Eastern path. In Muktananda's own words:

> I was assailed by all sorts of perverse and defiling emotions. My body started to move, and went on like this in a confused sort of way. . . . After a time, my breathing changed, becoming disturbed. Sometimes my abdomen would swell with air, after which I would exhale it with great force. Often the breath that I took in would be held inside me. I became more and more frightened . . . my mind was sick with fear. . . .
>
> My thoughts became confused, meaningless. My limbs and body got hotter and hotter. My head felt heavy, and every pore in me began to ache. When I breathed out, my breath stopped outside. When I breathed in, it stopped inside. This was terribly painful and I lost my courage. Something told me that I would die at any moment. . . . I could not understand what was happening, how it was happening, who was making it happen. . . .
>
> By now it was after 9:00. Someone had seated himself in my eyes and was making me see things. . . . It seemed that I

was being controlled by some power which made me do all these things. My intellect was completely unstable. . . . I heard hordes of people screaming frightfully . . . and saw strange creatures from six to fifty feet tall, neither demons nor demigods, but human in form, dancing naked, their mouths gaping open. Their screeching was horrible and apocalyptic. . . . An army of ghosts and demons surrounded me. All the while I was locked tight in the lotus posture, my eyes closed, my chin pressed down against my throat so that no air could escape.

Then I felt a searing pain. . . . I wanted to run away, but my legs were locked tight in the lotus posture. I felt as if my legs had been nailed down permanently in this position. My arms were completely immobilized. . . .

Then, from over the water, a moonlike sphere about four feet in diameter came floating in. It stopped in front of me. This radiant, white ball struck against my eyes and then passed inside me. I am writing this just as I saw it. It is not a dream or an allegory, but a scene which actually happened —that sphere came down from the sky and entered me. . . . My tongue curled up against my palate, and my eyes closed. I saw a dazzling light in my forehead and I was terrified. I was still locked in the lotus posture, and then my head was forced down and glued to the ground. . . .

I started to make a sound like a camel, which alternated with the roaring of a tiger. I must have roared very loudly, for the people around actually thought that a tiger had gotten into the sugarcane field. . . .

I am in a terrible state. I have gone completely insane. You may not be able to see it from the outside, but, inside, I am crazy. . . . My body began to twist. . . . Now, it was not I who meditated; meditation forced itself on me. It came spontaneously; it was in all the joints of my body. Then, suddenly, a red light came before me with such force that it seemed to have been living inside me. It was two feet tall and shone brightly. . . .

Every part of my body was emitting loud crackling and popping sounds. . . .

At this time, I understood nothing about the various experiences. . . .

Only afterward did I learn that they were all part of the process pertaining to [spiritual enlightenment]. . . . People who have experienced it call it the awakening of the Kundalini. The experiences I had had under the mango trees were due to the grace of my Gurudev Nityananda; they were all his *prasad* [blessing]. . . .

Sometimes I would jump and hop like a frog, and sometimes my limbs would shake violently as though shaken by a deity. And this was what was actually happening; a great deity in the form of my guru had spread all through me as Chiti [consciousness], and was shaking me with his inner Shakti [power]. . . .

The power of the guru's grace enters the disciple's body in a subtle form and does many great things. . . . Every day I had meditation like that. Sometimes my body would writhe and twist like a snake's, and a hissing sound would come from inside me. . . .

Sometimes my neck moved so violently that it made loud cracking sounds, and I became frightened. . . . I had many astonishing movements like this. Sometimes my neck would roll my head around so vigorously that it would bend right below my shoulders so that I could see my back. When the intensity lessened, I became peaceful again. But because I did not understand these *kriyas* [spontaneous yoga movements], I was always worried and afraid. Later, however, I learned that this was a Hatha Yoga process effected by the Goddess Kundalini in order for Her to move up through the spinal column into the *sahasrara* [upper psychic center].[13]

Thus, as is true in some forms of Western mysticism, the Hindu path endorsed by the Eastern gurus offers the possibility of temporary insanity and outright spirit possession, together

defined as expressions of one's emerging spiritual "enlightenment." Unfortunately, Western gurus who imitate the East are
not more encouraging. Ram Dass once said that psychosis is "far
out" and that mental hospitals are "groovy ashrams."[14] The
deceptions, follies, and other consequences of his own spiritual
path are detailed in books such as *Grist for the Mill*.[15] Further, the
"ascended masters" (spirits) who speak through "Guru Ma"
(Elizabeth Claire Prophet) of the Church Universal and Trium-
phant admit that their spiritual instructions have caused the
premature death of some students.[16]

But insanity or death is not the only hallmark of what Eastern
practices can offer sincere Western seekers. Possession is another. As we saw, Muktananda obviously was possessed by
something, and most gurus admit to spiritistic influences and/or
possession. Like mediums in general, they also attempt to make a
distinction between "good" (i.e., voluntary) possession and evil
(obsessional, involuntary) possession.

The Western Hindu sect of Da (Bubba) Free John and the
Dawn Horse Community provides an example of deliberately
cultivated possession for purposes of supposed spiritual enlightenment. Again, members do not view this as demonic possession
(something evil or dangerous), but rather as God possession (that
which is spiritually uplifting and safe). Thus, what is really
demonic possession is now reinterpreted as divine possession.
Some quotes by Free John show the results:

> There is no madness like the madness of real free-
> dom in God.[17]

> Motherhood is just a binding archetype . . . and it
> binds you. It is an illusion. Giving birth is no more
> Divine than taking a crap. . . . Motherhood is gar-
> bage. Children are garbage. It is all garbage. It is all
> distraction.[18]

Morality is referred to as "the usual moralistic horse . . ." and
his spiritual community had "marriages abruptly ripped to
shreds"[19] because:

Spiritual life is leading to the absolute undermining of your separate existence absolutely.[20]

One of the secrets of spiritual life is continually to violate your own contracts [e.g., personal morality, standards, marriage bonds, etc.]. If you do that with intelligence, with understanding, you will continually be free.[21]

Possession, as in the following examples, was commonplace. Note that these people did not originally seek to become possessed; it resulted simply from joining the cult. The following examples only convey a small portion of the reality described.

Example 1:
Bubba's eyes rolled up, and his lips pulled into a sneer. His hands formed *mudras* [yogic positions] as he slumped against Sal, who also fell back against other devotees sitting behind him. Almost immediately, many of those present began to feel the effects of intensified Shakti [spiritual power], through the spontaneous internal movement of the life-force. Their bodies jerked or shook, their faces contorted, some began to cry, scream, and moan. The whole bathhouse seemed to have slipped into another world. . . . I saw Bubba just enter into Sal, just go right into Sal. From there he went out over everybody else, and then everybody else started going crazy. Sal fell onto me, into my lap, and then everybody else started howling and so forth.[22]

In a later incident:

Then he turned to me, looked at me, and said, "You remember the agreement we made?" I said, "Yeah." So then he said, "Are you ready?" And I told him, "Yes," I was. At that point he entered the body completely, down to the cells, I could feel the entry taking place. It is a form of possession, only not by anything demonic, but by the guru. It is almost like anaesthesia, or like a form of radiation. After the entry was complete, he put his head against mine, and went into a yogic process, and we drifted out of the body altogether.[23]

Example 2:

We started having Satsang [spiritual teaching] and the Force was manifesting through me. It was really strong. My hands and my feet were both manifesting the Force, and everyone in the room was freaking out. It was coming through my eyes too. I remember looking at one girl and not having any control. I didn't want to do this to anybody. . . . I felt utterly possessed, my body was possessed, and my hands started to move, and I couldn't control them. I had no control at all. My face started taking on expressions.[24]

Example 3:

Then Sal began to speak. The intensity rose: animal sounds, screams, *kriyas*. It was difficult to hear what was being said. The fear of insanity. The rain got harder, the wind rose. . . . People were screaming and howling and weeping, emitting strange grunts and snarls, their bodies jerking, writhing and assuming yogic *mudras*.[25]

Example 4:

Then Bubba put his hand on the top of my head and I felt the Divine Force, literally, this tremendous Light and Force, coming down and filling my whole body, consuming me, as if it was turning every part of me inside out. The Force of the Divine was so great, my body assumed tremendous force, there was this tremendous expansion of the chest, much more than I could probably ever attempt to do, and of the arms. It was as if I were fighting something, and I literally was. It was my psyche being ripped out. I was very reluctant, and I was holding on, and so the Divine Force was actually pulling it out from the top of my head. It was coming down and the psyche was trying to . . . it was like being exorcised. It was almost unbearable, but it was never painful. It's just tremendous intensity. At that point I felt the psyche being drawn out. I knew that my marriage had dissolved. I also knew that my ordinary life, my coming from the ordinary point of view had absolutely dissolved. I knew there was nothing but the Divine. . . . I felt twitches, you know, like my mind was being dissolved at this time. Again it was very intense. It was so intense I kept pushing his hand like I wanted it and needed it on top of my head. And I pressed against his forehead. I felt like the top of my brain was being ripped off, and I needed more force to deal with this. Then the assumed region of my mind started to dissolve, literally dissolve.[26]

Perhaps the most common practice advanced by Eastern occultism is some form of yoga and/or meditation. In our critique of New Age medicine, *Can You Trust Your Doctor?*, we have documented the multiple dangers of most meditation practice. Here, we will concentrate on yoga.

Although many Americans practice yoga as mere exercise, few have any idea of where such practice may take them. In the literature we have read numerous accounts of yoga or meditation-induced insanity and demonization even from seemingly innocent practice. But again, the altered states that yoga/meditation produce—even the periods of madness—are now frequently defined as positive spiritual experiences capable of leading one to religious enlightenment.[27]

For example, that yoga practice can break down the mind and body is not surprising. The true goal of yoga is to destroy the person (who is only a false self, an illusion) so that the impersonal Brahman (the alleged real self) may be experienced.

Yoga authorities Fuernstein and Miller identify "the Yogic path as a progressive dismantling of human personality ending in a complete abolition. With every step (*anga*) of Yoga, what we call 'man' is demolished a little more."[28]

Moti Lal Pandit observes:

The aim of Yoga is to realize liberation from the human condition. To achieve this liberation, various psychological, physical, mental, and mystical [occult] methods have been devised. All those methods

are anti-social (sometimes even anti-human) in that
Yoga prescribes a way of life which says: "This mortal
life is not worth living."[29]

Because yoga is ultimately an occult practice (e.g., it characteristically develops psychic abilities), it is not unexpected that
the characteristic hazards of occult practice—for example, physical diseases, mental illness, and demonization[30]—could be
encountered. We believe that these hazards are encountered
because yoga is an occult practice and not because yoga is
allegedly performed in an incorrect manner.

Most people (including most Western medical doctors)
wrongly assume that yoga is harmless. They rarely consider yoga
per se as relevant to any illnesses they may encounter in their
patients. But we are convinced that many perplexing physical
conditions, including some deaths, are related to yoga. For
example, Swami Prabhavananda warns about the dangers of
yogic breathing exercises:

> Now we come to breathing exercises. Let me cau-
> tion you: they can be very dangerous. Unless properly
> done, there is a good chance of injuring the brain.
> And those who practice such breathing without
> proper supervision can suffer a disease which no
> known science or doctor can cure. It is impossible
> even for a medical person to diagnose such an ill-
> ness.[31]

Shree Purohit Swami's commentary on Pantanjali's *Yoga
Sutras* warns:

> In India and Europe, I came across some three
> hundred people who suffered permanently from wrong
> practices. The doctors, upon examination, found
> there was nothing organically wrong and conse-
> quently could not prescribe [treatment].[32]

Perhaps such phenomena explains, in part, why many yoga
authorities openly confess the dangers of yoga practice. As

noted, these dangers are often said to arise from "wrong" methods. But, in fact, no one has ever objectively identified the specific mechanics of "correct" or "incorrect" yoga; "incorrect" yoga practice in one tradition is often "correct" practice in another.[33]

Below we cite some of the hazards of yoga as noted by yoga authorities.

United Nations spiritual adviser and spiritist[34] Sri Chinmoy, author of *Yoga and the Spiritual Life*, observes: "To practice *pranayama* [yogic breath control] without real guidance is very dangerous. I know of three persons who have died from it."[35]

Yoga authority Hans-Ulrich Rieker admonishes in *The Yoga of Light*: "Yoga is not a trifling jest if we consider that any misunderstanding in the practice of yoga can mean death or insanity," and that in kundalini yoga, if the breath or prana is "prematurely exhausted [exhaled] there is immediate danger of death for the yogi."[36]

Gopi Krishna, another yoga authority, also warns of the possible dangers of yoga practice, including "drastic effects" on the central nervous system and the possibility of death.[37]

The standard authority on hatha yoga, *The Hatha Yoga Pradipika* (Chapter 2, verse 15), cautions: "Just as lions, elephants, and tigers are tamed, so the prana [breath; actually prana is the alleged divine energy underlying the breath] should be kept under control. Otherwise it can kill the practitioner."[38]

Hindu master Sri Krishna Prem cautions in *The Yoga of the Bhagavat Gita*: "As stated before, nothing but dangerous, mediumistic psychisms or neurotic dissociations of personality can result from the practice of [yoga] meditation without the qualifications mentioned at the end of the last chapter."[39] He warns, "To practice it, as many do, out of curiosity . . . is a mistake which is punished with futility, neurosis, or worse ['even insanity itself']."[40]

Swami Prabhavananda's *Yoga and Mysticism* lists brain injury, incurable diseases, and insanity as potential hazards of wrong yoga practice;[41] Ulrich-Rieker lists cancer of the throat, all sorts of ailments, blackouts, strange trance states, or insanity from even "the slightest mistake."[42]

In *The Seven Schools of Yoga*, Ernest Wood warns of "the imminent risk of most serious bodily disorder, disease, and even madness."[43]

In conclusion, those who practice the occultism of the East also warn of its dangers. This is why those who seek the so-called "wisdom from the East" frequently get more than they bargained for.

10

What Theologians Say

We have now examined the opinions of a number of authorities and practitioners as to the dangers of psychic or occult activity, but we have not yet entered the domain of the theologian. It is to this we now briefly turn.

The late Dr. Kurt Koch was a German theologian with extensive personal experience in counseling the occultly subjected. He reports that in his 45 years of experience he "has heard some twenty-thousand terrible cases."[1] Unfortunately, he points out that many therapists simply refuse to recognize a problem exists and so perpetuate the problem through false diagnosis and resulting unworkable solutions.

Those in countries where occultism is more prevalent have complained to him of "the arrogant attitude of Western scientists and how they simply explain away all mediumistic phenomena as harmless without really knowing the slightest thing about the background or the effects of these phenomena."[2]

> Yet in my forty years of Christian work, and as a result of having counselled something in the region of 20,000 individual people, I have personally come across thousands of cases in which it was the contact with occultism that was the root cause of the problem, and the oppression that was the direct result of this contact. In the light of this, I have often wondered why the scientific research workers of today have

159

been unable to produce any form of argument or proof in support of their dogmatic *a priori* assumptions.[3]

He noted that in the case of the drug thalidomide, the harmful effects were in the ratio of one thalidomide child for every 10,000 doses given. Who today would risk taking thalidomide, even at the ratio of 1:10,000? And yet:

> Now, if we were to consider the number of cases in which occultism has had a damaging effect on people, our ratio would work out to something in the region of *nine out of ten cases*. I could support this fact by means of many thousands of examples. Yet scientists persist in saying "The problem does not exist." If one's counselling work were dependent upon narrow-mindedness like this, one would be driven to despair[4] (emphasis added).

According to Koch's experience, occult involvement is 9000 times as dangerous as taking the drug thalidomide. Thus, when researchers and alleged authorities make statements like the following, one can but wonder about the quality of the data upon which they base their assumptions.

Researcher Guy Playfair asserts in *The Unknown Power*, "I have nothing against occultism, which is no more harmful than science fiction, and can be just about as entertaining."[5] Parapsychology professor Han Holzer alleges, "For the record, no psychic healer ever caused anyone any physical harm."[6] Parapsychology authority Dr. Louise E. Rhine answers the question, "Are automatisms (e.g., automatic writing) harmful?" with "Taken in moderation, they probably are not."[7] Another parapsychology authority, Ian Stevenson, M.D., who is known worldwide for his research on supposed reincarnation experiences, declares, "I see no reason why interested persons should not try to develop themselves as automatic writers if they feel so inclined."[8] One well-respected psychologist told us, "You are a fool if you really believe spiritual occult practices have any dangers attached to them."

Compare the above with Dr. Koch's conclusions on those actively involved in the occult:

> The family histories and the end of these occult workers are, in many cases known to me, so tragic that we can no longer speak in terms of coincidence. . . .
>
> In our section on magic charms we have already given many examples of the tragic end of magic charmers. In many instances we see suicide (e.g., Exs. 36, 61, 65, 66, 114), fatal accidents (e.g., Ex. 66), psychoses (e.g., Exs. 54, 61, 63, 65), or horrible death-bed scenes (e.g., Exs. 65, 82). Besides the instances recorded in this study, there are numerous other examples of this kind well known to me, e.g., the leader of a spiritist group in South Wurttemberg who hanged himself, and the leader of another group who ended his life in an asylum. Perhaps we should also mention here some examples from literature. The famous medium Dr. Slade suffered two apoplectic fits; a pioneer in the field of psychical research, Crawford, who made experiments with the medium Kathleen Goligher, took his own life in 1920. In the literature of psychical research we continually find reference to such happenings.[9]

In the case of those passively involved, the consequences are no less disturbing. Koch observes that in many instances "occult subjection has been seen in relation to psychological disturbances which have the following predominant characteristics:

a) Warping and distortion of character: hard, egoistic persons; uncongenial, dark natures.
b) Extreme passions: abnormal sexuality; violent temper, belligerence; tendencies to addiction; meanness and kleptomania.
c) Emotional disturbances: compulsive thoughts, anxiety states.

d) Possession: destructive urges, fits of mania; tendency to violent acts and crime; inhabitation by demons.

e) Mental illnesses.

f) Bigoted attitude against Christ and God: conscious atheism; simulated piety; indifference to God's word and to prayer; blasphemous thoughts; religious delusions.

g) Puzzling phenomena in their environment.[10]

In *Occult Bondage and Deliverance* and elsewhere he argues that every sin connected with the occult cuts a person off from God, and that the effects of this transgressing of God's laws make themselves felt in different areas of a person's life.

These areas involve 1) moral character, 2) spiritual volition, e.g., moderate to severe difficulty in turning to Christ (such persons "begin to show signs of all sorts of emotional disturbances"—suicidal thoughts, severe depression, etc.), 3) family—families in which the occult has been practiced "are much more prone to mental illness and mental abnormalities than other families," and 4) the development of mediumistic abilities.[11]

Koch also gives numerous examples in *Between Christ and Satan*:

We will just briefly summarize these effects, although it must be pointed out that the list only represents a frequency pattern, and it cannot be assumed that these effects are always the result of occult practices. Nevertheless, people infected or burdened by fortune-telling and occult phenomena very frequently suffer in the following ways:

The characters of such people reveal abnormal passions, instability, violent tempers, addiction to alcohol, nicotine and sexual vices, selfishness, gossiping, egotism, cursing, etc. . . .

Medically speaking the families of those involved in fortune-telling reveal in a remarkable way such things as nervous disturbances, psychopathic and hysteric symptoms, cases of St. Vitus' dance, symptoms of paralysis, epileptics, freaks, deaf-mutes, cases of mediumistic psychoses, and a general tendency towards emotional and mental illnesses, etc.[12]

... I would like to point out that in my own experience numerous cases of suicides, fatal accidents, strokes and insanity are to be observed among occult practitioners.[13]

It is known particularly in the field of psychiatry that prolonged activity with mediumistic forces produces symptoms of schizophrenia. This has been termed mediumistic psychosis. Psychology too has drawn certain conclusions on the matter, and Professor Bender, a psychologist of the University of Frieburg in his booklet entitled "Parapsychology—Its Results and Problems," has warned people in these words: "Thousands of people base their hopes on the deceptive statements of spiritistic practitioners and subsequently become dependent upon the advice they receive from the 'other side.' I have quite a number of patients who have suffered serious psychic disturbances through the misuse of such practices. Their personalities have been split and they have been utterly confused by the spirits on which they have called."[14]

The above represents only a few of Koch's relevant comments, although literally hundreds of examples are detailed throughout his various books.[15]

The findings of other reputable theologians produce similar conclusions. Dr. Merrill F. Unger (Ph.D., John Hopkins University; Th.D. Dallas Theological Seminary) is the author of four books on occultism and demonism. He observes:

Both psychiatry and psychology recognize the adverse effects of spiritistic activity upon the mind.

Symptoms of split personality appear after sustained dealings in the occult. Psychiatry defines the resulting disorder as mediumistic psychosis.[16]

Elsewhere he points out that occult initiates commonly

develop antipathy toward true spirituality and reject the Bible as the authoritative word of God. They tend to relax moral standards and to make morality a relative matter. . . . Those who become involved in spiritualism or in occultism in general become mentally oppressed or enslaved by inexplicable forces. Often they suffer from strong depression, melancholia, psychopathic disorders, and severe psychoses. Suicide is common in occult circles, as are horrible deathbed scenes among practicing occultists, especially when no one is at hand to carry on their occult practices.[17]

In *Demons in the World Today* and *What Demons Can Do to Saints*, Unger lists many examples of the terrible harm caused by occult practices.[18]

Dr. John Warwick Montgomery, editor of *Demon Possession* and author of some 50 books, reveals in his *Principalities and Powers*:

There is a definite correlation between negative occult activity and madness. European psychiatrist L. Szondi has shown a high correlation between involvement in spiritualism and occultism (and the related theosophical blind alleys) on the one hand, and schizophrenia on the other. Kurt Koch's detailed case studies have confirmed this judgement. . . . Being a genuine Christian believer is no guarantee of exemption from the consequences of sorcery and black magic. . . .

The tragedy of most sorcery, invocation of demons, and related practices is that those who carry on these activities refuse to face the fact that they always turn out for the worst. What is received through the Faustian past never satisfies and one pays with one's soul in the end anyway.[19]

In *Demon Possession and the Christian*, theologian Dr. C. Fred Dickason details many examples of what occult practices can do to Christians who are foolish enough to disobey God in this area.[20] Problems of demon influence or possession may result from practices engaged in before conversion and this may even extend to the sins of one's ancestors: "I have found this avenue of ancestral involvement to be the chief cause of demonization. Well over 95 percent of more than 400 persons I have contacted in my counseling ministry have been demonized because of their ancestors' involvement in occult and demonic activities."[21]

Theologian and psychologist/psycholinguist Dr. Clifford Wilson emphasizes the following:

There are many evidences that dabbling in black magic is dangerous. Alcoholism, drug addiction, prostitution, insanity and other abnormal conditions are all too often the fruits of such involvement. Even financial disaster can follow those who have been snared and seek to extricate themselves by their own power.[22]

All this explains why Dr. Alfred Lechler, a Christian psychiatrist with wide clinical experience, can argue that even in our modern era of scientific advance and cultural achievement, "Demonic subjection is a surprisingly common occurrence."[23]

The testimony of scholars like Koch, Unger, Wilson, Dickason, Lechler, and Montgomery cannot simply be swept under the rug. The overall counseling experiences and/or scholarly research of these and other men stand as a testimony to the dangers of occult practice. In our next section we will document this by specific categories.

11

Suicide, Murder, and Death

*Nine associates of channeler Terri Hoffman have
committed suicide or died in accidents since 1977.*
—AP Newswire, Dallas

Suicide seems to be a recurring theme in the world of the
occult, especially in the case of those who attempt to leave their
former practices. Dr. Koch observes that "suicides are a familiar
phenomenon in the realm of the occult," [1] and he provides numerous examples throughout his books. He points out that in his own
country the province of Schleswig-Holstein has the highest suicide figures of all West Germany and is also one of two provinces
having the largest number of magic charmers. [2]

Many times there is a deliberate attempt by the spirits to
induce suicide in an unwary person. If people are trying to leave
the occult, they are told they will never be able to and that the
only escape is to take their own life. Or they may become
enamored with blissful descriptions of the wonders of the "next-
life" and be lovingly urged to "come join us." Former witch-
turned-Christian Doreen Irvine was subjected to repeated pres-
sures to take her own life in her attempt to escape from witchcraft. [3] Another individual noted that "many attempts have been
made to lead me astray and to cause me great physical and mental
harm. . . . On numerous occasions these spirits sought verbally to
convince me that suicide was the only answer." [4] The authors have
talked with half a dozen people who felt strangely compelled to

take their own life after beginning occult practice. In *The Christian and the Supernatural*, liberal theologian and occult supporter Morton Kelsey reveals:

> Two researchers working with the problem of suicide in Los Angeles were amazed at how often, in the course of their interviews, people who showed suicidal tendencies referred to contact with the dead.[5]

John D. Pearce-Higgins, vice chairman of a Christian psychic society, mentions a case of two girls engaging in automatic writing:

> At first it went fine; the student appeared to contact her dead father, who appeared to know all about her, and gave good evidence. Then a friend of her father came through and claimed to have been her "guardian angel" for many years. Presently, having got her hooked by what appeared to be good evidence, the messages came "Life does not hold much for you really, dear, it is such a lovely world over here, you had better come over and join us." So the girl threw herself under a bus. Mercifully, she wasn't killed; she was taken to a hospital and after a year, although she was well enough to come home, she was not free of the compulsion to write of obsessive ideas. The other girl got roughly the same advice from her "father"— but now she took fright and consulted the curate, who brought me in.[6]

In "Psychosis in the Seance Room," parapsychologist Hans Bender mentions four cases of people who were told to commit suicide by the spirits they contacted. The first case involved a husband and wife who joined a psychic development class:

> The instructions of the "spirit doctors" regarding the treatment of her sick child, she thought quite

foolish, but her husband, who believed unswervingly in the reality of these experiences, wished to carry them out in every detail. Things came to a head when the leader of the circle expelled the young woman, thus sharpening the conflict in her marriage. The young wife, thoroughly confused, divided between faith and doubt, attempted to apply the mediumistic practices she had learned during the seance. She began to write automatically and suddenly heard voices demanding that she take her own life. She was barely prevented from throwing herself from a balcony while saying "it was a force that I had to obey."[7]

In the second and third incidents, two married sisters attempted suicide as a result of seance practices and automatic writing. Both were hospitalized at the psychiatric clinic at Freiburg. In both cases "schizophrenic tendencies seemed to be apparent." In the case of one of the sisters, "eventually she heard spirit voices, not only while engaged in automatic writing, but everywhere all the time. These voices grew louder and more emphatic. They commented upon her behavior; gave her meaningless orders that she tried to resist; and alternated between quiet or vulgar and destructive tones.

"When she entered the hospital, the patient at first refused to provide any information whatsoever. She maintained that the spirits had ordered her to remain silent. Also, at the behest of one spirit, the patient once tried to cut her wrist with a piece of glass."

In the fourth case, that of a 25-year-old teacher, mediumistic psychoses developed after automatic writing. She was eventually urged to sacrifice her life, threw herself into a river, and was "rescued much against her will." Bender notes that oftentimes even mediums "find themselves led astray by the suggestions of allegedly high level discarnate entities."[8]

Former medium Victor Ernest refers to two women Satanists who had attempted unsuccessfully to disrupt his church service by physically attacking him. He reports:

Ten days later I received a telephone call from a woman who claimed that she and a friend had turned on satanic power in the Sunday service. She told me they had left the service frightened by the Bible text and message.

After the service, she said, Satan had come to their homes to induce them to commit suicide. Mrs. S., the woman calling me, overcame an impulse to leap into the Mississippi River, but she succumbed to the next temptation and took an overdose of sleeping pills. She had been near death for several days.

When she recovered, Mrs. S. learned that her friend had been committed to a mental hospital. That news so frightened her that she was prompted to call me. We set up a counseling appointment for the next morning.

I saw immediately that she was demon-indwelt. The only way she could say the name of Jesus was in blasphemy. She told me the demons had caused her to steal casually, sell her body for extra income, and disturb gospel services for entertainment. She and her friend—she told me later—regularly met on the banks of the Mississippi to worship Satan. They would prostrate themselves before their altar and pray to Satan that they might be chosen to bear the anti-christ into the world.[9]

The woman was later exorcised and became a follower of Christ. How many modern suicides are the result of occult practices no one can say. There are many other reports, new and old, of spirits attempting to manipulate a person to suicide.[10]

But there are other ways to die as a result of seeking the spirit world or other occult practices.

Professor Ed Gruss lists several cases of Ouija-board-inspired murders.[11] Pedro McGreggor in *Jesus of the Spirits*, relates a case where four people were murdered by the actual spirits themselves.[12] Dr. Nandor Fodor discusses many more incidents in his

Encyclopedia of Psychic Science. For example, a Franklin B. Evans was executed in Concord, New Hampshire, for the murder of a 12-year-old child. In his confession made just before his execution, he said that "for some days before the murder, I seemed to be attended continually by one who seemed to bear a human form, urging me on to the deed. At length it became fixed in my mind to take her life."[13] Fodor relates another case where a spirit persecuted one women for almost a year, setting fire to her house and even stabbing her in the back with a knife![14]

Death magic also has a long tradition where occultists attempt to command spirits to kill other people.[15] Dr. Koch observes that persecution and defense magic are "among the most common forms of magic."[16] The compilation *Demon Experiences in Many Lands* quotes three missionaries in Madras, India, who "won two men to Christ who were doing black magic using it to kill people."[17] Koch refers to one woman whose "specialty was in causing sickness and in death magic; she has already committed several murders which the police had been unable to solve."[18] He refers to another woman who used *The 6th and 7th Book of Moses*, *The Spring Book*, *The Spiritual Shield*, and many other dangerous texts. She:

> experimented in the area of magic persecution and death magic and she even boasted of having caused the deaths of her husband and daughter. She would inflict her enemies with diseases and claimed that she was able to cause eczemas, diarrhea, heart trouble, itching, stomach pains, swelling of the body and other things. After causing the death of all the members of her family, according to her own words, she then took on the job of a district nurse.[19]

Noted UFO/psychic investigator John Keel has personally researched on-site cases around the world. He observes:

> In demonology, practitioners of witchcraft and black magic traditionally end up as victims of the very

forces they hoped to control. Strange tragedies stalk
them, and they fall prey to the phenomenon of possession. That is, some outside force seems to possess
them, destroys their will power, and forces them to
carry out anti-social acts ranging from arson to murder. This same kind of possession is apparent in many
UFO contactee cases. There have been a number of
senseless murders in which the killer's only defense
was that he had been ordered to commit the act by
"Martians."[20]

Another noted UFO researcher, astrophysicist and parapsychologist Dr. Jacques Vallee agrees. For example:

In the Soviet Union, not so long ago, a leading
plasma physicist died in strange circumstances: He
was thrown under a Moscow subway train by a mentally deranged woman. It is noteworthy that she
claimed a "voice from space" had given her orders to
kill that particular man—orders she could not resist.
Soviet criminologists, I have been reliably informed,
are worried by the increase of such cases in recent
years.[21]

Jack Roper, the director of a Midwest countercult organization, has produced a computerized data base on Satanism,
witchcraft, Druidism, and other forms of paganism which lists
hundreds of organizations involved in such activities. The introduction also lists several incidents of criminal occult activity, for
example, 1) a physician involved in Satanism under investigation
for multiple murders and 2) a student who murdered his school
principal because his *animal* sacrifices to the devil were apparently not sufficient.[22]

In his ominous *Cults That Kill: Probing the Underworld of
Occult Crime*, award-winning journalist Larry Kahaner supplies
firsthand accounts of hideous torture, child molestation, murder,
crime and cruelty that are almost impossible for the uninitiated

to imagine. His purpose in writing this carefully researched book was "to show the far-reaching breadth of this type of crime."[23]

But even dabbling on the "innocent fringes" of occultism may carry a heavy price tag, at least for some people. Perhaps several hundred deaths have now been connected to imaginative games that role play occult realities, such as Dungeons and Dragons.[24] Dungeons and Dragons alone has sold some ten million sets and has led many teenagers and adults into active occult practice.[25] Further, "There is many a psychiatrist who will testify to having to work with disturbed children whose trouble began with a fascination aroused by such fantasy games."[26]

In an age of occult revival and reality, even Halloween practices can present a problem:

> In the opinion of Dr. David Enoch, former senior consultant psychiatrist at the Royal Liverpool Hospital and the University of Liverpool, Halloween practices open the door to the occult and can introduce forces into people's lives that they do not understand and often cannot combat.
>
> Much damage is done by Christians who mix up Christianity with the occult by encouraging this practice, which is pagan at heart. For too many children, this annual preoccupation with evil leads to a deepening fascination with the supernatural, witches and the possibility of exercising power over others.
>
> In the United Kingdom, the Association of Christian Teachers has produced a leaflet entitled *Hallowe'en* in response to this popularization of something intrinsically evil. They underline three reasons for concern about Halloween as an educational exercise.
>
> 1. If we suppose that witches and spirits are nonsense, why, then, encourage children to celebrate their mythical frolics and perhaps take them seriously? Paganism is hardly a cultural mainstay of all that is best in our society.
> 2. Suppose that in our folklore, witches and demons merely represent moral evil. Hallowe'en then

tends to celebrate evil in the ascendant by the
reversal of moral standards. If Nazi figures were
regularly presented for children's admiration and
affection there would soon be a public outcry. But
lovable little witches are brought out every autumn. This disturbs the polarization of good and
bad, right and wrong, in children's minds.

3. Hallowe'en does in fact encourage an interest and
fascination in the occult and this invariably leads to
more serious involvement and damage to the individuals concerned.[27]

The Washington Post provided several illustrations of the tragedy resulting from the revival of occultism in China, which it
alleges is now "running rampant" as admitted even by Communist leaders.[28] The article briefly describes the conditions surrounding eight murders, three deaths, and two suicides related to
occult practices. It also observes that literally millions of Chinese
are ruled by superstitions and occult beliefs.

In our eight years of research on over 70 religious sects in
America, we noted a theme of unquestioning obedience to the
authority figure, "whether right or wrong." Unethical or criminal activity is justified on pragmatic grounds, and many disciples
spoke of a willingness to either kill themselves or other people
should their spiritual leader demand it.

We all remember the horror of Jonestown and the murder of
Rep. Leo Ryan. Former members of Jim Jones' People's Temple
admitted they signed a statement declaring they would "kill,
destroy or commit any act necessary" to further the plans of
Jones.[29] As a result, 900 murders and suicides in the Guyana
jungle shocked the nation. But how many people were ever aware
of Rev. Jones' connection to the occult? An article in *Christianity
Today* indicated Jones apparently "believed he was 'guided' by a
supernatural 'spirit,'" and researcher Dave Hunt refers to Jones'
early involvement with South American spiritism.[30]

Ironically, in a 1981 interview, Leo Ryan's own daughter spoke
of her devotion to the late Indian guru Rajneesh. She stated, "I've

heard other people say if Bhagwan asked them to kill themselves, they would do it. . . . . If Bhagwan asked them to kill someone else, they would do it. I don't know if my trust in him is that total. I would like it to be, and I don't believe he would ever do that."[31] But as we document in Chapter 13, even Rajneesh teaches there is nothing really wrong with murder as long as it is done "properly" in "higher consciousness."

Regardless, death may also occur from many other causes related to occult activity. For example, death may result from the psychic vampirism of a seance. This has long been noted, with probably hundreds of cases occurring since the beginnings of modern American spiritism in 1848. Mediums require that those present at seances allow themselves to become vampirized by the control spirit who utilizes their energy as well as the mediums' for its own purposes. In one case with medium d'Esperance, "The draw on the sitter proved fatal. The [ectoplasmic] phantom was grabbed, and an old lady, the mother of the spirit grabber, who apparently contributed most of the ectoplasm, was so seriously injured, that after much suffering, she died from the consequences (*Light*, Nov. 21, 1903)."[32]

Former medium Raphael Gasson warns:

> During this process of entering and departing from the medium's body, the spirit demands absolute silence on the part of the sitters, as a sudden noise, movement, etc., may result in the medium receiving a violent shock to his system and may even go so far as to cause him to lose his life. Mediumship then is certainly not a thing to tamper with unless one is prepared to risk everything for it. . . . At my last seance . . . all I could recall upon regaining consciousness was that . . . the spirits were trying to take my life by preventing me returning to my body.[33]

Occultist Brennan offers another example in a different area:

> But fascination is not the only danger. Any reader with experience of mental illness knows the strength

of psychic forces. On some levels of the Astral, these forces are met head on. The effect on an unprepared personality can be staggering. Dream deaths have actually been recorded in the Philippines.[34]

Sometimes even the dying process itself carries an added weight of agony. "Many occultists and magic workers, especially those who have cultivated the black arts and signed themselves over to the devil in their own blood, die horrible deaths. This is especially true when a ready successor is not provided to carry on the nefarious practice."[35] Occult literature and biographies supply many illustrations of this fact, known only too well by the tortured family members of the dying.

In conclusion, when life is so precious and death so consequential for those outside of Christ, it is nothing short of lunacy to risk one's life by tampering with the occult. But for those still living, there can be yet other consequences of occult activity.

12

Psychiatric Illness and Related Problems

Most mental illness stems from causes other than the occult. For example, of perhaps 20 different causes of depression, Koch lists only one relating to the occult. Thus:

> Those who are not familiar with the medical aspect of emotional disorders are in great danger of making false diagnoses and therefore giving the wrong treatment. . . . I must again warn against ascribing all mental disorders to occult causes. Only a small percentage of emotional disorders have occult roots. . . . It is, however, often difficult to separate the two areas and to say whether a particular problem is spiritual or medical.[1]

This underscores the importance of proper medical testing, counseling, and spiritual discernment before making a final diagnosis (see Chapter 17 and Appendix H). If even committed Christian psychiatrists can have a hard time distinguishing mental illness from occult bondage, this is surely an area needing caution and wisdom. This is even more true in a phenomenon such as multiple personality disorder where distinguishing occult causes and/or possession by spirits from true multiple personalities can be difficult at best (cf. James G. Frieson, *Uncovering the Mystery of MPD* [Here's Life, 1991]). In addition, independent mental problems and emotional disorders arising from occult bondage may often exist simultaneously.

Nevertheless, with so many people turning to the occult today, resulting emotional problems are on the rise.

Mediums and other channelers, for example, are often known to have psychological disturbances; so are psychics, witches, and Satanists. For example, Dr. Jeffrey Russell of the University of California at Santa Barbara observes, "Satanism . . . has had a great effect on people of unsound mind. Some people have been psychologically damaged by it. There's no doubt about that."[2] Occultists and their victims frequently end up in mental institutions when the experiences they have encountered push them over the edge. Dr. Koch refers to a New Zealand psychiatrist who "claims that 50% of the neurotics being treated in the clinics in Hamilton are the fruit of Maori sorcery."[3] He also says he knows of Christian psychiatrists who believe that sometimes over half of the inmates at their psychiatric clinics are suffering from occult oppression rather than mental illness, but that this occurs only in areas where occultism is extensively practiced.[4]

In "Mental Health Needs and the Psychic Community," the late psychic researcher D. Scott Rogo warned, "The types of negative reactions people initially have to their psychic experiences may lead to permanent psychological damage if not immediately treated."[5] Rogo further observes that three of the most typical negative reactions to having a psychic encounter are 1) alienation from social relationships, 2) fear of impending insanity, and 3) a morbid preoccupation with psychic experiences.[6]

A four-day symposium of the American Academy of Religion, the Society of Biblical Literature, and the American School of Oriental Research also noted the dangers of the occult in relation to mental health. In a paper delivered before the symposium, Roger L. Moore, a psychologist of religion at Chicago Theological Seminary, observed that there are "haunting parallels" between the paranoid schizophrenic and the deeply involved occultist. He warned that "participation in the occult is dangerous for persons who are the most interested in it because they are the least able to turn it on and off. . . . And a lot of them have become paranoid psychotics."[7]

Alice McDowell Pempel of Cornell University delivered another paper on the consequences of drug-induced altered state of consciousness (ASC), and noted the "possibility for madness is ever present" if those who meet up with monsters and demons in these states view them as real.[8] Of course, psychic and occult practices characteristically induce altered states of consciousness and this in itself poses risks. Psychiatrist Arnold M. Ludwig points out, "As a person enters or is in an ASC, he often experiences fear of losing his grip on reality and losing his self-control."[9]

Psychotherapist Elsa First warns that cultivating ASCs may result in a "permanent alienation from ordinary human attachments."[10] Medium Wanda Sue Parrott also notes the ease with which psychics may lose a grip on reality:

> What is the greatest threat to human well-being in the world of psychic phenomena? I would say from experience, *fear.* Fear of losing one's sanity and self-control are nearly as common as fear of losing one's soul.[11]

The fear of insanity seems to be a genuine concern, for as former witch Irvine alleges, "Be warned: those who walk down the dark road of witchcraft lose their reason, often going completely insane. . . . Minds are twisted and warped."[12]

Psychic Harmon H. Bro refers to the occultly influenced mental conditions of some people—conditions which overcome their sanity as they seek to become more and more psychic: "I shall not soon forget the power-driven widow who frantically burned incense in her bedroom to rid it of 'evil entities' and aimlessly constructed 'aura-charts' of angels as she withdrew from her friends and family into a hate-supported schizophrenic world."[13]

Psychical researcher Robert H. Ashby, author of *A Guidebook to the Study of Psychical Research*, relates one case of a Ouija-board-induced breakdown. The spirit ("Joe") started out typically with a surprising knowledge of personal details of the participants' lives. He was very witty and entertaining besides. But once the person was in emotional dependence on advice from the board, the message changed:

> (The) next stage was frankly sexual propositions that soon had the girls disturbed; but when they asked that he (the spirit) stop this, the messages became threatening, the warnings including something "Joe" termed "psychic rape" if they did not comply with his wishes. At this point, Wendy was so frightened that she stopped sitting at the board. Linda, however, was so "hooked" that she felt it more dangerous to stop than to continue, for Joe ordered her fiercely to keep on with the ritual. Eventually, the climax arrived when Joe told Linda that she must drop out with him, for they were, he assured her, "soulmates" from former lives. The punishment if she did not do his bidding was serious physical disfigurement or even death at his hands. . . .
>
> Linda became a recluse, unwilling to seek psychiatric help (Joe had warned her against that), afraid to continue school, and sinking steadily into a desperate mental state. . . . Linda refused to see me because Joe had whispered to her that he would kill her if she did.
>
> The pattern outlined above . . . is all too common in Ouija board experiences.[14]

Raymond Van Over, a former editor of the *International Journal of Parapsychology*, refers to one girl, who, through her occult involvement felt:

> She was being attacked telepathically by a vampire who was after her blood. His voice kept cursing her and telling her disgusting things to do. One didn't need to be a psychiatrist to see that she was deeply disturbed and on the verge of a breakdown. . . . She suffered a complete mental collapse.[15]

Anita Muhl, M.D., is an authority on automatic writing. She refers to one actress who became interested in spiritism by this method, and was finally admitted to a mental hospital. In the hospital she felt she had been taken over by the spirit of her dead father:

> That same evening the patient suddenly threw herself to the floor and went through numerous gross symbolic movements. . . . She spoke of being thrown to the floor by occult powers.[16]

The actress subsequently went through several releases and readmittances to the hospital and, after a year, was discharged with a diagnosis of "Paranoid Condition—Much Improved." For the next year, she continued to develop mediumistic powers and believed she was healed of numerous physical ailments by her spirit controls. But while lecturing in another city, she spontaneously fell into a trance on a crowded street. She had to be taken to a hospital first and then to a mental institution where she developed feelings of grandeur and experienced other traumas. Eventually released, "she continued to lead a miserable unadjusted life."[17]

Although advocating automatic writing as a possible tool for psychotherapy(!), even Dr. Muhl confesses that when used for working off fantasies, when the material is destructive (which is often the case), the person is "apt to become more and more unstable and sometimes psychotic."[18]

For example, Dr. Muhl herself gives numerous case histories of the problems associated with automatic writing, pointing out that the messages "often prove dangerous" and cause a tendency to schizophrenic reactions. "The subject begins to lose interest in everyday contacts and responsibilities and often becomes delusional and hallucinated. I have seen many a fine business and professional man lose his grip through too intense interest in automatic writing." The person becomes "less and less able to face reality" and these automatisms "frequently precipitate a psychosis."[19] She says that any other use of automatic writing besides for therapy (!) is "very dangerous."[20]

It is both ironic and unfortunate that hundreds of psychotherapists today see benefits to automatisms and other forms of the occult in counseling. Use of these practices (including automatic drawing, speech, painting, musical composition; tarot card therapy, shamanism and sorcery, ASCs, pendulums, meditation, psychosynthesis, etc.)[21] is dangerous and should be avoided.

In conclusion, we have to date seen that the possibility of death or insanity constitutes two potential hazards of occult practice; these, of course, represent personal dangers. But the occult carries with it dangers of another variety that impact society more directly. In our next chapter we examine some of the moral and social implications of occultism.

13

Sexual Immorality and Other Personal and Social Consequences

In Chapter 2 we briefly discussed the monistic philosophy of the occult and how such a belief ultimately rejects moral categories, such as good and evil or right and wrong. Characteristically, this anti-moral philosophy is undergirded by occult states of consciousness which seem to support a monistic perspective. As one psychic told us, "Once I *experienced* cosmic consciousness, I *knew* conventional morality was just an illusion."

Monism teaches that "God is One"—that ultimate reality is one impersonal, undifferentiated, divine essence. What this means is that just as humanity itself is ultimately meaningless (as separate individual persons) then humanity's morality must also be meaningless. Human morality is simply a product of "unenlightened" and "deluded" thinking; morality *per se* does not exist.

Thus, in the occult we find not only the rejection of the image of God in man concerning his personality, but often the attempt to *defile* the image of God in man concerning his morality (his conscience). Moral thinking is held to be as destructive of higher consciousness and true reality as any other binding and illusory activity.

Of course, the repudiation of morality is not always immediately evident to those who join Eastern sects or occult groups. People must slowly be reconditioned to accept such radical denials. Again, this is often a result of repeated cultivation of occult states of consciousness and the gradual adoption of anti-moral philosophies—usually encouraged in the name of "God" and "higher spirituality."

In essence, in the long run, to adopt occult beliefs and practice is to vaporize absolute moral standards, both philosophically and experientially.

The rejection of morality goes hand in hand with the occult, and this fact is noted by many commentators. Dr. Unger observes: "People who deal in the occult are often found to be immoral."[1]

Of course, occultists may claim to be moral people, but their own philosophy and lifestyle reject their claims. For example, in a special week-long segment on a Los Angeles news show, Ziena LaVey, the daughter of Satanist Anton LaVey, claimed that "True Satanists are very moral people." But she then proceeded to discuss the necessity for engaging in the "seven deadly sins" (e.g., pride, lust, greed, etc.) for proper mental health.[2]

Another example is the overriding philosophy of famous occultist Aleister Crowley which was "the whole of the law is 'Do what thou wilt.'" Crowley was grossly perverse and had a reputation as "the most wicked man in the world." He even named himself "The beast-666."[3]

In a similar manner, Eastern gurus who accept the monism of *advaita* Vedanta characteristically deny the moral distinctions of good versus evil as part of the *maya* (illusion) of the world. With other occultists, they accept that biblical morality is an illusion stifling spiritual advancement. This is why Rajneesh says (commenting on Christian faith), "The greatest deception is the deception of devotion to God."[4] Such a belief presupposes a dualistic reality (God and man as real, distinct categories); hence, it is deception within the premise of monism. It is the greatest deception because it prevents man from realizing he is one essence with God if he thinks he must be devoted to God, especially a holy and righteous God.

Thus, Rajneesh teaches that "to emphasize morality is mean, degrading; it is inhuman" and that literally "everything is holy; nothing is unholy."[5] Here we see that one of the purposes of the Eastern monistic path is to get the disciple to understand that, after "enlightenment" *everything* he does is "holy," whether good or evil. Because nothing is truly evil, Rajneesh even acknowledges *murder* as a potentially meditative act (i.e., something "good" or "holy")—assuming, of course, it is done in "higher" consciousness.

In commenting upon the lesson of the *Bhagavad Gita* (a Hindu scripture) he says: "Even if you kill someone consciously, while fully conscious [i.e., "enlightened"], it is meditative. . . . Kill, murder, fully conscious, knowing fully that no one is murdered and no one killed. . . . Just become the instrument of Divine hands and know well that no one is killed, no one can be killed."[6]

No one can be killed in this philosophy because no one really exists to be killed. All duality (e.g., people) is illusion and only the impersonal, undifferentiated God is real. In a letter to the editor, even Charles Manson once said, "I've killed no one."[7] Given the influence of monism upon him, this attitude is not surprising.

Some of the most evil and dehumanizing acts occur in this area where morality is rejected and occultism practiced, and books have been written cataloguing the horrors. Of course, there is a limit to what can be discussed in a public book, especially a Christian book. What we mention is the tip of the iceberg.

If we really believe that man as man is only an "illusion," and that morality is irrelevant, then is it surprising to discover that those who hold such views are willing to accept the mistreatment, brutalization, or even demonization of other men and women?

Virtually any evil—from deliberate deception to criminal activity—is capable of rationalization within monistic occultism. Thus, "What you would normally think to be right or wrong no longer has any place."[8]

If morality is ultimately an illusion, then to achieve true enlightenment, to inhabit true reality, one must go beyond the idea of good and evil. Again, theoretically, once a person becomes truly "enlightened," any actions (even evil actions) become "spiritual" actions—for the "enlightened" individual is, by definition, incapable of committing evil. He cannot possibly commit that which does not exist. Thus, the following teachings as cited by gurus, astrologers, psychics, and other practitioners are commonplace in the occult.

> Our concepts of sin and virtue . . . alienate us from our true Self. . . . That which you see as impure is pure. . . . You imagine [ideas of] sin and virtue through ignorance.[9]
>
> Moral obligation is a myth, a detriment to spiritual advance.[10]
>
> If you are possessed by that higher sense of wisdom, nothing is bad.[11]
>
> In the Christian tradition, the being called Satan or the Devil is the epitome of wisdom and his actions are the true expression of an enlightened conscience.[12]
>
> [God] sees your good and evil thoughts and actions but they do not matter to him.[13]
>
> My ashram [spiritual community] makes no difference between the Devil and the Divine. . . . I use all sorts of energies. And if the devilish energy can be used in a divine way, it becomes tremendously fruitful.[14]
>
> Obedience [to God] is the greatest sin.[15]
>
> I don't believe in morality . . . and I am bent on destroying it. . . . I believe in consciousness, not conscience.[16]
>
> The person who has deep compassion is not going to be bothered about whether he tells a lie or a truth. . . . All [spiritual teachers] have lied. . . . Through lies, by and by a master brings you toward light.[17]
>
> Good and evil have no absolute reality.[18]
>
> Really, good and evil are one and the same.[19]

Even in light of the modern AIDS plague, the teachings of occultists concerning sexual permissiveness continue: "[Homosexual love] is natural . . . far easier, far more convenient."[20]

"Sex relations are [a divine process, in or out of marriage] . . . a random and loving occasion without [any] contracts [obligations]."[21]

But in the area of sexual behavior, even occultists sometimes give warnings. Yoga authorities Sri Krishna Prem and Arthur Avalon both severely caution mixing sex and certain forms of the occult, in this case, hatha yoga. Prem says it is safer to play with dynamite and Avalon says that intercourse during the early stages of hatha yoga "is likely to prove fatal."[22] Why is anyone's guess, but paradoxically, occultism and sexual promiscuity go hand in hand.

For example, Harmon H. Bro refers to one man,

> a well-trained Viennese psychiatrist, a man who effectively had healed many neurotic patients but whose ventures in automatic writing led him into grandiose delusions, then homosexual practices which eventually destroyed his professional usefulness and personal happiness.[23]

The increasingly influential Tantric philosophy and related disciplines are bound up in the idea of the "enlightenment of sexual power" and offer justification for all kinds of illegitimate and perverse sexual activity. The late Hindu Tantrist Bhagwan Shree Rajneesh, once headquartered in Oregon, was well-known for his free-sex teachings which also condoned beatings and rapes (see Tal Brooke, *Riders of the Cosmic Circuit*, available from SCP, P. O. Box 4308, Berkeley, CA 94704). As Rajneesh pointed out, Tantrists do not make love to one another so that they become united as one; rather they merely use each other as "doors" to higher consciousness to allegedly discover their own completeness as androgynous entities. But in the process the very nature and purpose of sexual complementarity is cheapened and perverted. Many other gurus endorse bisexuality/homosexuality or are themselves bisexual (e.g., Ram Dass) or homosexual (e.g., Sai Baba—again see Tal Brooke, *Riders of the Cosmic Circuit*).

One West Coast actress stated:

> I thought my guru was God's next of kin, until I
> discovered he made my girlfriend pregnant at the
> same time he was sleeping with me.[24]

The collective personal tragedies wrought by occult sexual license can hardly be fathomed. They can perhaps be gauged by
books such as Tal Brooke, *Riders of the Cosmic Circuit*; Brad
Steiger, *Sex and Satanism*; and Ankerberg and Weldon, *The Myth of
Safe Sex: The Devastating Consequences of Violating God's Plan*.

Sexual promiscuity and perverted sex go hand in hand with
the occult so regularly that occult activity surely carries a greater
proportional share for the debilitating sexual conditions in modern culture.[25] Remember, tens of millions of people today follow
the New Age Movement, Eastern gurus, and other forms of the
occult.

In occult circles, a person may be told that for many lifetimes
he or she was a member of the opposite sex, justifying bisexual
and homosexual appetites. (As we documented in *Astrology: Do
the Heavens Rule Our Destiny?* [1989], some astrologers and
other occultists cater specifically to the homosexual community
and encourage homosexual licentiousness.) An individual may
also be told that he or she has not married the proper "soul mate"
and that unless joined sexually with that person, the karmic
"imbalance" will have to be paid in more difficult ways, justifying adulterous exploits or divorce.[26]

Recently the famous actress Sharon Stone was told by a
psychic that her true "soul mate" from a previous life was the
husband of another woman. He left his wife for the actress, and
they are now engaged to be married (*Hard Copy*, April 6, 1993).

In Eastern religions and many Western cults and sects, monistic philosophies can be used to obliterate sexual distinction since
male-female roles constitute part of the *maya* (illusion) of duality.
Perhaps this is one reason why so many gurus accept bisexuality.
Or, in reincarnation philosophies, one may be informed through
psychic means that one has a male body but a female spirit, or
vice versa. Sexual preference is anybody's guess at that point.

Indeed, of 54 gurus examined, 39 were found to be sexually active—over 70 percent.[27, 28] Close to 90 percent of the sexually active gurus had "at least occasional sexual relationships with one or more students."[29] Of the married, many were adulterers and "some are homosexual and some are bisexual in preference."[30] In those cases where gurus had sex with their women disciples, approximately 50 percent of the women were in some way damaged by the incident. Being seduced by the guru was "a source of great suffering."[31] And these are only the admitted confessions.

According to the Associated Press, on June 2, 1986, Guru Prem Paramahansa, 38, was found guilty in Torrance, California, of eight counts of unlawful sex, over a 17-month period, with an eight-year-old girl (in 1982 to 1983).

The *Chicago Tribune* of August 16, 1982, ran an article on the 400,000-member Ananda Marga Yoga Society titled "Guru Sect is Probed for Terrorism, Murder," detailing CIA and FBI investigations into the sect. Writer Bernard Bauer noted that for 27 years, "The cult has left a trail of blood around the world."

The ISKCON or Hare Krishna community has been under federal investigation. Over the years there have been many reports in the *Los Angeles Times* and other papers on alleged criminal activity at the sect's various headquarters (for example, the Gurukula School in Dallas, Texas, and the "New Vrindaban" community in West Virginia). Concerning the latter, the investigative news show "West 57th Street," on October 31, 1987, reported allegations concerning the murder of former members, wife beating, child molesting, and the sale of illegal drugs such as cocaine and heroin.

Again, given the forceful denial of absolute standards of right and wrong, is any of the above really so surprising? But there is more. In some forms of occult enlightenment, the basic ethical categories of right and wrong must be transcended in another manner: through the intentional violation of moral values by the *deliberate* practice of evil.

As Rajneesh and many Satanists have stated, the goal is to completely erode the conscience. Since man is created in God's image, and a strong part of that image involves conscience, it is not surprising that the destruction of the conscience is part of the process of the destruction of the individual. Once the individual and his conscience are seared away and only a "void" remains, is it surprising that what enters and sets up house could be demonic? In other words, should anyone be surprised that the *deliberate* practice of spiritual evil would lead to further spiritual evil along the lines of demonization? We earlier cited the disciples of Da Free John as an example. But this can be multiplied in dozens of occult groups:

> The effect of this level of practice becomes chillingly clear in the inner rings of the Rajneesh camp. We listen to ex-Neeshlings [ex-followers] unfold horrific tales of breaking the boundaries—of bizarre behavior, of beatings, rapes, and worse in the intensive training courses. We see a shockingly effective effort to break down human identity through a calculated violation of the taboos of human morality.... This is more than random vileness. Such thoroughgoing violation of taboo eventually erodes one's humanity—it "reams out" the physical envelope of a human being and leaves a void where the person should be. This extinction of identity makes possible the entry of demonic entities in a unique and total way.[32]

As another illustration, the *San Francisco Chronicle* ran an article about guru Da Free John being sued for $45 million by a former member alleging sexual abuse, assault, brainwashing, and imprisonment. Another member alleged that devotees were ordered to make pornographic films and that "everything that was done was interpreted as a lesson about your own lack of spirituality."[33]

But is it so surprising that those who worship evil gods will themselves soon come to glorify evil? The Hindu god Indra says in the *Kaushitaki Upanishad*:

The man who knows me as I am loses nothing
whatever he does. Even if he kills his mother or his
father, even if he steals or procures an abortion,
whatever evil he does, he does not blanch if he knows
me as I am.[34]

In the Bhagavad Gita 9:30 Krishna declares, "Even if a devotee commits the most abominable actions, he is to be considered saintly because he is properly situated" (i.e., in "higher"
consciousness). Transcendental Meditation peacemaker Maharishi Mahesh Yogi comments on Arjuna in the *Bhagavad Gita* that
he must attain "a state of consciousness which will justify any
action . . . and will allow him even to kill in love in support of the
purpose of evolution."[35]

As we noted earlier, the Manson clan was also influenced by
Eastern/occult philosophy and also knew of this "love." Susan
Atkins explained her murder of Sharon Tate with, "You really
have to have a lot of love in your heart to do what I did to Tate."
Sandra Good put it simply as, "There's no wrong. . . . You kill
whoever gets in your way."[36]

Should we forget the horrors? The eight-month-pregnant
Sharon Tate repeatedly stabbed in the stomach; Voytek Fry-
kowsky—shot twice, hit over the head 13 times, stabbed 51
times; Rosemary La Bianca—41 knife wounds; Leno La Bianca
12 knife wounds, punctured with a fork seven times, a knife in his
throat, a fork in his stomach, and on the wall in his own blood,
DEATH TO PIGS.[37] "The more you murder, the more you like
it," Atkins boasted.[38]

Spiritism and Immorality

Now let us consider spiritism—or more popularly, channeling. Spiritism is increasingly advocated today and often claims
to be morally based. Thus, in the minds of most practitioners,
"Spirit guides are usually perceived as beings on a high level of
consciousness development, with superior intelligence and extraordinary moral integrity."[39] The spirits themselves may appear moral, especially in something like so-called "Christian"

spiritualism where the spirits are seeking to reach those with at least a nominal Christian perspective. For example, in his life as a medium, Victor Ernest recalls that, for the most part, the spirits he spoke to were very moralistic. "Amoah and Emoah, my control spirits, lectured me often on what was wrong in my thoughts, morals, and manners. They even stressed physical health and cleanliness."[40]

Unfortunately, this is another ruse whereby the spirits only seek to entrap people by appealing to their moral character. With the morally inclined, the spirits may indeed be moral, at least initially. But the fact is that spiritism—in all its forms—sooner or later leads to moral demise. This, too, is the goal of the spirits.

In her comprehensive *Modern American Spiritualism*, medium Emma Harding noted:

> One marked result of spirit influence has been to externalize character, and develop into sudden prominence the hidden traits, perhaps scarcely known to their possessors. . . . It is certain that latent evil tendencies are not unfrequently matured into ugly prominence by the effects of [spiritism].[41]

In *The Haunted Mind*, psychoanalyst and authority on the psychic Dr. Nandor Fodor also observes the sexual perversity possible through mediumism:

> That in mediumship sexual energies may furnish the fuel for many physical, and perhaps also for mental, manifestations, is established by the scientific findings I have quoted. . . . I have known male mediums who were homosexuals. One in England was jailed because his spirit control persuaded a young boy to yield to him. . . . While it is not more shocking for a medium to be homosexual than for any other man, an unusual element emerges when a male medium has a female control and this female control, in a "materialized" shape, tried to make love to the male sitters.[42]

John A. Keel is the author of several books on UFOs and other occult phenomena. He spent a great deal of time personally investigating occult ritual and practice:

> Sex is heavily intermixed with cultist rites and beliefs, particularly in black magic, witchcraft, and even spiritualism. A number of famous spirit mediums admit to the practice of having sexual intercourse just before a big seance.[43]

M. Lamar Keene was a fraudulent medium for 13 years. He eventually renounced his deceptions, but he also noted that the general outlook among mediums was frequently immoral:

> Some of the mediums I knew were virtually psychic prostitutes. In the seance room Brenda Hummel took on all comers. For a price. One whole family of second-generation mediums, male and female, were invited to leave Camp Chesterfield [a spiritist haven] because their sexual escapades in the seance room were too open and notorious.[44]

Keene emphasizes the amoral attitude of most mediums, and states it is legitimate to ask

> just how common such sexual seances really are. More common, perhaps than even I suspect. To me, of course, sex in the seance room is merely a logical, though particularly nasty, extension of the basic fraudulent mediumship: Give the customer what he (or she) wants. What it is doesn't matter; what it pays does.[45]

The late Olga and Ambrose Worral were both "Christian" mediumistic "healers" having wide experience with the spirit world. In an interview they stated: "We have had overwhelming evidence of lower spirit entities possessing the minds of those still living as a means to sensually experience physical appetites and feelings again."[46].

They observe the spirit first poses as a highly evolved, moral spirit and assures the person they have an important job for him to perform. Then the spirit's entire character undergoes a change and it begins to make sexual remarks and to stimulate the person sexually. The voice never lets up, night or day, and "tries to upset relations between husband and wife, and urges whoever it controls to commit suicide so the two can be together in the same dimension."[47] In their work, the Worrals encountered so many cases like this that they believe the situation is very serious. And yet as mediums themselves (operating out of a Methodist church) they continued to advocate spiritism.

Carolee Collins refers to one case:

> A heretofore reasonably happily married man, father of several children, was informed that he had been married in another life to an attractive woman whom he met in the psychic's "clinic," and that they were "soulmates" destined always to be together. The woman was married and had a family but the two left their spouses and promptly set up housekeeping together—because it had been legal in a previous existence and was their destiny![48]

Cosmic Rationalizations·

Of course, in occult/Eastern philosophies there exists a host of spiritual rationalizations which allow both the leader and disciple to sidestep their own immorality, failures, or greed. The blame for any resulting sin or disaster can be placed upon the interference of "malevolent spirits," the necessity of "karmic justice," spiritual "testing," or the failure of other people to properly "attune" themselves psychically as instructed. Collins refers to one case where "ascended masters," speaking through a medium,

> maintained that members of this entire inner group were over the centuries constantly reincarnating into

different relationships with each other. . . . And so each of them in turn had been mother, father, sister, brother, aunt or uncle, wife or husband, to all the others. And because Karen had at one time or another been legally wed to each of the men in the congregation, no one would dare to castigate her if she now slept with most of the good-looking ones. The wives, and Karen's husband, were told that it was their karma to endure whatever life handed them, and if the prettiest girl in the crowd got most of the goodies, that was their tough luck.[49]

Raymond Van Over confesses:

> This is danger number one: occultism offers ready and convenient means by which those already disturbed—or those on the borderline—can justify or rationalize their neurotic needs. The deeper their involvement in occultism, the more likely it is that such people will utilize its teachings and symbolism in a psychotic way.[50]

And so it has always been. For example, *Current Opinion* of June 1914 (Vol. 56) had the following editorial commenting on Dr. John Raupert's book, *The Dangers of Spiritualism* (1901):

> Throughout the whole of his experience he obtained proofs that the character of these spirits is immoral and of blighting influence upon their victims. Although for a time they dictate high moral principles, especially to those who indulge in automatic writing, these invariably degenerate into sinister, blasphemous, or obscene suggestions. Hints are thrown out that morality is a matter of conventionality, that certain instincts are implanted in us in order to be gratified. Mr. Raupert asserts that he has known many women ruined utterly in body and soul by these

debasing immoralities, urged upon them when their will-power had been destroyed by opening the doors of their mind to evil suggestion.

The ravages of such an experience upon the nervous system are well known to those who investigate the causes of insanity. The growth of a morbid tendency among persons addicted to amusements of the mediumistic sort has long been familiar to psychologists. The subconscious associations seem to usurp the functions of the normal processes in those addicted to a haphazard pursuit of "black magic."[51]

The "Shanti Nilah" spiritual retreat center in Southern California is another illustration of sex and the occult. Headed by a psychic healer and the well-known spiritist Dr. Elizabeth Kubler-Ross (the famous authority on death and dying), the center attracted negative publicity for its many tales of sexual promiscuity—ostensibly with spirit entities or, in other words, the phenomena known historically as the "incubi" and "succubae."[52]

Perhaps this is one of the most unsavory activities in the area of occult sexuality: sex with "male" or "female" demons. This has a long tradition in witchcraft and other forms of the occult, and regardless of how it is done, the experience is reported as a physical one. John Weldon has talked with a former witch who experienced such phenomena personally, while she was clearly in a waking state. It is also mentioned by Drs. Koch, Unger, Vallee, Fodor, and many other researchers.[53]

For example, witch Doreen Valiente in *An ABC of Witchcraft Past and Present* discusses one case she personally knew of, noting, "Psychic researchers have encountered similar phenomena, sometimes with the added horror of alleged vampirism."[54]

There are also reported cases in Catholic monasteries. Dr. Vallee observes that "the most remarkable cases of sexual contact with nonhumans are...in the archives of the Catholic Church" and he proceeds to list examples.[55] Given the claim that (according to Investigative Reports TV series "Sins of the

Fathers") widespread homosexuality and, to a much lesser degree, pedophilia exist in some Catholic seminaries and among priests today (25 to 50 percent of priests were estimated to be homosexually inclined), one can only wonder if this phenomena has already returned.[56] There are also cases of sex with alleged UFO occupants (e.g., the Villa Boas, Shane Kurz, and Cordelia Donovan incidents), which essentially parallel the incubi-succubae.[57]

Psychiatrists rationalistically view these experiences as sexual "dreams," but this does little justice to the data, especially when people report them in a waking state.

Dr. Koch comments on this bizarre experience and supplies examples from his own counseling ministry.

> We now come to discuss [spirit] phenomena in the form of sexual experiences, which is surely the most repellent area of pastoral work. There are, namely, some severely troubled people who have nocturnal sexual [spirit] experiences, and are tormented by them. This is not a matter of "wet dreams" or of the sexual hallucinations of schizophrenics, but of experiences in a waking state. In the history of religion this phenomenon is known as incubi and succubae. These are male and female seducing demons. In the Bible there is such a story recorded in Genesis 6:4. There we read how sons of God united with daughters of men. This would be the phenomenon of angel marriages.
>
> Among the ancient peoples we can point to such conceptions too. The Babylonians and Assyrians had myths of so-called night maidens (ardat lili), which continued in Jewish tradition as lilith. In the Christian era this motif of demon marriage continued. In the Legend of St. Antony, the devil appears in the form, among others, of an enticing woman. The theme continued in the popular beliefs of the middle ages. In *The 6th and 7th Book of Moses* it is reported (6, 6) how

the demons make sexual assaults on people at night in the form of beautiful maidens or young men. In our day the phenomenon is constantly appearing in pastoral interviews. A few examples will illustrate in a striking way the mental distress of those afflicted.

Ex. 84—A woman often experiences nocturnal visitations. In a waking state she sees five wild boars charging at her, with intent to violate her. The woman cries loudly for help. Her husband finds it hard to calm her. He does not see the boars; he only hears strange noises.

Ex. 85—A friend of mine who was a missionary in China reported similar things among the Chinese. We have here a problem well known in the history of missions, that of fox-possession. Girls who are by day perfectly normal psychologically, and go about their work quite regularly, are at night sexually plagued by apparitions. Figures appear with the head of a fox. As soon as the figure draws near, the fox-head changes into the handsome face of a man. These girls suffer dreadfully from these nocturnal visitations. It is worthy of note that girls who turn to Christ are delivered from this. Christian Chinese girls are not subject to this affliction.[58]

Thus, he emphasizes, "From the pastoral point of view it is significant that faith in Jesus Christ puts an end to these sexual [spirit] apparitions."[59]

Dr. Unger also observes:

Perhaps the most terrible and revolting form of demonic oppression is what is known in the history of religion as incubi and succubae experiences. This is the assault by an unclean spirit upon its enslaved victim for the purpose of sexual lust. Both men and women have been attacked and molested by "seducing male and female demons." Such fully established phenomena show that angelic-human union, a major cause of the flood (Genesis 6:1-4; cf., 2 Peter 2:4; Jude 1:6-7), has its parallel in occultism today.[60]

In another account described by Dr. Fodor:

> Twice she had a waking experience at night of an unbelievably more frightening nature. She was visited by an incubus—a phantom or demon who behaved like a man and felt like a corpse. She saw no face and was paralyzed with fear[61] (see example in footnote).

Satanism and Witchcraft

Now let us turn to Satanism and witchcraft. Here, we see that sexual depravity is even more frequently found (sadomasochism, bestiality, ritual murder, etc.). We agree with Dr. Unger who warns, "For those who surrender themselves to worship and serve Satan, the moral degradation and perversion are horrifying."[62]

For example, in *Freed From Witchcraft*, former witch/Satanist Doreen Irvine discusses the rationale for her previous lifestyle:

> Lucifer must be highly esteemed in all situations, even while at work or in private. Lucifer sees, as he is with Satanists always, and he must be obeyed. Lying, cheating, swearing, free lust—even murder—are condoned. . . . The chief Satanist didn't care about my prostitution. He believed the more evil he condoned or achieved on earth, the greater would be his reward. . . . I had witnessed evil and ugly orgies in the Satanists' temple, but I was to see far worse in the witches' coven. . . . All meetings included awful scenes of perverted sexual acts, as sex plays an important part in witchcraft. Many black witches were lesbians or homosexuals. Sadism was practiced frequently. Some even cut themselves with knives and

felt no pain. Some swallowed poison, and no ill effects were experienced at all. Imagine over one hundred black witches all taking part in such perversions at the same time. . . . I added to my knowledge of evil every day. . . . I practiced more wickedness in a single week than many would in an entire lifetime.[63]

Psychologist Dr. James D. Lisle believes that in the case of the various types of black magic (e.g., Satanism, witchcraft):

You can never be sure a person involved in this won't step over the line into infant sacrifice or canni-balism. We have evidence that it happens. The people who get involved in a thing like witchcraft have a developing tunnel vision about the world and life. It is a continually narrowing thing that cuts them off from what is going on around them.[64]

R. J. Rushdoony, in a review of J. B. Russell's historical study, *Witchcraft in the Middle Ages*, perhaps unveils our future destiny as a nation, as increasing segments of our culture continue their quest for occult power and knowledge:

Because of its radical homocentricity or humanism, witchcraft is radically hostile to law and as a result is religiously antinomian. Russell documents this antinomia-nism repeatedly (pp. 26, 68, 94, 128, 133, 141, 168, 177, 224). This antinomianism manifested itself in a hostility against the Church (burning churches and killing priests) and against the people who by name stood for the law of God, the Jews, who were readily and brutally slaughtered by the antinomians, and also by the Inquisition. The sub-versive Joachimite movement fostered such popular ac-tivities. As Russell shows, "The antinomians, by arguing that all action was virtuous and that Satan was God, ad-vanced the cause of rebellion, libertinism, and Satanism" (p. 142).

The practical consequences of this antinomian activity, e.g., rebellion, libertinism, and Satanism, were militant action against the social order and a variety of illegal and hostile practices. These included human sacrifice (pp. 67, 88ff., 251, 263); Russell is careful to consider the possibility that such charges against witches may have been false, but he concludes that they were clearly true. The purpose was magical, and hence human sacrifice was often followed by cannibalism (pp. 69f., 81, 125, 239f., 251), adding, "Witches sacrificed or ate children or made them into magical slaves or powders, but they did not abuse them sexually" (p. 263). Not only was libertinism common to witches, because of their antinomianism, but also homosexuality (p. 95). "The essential element" in witchcraft during the medieval and later eras "is defiance of Church and society on behalf of the power of evil" (p. 101). The witch "takes pleasure in corruption of all that a peaceful and just society holds dear" (p. 276).

Witchcraft is a product in part of a rejection of all existing institutions and the "establishments" which are a part of them, and, together with this, a rejection of all religious and moral standards in the belief that the universe is meaningless, chaotic, and purposeless. Witchcraft thus demands the rejection of the existing order and values. Russell quotes Lynn White, who states of Witchcraft, "It is a drastic and spectacular way of rebelling, a repudiation of things as they are. It is an ultimate denial, a form of nihilism which is demanded by mentally and emotionally unstable people in any time of rapid change" (p. 278).

The return of magic and witchcraft concerns Russell. It is a return to the vicious and the dark in the human soul, more fearful now perhaps because we are a more secular culture and less restrained. We see again the rise of nihilism and mindless violence, for, in its deeper sense, Russell holds, "witchcraft springs out of hostility and violence that are at the same time as old as man and as contemporary" (p. 289).[65]

Obviously, any philosophy which rejects morality and can justify every conceivable evil must be rejected by society as a whole. No society can long survive when moral standards are torn asunder, especially in the name of God and religion. If our nation does not change its path soon, our children and grand-children will live to see an America unrecognizable by our standards.

Social Withdrawal

But if the occult can cause moral withdrawal, it can also lead to social withdrawal, which carries its own ethical price tag. Here we see that occult activity can lead to an indifferent attitude toward life—one which neglects larger social concerns in favor of personal ones.

Berkeley psychologist and psychic counselor Freda Morris refers to a typical case of a girl whose "life closed off. She became increasingly depressed and disinterested in anything. Finally she was no longer able to work." This continued for four years.[66]

Cultivating OBEs (out-of-body experiences) is a frequent fruit of occult activity and also bears significant responsibility for inducing isolationist tendencies. Although Robert Crookall has conducted most of the modern studies in astral travel, Robert Monroe is perhaps the most popular advocate. He is well aware of the dangers of the practice. For example, in *Journeys Out of the Body*, he refers to an area in his astral travels which "is a grey-black hungry ocean where the slightest motion attracts nibbling and tormenting beings."[67] In common with many occultists, he also observes that his astral wanderings are not done through his own will. He has "helpers" who are with him and seemingly control his travels:

> They are rarely "friendly" in the sense that we understand that term. Yet there is a definite sense of understanding, knowledge, and purposefulness in their actions toward me. I feel no intent on their part to bring harm to me and I trust their directions.[68]

Significantly, Monroe observes one particular consequence of attempting astral projection—a consequence also found in the "psychic transformation" of various New Age human potential seminars, the "God-Realization" sought in innumerable Hindu sects, and occult "enlightenment" in general. One becomes "a god" and views the world in a totally new way. One is now beyond the petty concepts of good/evil, right/wrong, compassion/love, etc.

But such experiences can also produce cold and callous human beings. Even Monroe warns:

> A note of caution is in order here for those who are interested in experimenting, for once opened, the doorway to this experience cannot be closed. More exactly, it is a case of "you can't live with it and you can't live without it." The activity and resultant awareness are quite *incompatible* with the science, religion, and mores of the society in which we live[69] (emphasis added).

Another illustration of how occult experiences can lead to ethical or social indifference is seen in a woman we met many years ago. At the urging of "Michael," a self-styled messiah, this woman left her husband and two sons, ages five and eight. Michael had previously experienced spontaneous kundalini arousal (the occult transformation activated in yoga and often in most other occult practice). This powerful experience led him to believe he was specially chosen of God. When he met this woman, he demanded she become his disciple if she were really serious in her desire to "serve God."

After abandoning her family to follow Michael, the resulting suffering to her husband and young children was unimaginable. "Michael's" only response to a personal plea from the woman's husband was that his kundalini experience had so elevated his consciousness (he now claimed to be Christ reincarnated), that he was, in effect, above the petty considerations of "lower" beings or their terribly mundane values and concerns. He could never view the world in the "old" way again, and had no regrets about encouraging a mother to leave her husband and children to follow him. That was entirely her gain, not her family's loss.

Such callousness is not at all atypical for those who have undergone occult transformation. The authors know personally of similar incidents and have read of other far more brutal examples.

But even milder forms of occult practice can lead in this direction. Transcendental Meditation founder Maharishi Mahesh Yogi declared that his meditators will eventually reach a state where they are "far above the boundaries of any social bond or obligation," and that "indifference is the weapon to be used against any negative situation in life." Hence:

> Because his self is fixed in the universal Self, there is nothing he could gain from another. His Self is uninvolved in every way—it is uninvolved with activity and it is uninvolved with the selves of individual beings. His own Self is the Self of all beings.

And he also claims:

> This world of joys and sorrows, of man's great enterprise and ambition, is for them like a world of dolls and toys with which children play and amuse themselves. Toys are a great source of excitement for children, but grown-ups remain untouched by them.[70]

Thus, Oxford professor R. C. Zaehner discusses the final state of the "God-realized" soul:

> The Absolute (Brahman or the universal Self) is wholly indifferent to what goes on in the world. "He does not speak and has no care." "He neither increases by good works, nor does he diminish by evil ones." Similarly in the case of the man who has realized that in the ground of his being he is identical

> with the Absolute, these two thoughts do not occur to
> him—"So I have done evil" or "So I have done what is
> good and fair." He shrugs them off. . . . This because,
> seeing the Self in himself and all things as the Self, he
> will be indifferent to all actions, good and evil, which
> take place in the phenomenal world.[71]

Philosophy professor and parapsychologist, Dr. Bob Brier describes one correspondent whose life is an epitaph for thousands of others: "Wyszynski is a man whose everyday reality is what other people call fantasy. He has acknowledged and accepted the existence of occult powers and they have consumed him."[72]

In conclusion, we have now briefly examined some of the moral and social implications of psychic/occult activity. We have seen it is personally dangerous; now we know it also carries grave moral and social consequences. (For a look at the economic consequences, see "Magic, Envy and Foreign Aid" in Gary North, *Unholy Spirits*, Chapter 8.)

But few people seem to realize there are other areas in which psychic activity may bring harm, including harm to one's own children and family members. It is to this consequence we now turn.

14

Hereditary Coherence and Other Forms of Transference

Dear ASPR:

Please tell me everything about ESP. I want to be a scientist. P.S. I am 9.[1]

The above letter to The American Society for Psychical Research (ASPR) was cited in *The Christian Parapsychologist* (the journal of the Churches Fellowship for Psychical and Spiritual Studies—an organization seeking to integrate Christianity and parapsychology). It represents an unfortunate sign of the times. Thousands of teens and even preteens have become interested in the psychic realm due to the influence of the modern occult revival. Hundreds of educators are obliging them. (See our book *Thieves of Innocence*, Harvest House, 1993.) For example, the Director of Education for the ASPR confessed the following:

> At the American Society for Psychical Research we receive letters, telephone calls, and visits from young people of all ages. They come from elementary schools, junior high and high schools, college and postgraduate levels, from people with degrees and even careers in other fields; from teachers, guidance counsellors, information centres, administrators. . . . These inquiring young people . . . are highly motivated. A high school student wrote: "I am almost consumed by the desire to work and study in parapsychology. Yet I do not know where to start. . . .

Please help me." . . . More and more young people
are becoming interested in parapsychology—to study
and to make a career in the field. . . . It seems to them
that this is "where it's at."[2]

One reason for the increase in interest in these matters is
undoubtedly the positive media exposure to the world of the
psychic, the educational efforts of organized parapsychology
institutions to legitimize its "scientific" nature, and the growing
influence of the New Age Movement.

But there is another aspect that cannot be overlooked and
which should be considered relevant: As surprising as this will be
to some, it is the sins of the parents. Can parents' occult activity
really have some effect in predisposing their unborn children, or
even their children's descendants toward occult interests? Further, can occult activity bring unintended harm to one's children
and other family members?

We know that certain sins committed by the parents in the
physical realm can seriously affect—even deform or kill—an
unborn child. This would include alcohol or drug addiction and
many sexually transmitted diseases like herpes, syphilis, and
AIDS. We also know that the physical and emotional sins of
parents can also leave lasting scars on their children as in incest,
emotional withdrawal, and physical abuse. Can we be sure, then,
that the spiritual area is exempt from visiting the sins of the
parents on the children? Why are some children "born" psychic?
Further, can parents' occult practices influence an unborn child
emotionally? If in rare cases a child can apparently be *physically*
marked in the womb from occult practices, what other kinds of
psychic or spiritual "markings" might be caused by such activity?[3]

That the occult involvement of one's parents can predispose a
child to the occult or result in psychological disturbances should
not be thought impossible. Widespread reading in occult literature reveals this as a common theme. Further, according to the
Scripture, occult activity is one proof of hatred for God. Exodus
20:5,6 declares that the sins of those who *hate* God are carried to
the third and fourth generation:

You shall not bow down to them or worship them [false idols/gods]; for I, the LORD your God, am a jealous God, punishing the children for the sin of the fathers to the third and fourth generation of those who hate me, but showing love to thousands who love me and keep my commandments (NIV).

As Dr. Koch has noted:

It is indeed a fact established by some 600 examples from pastoral experience with those involved in the occult, that prolonged occult practice creates a corresponding psychological constitution, a susceptibility, an inclination, a breeding-ground for various psychological disorders. In a long series of cases it has been possible to establish that occult subjection is an especially marked psychological constitution lasting through four succeeding generations of the same family.[4]

He gives many examples which are indicative of the impact one person can have on his own family and even succeeding generations. We will cite relevant details from just five cases mentioned in his *Christian Counseling and Occultism*:

(Case 60) Although she had a [magical] charm for every disease of man and beast, she was unable to control the psychological sufferings of her own posterity. From her own children down to her grandchildren, an enormous variety of psychological disorders are to be observed. . . .

(Case 61) Her grandmother was a charmer for many years. Her oldest son, the father of the girl who came to me, was harassed by suicidal thoughts. The second son hanged himself. This first granddaughter had fits of mania. . . .

(Case 62) After years of successful healing practice, his own mind became disturbed. He was taken to a mental institution. Two of his children suffered the same fate. The whole family had psychological disturbances for several generations.

(Case 63) Her grandfather worked with magic books and conducted occult experiments. Finally he became blind. He burned his magic books and warned his children that they must not continue his occult practices because he had become blind as a result of them. In the following generation an astounding picture of psychological abnormalities presented itself. The son was an alcoholic. The granddaughter is a clairvoyant. . . . Five of his grandchildren are mentally abnormal . . . some with psychoses.

The fifth case is cited at length as an illustration of the extent of damage that can be caused in what Koch refers to as "the terrible balance sheet of this family": four cases of mental illness and nine terrible deaths—

(Case 65) The great grandfather (first family member) was an expert in the field of occult practice. . . . This man died in dreadful pain and amid the spread of a penetrating odor. His sister (second family member) sensed a change in her emotional equilibrium, became insane, suffered manic attacks, heard voices, committed compulsive acts, and ended in a mental institution. In the generation of the grandparents, the magic and psychic activities continued. The grandmother (daughter of the second family member) had fits of manic and destructive fury. She demolished the furniture, and twice she was in the same mental hospital as her mother. Her sister (fourth family member) had visual, acoustic, and tactile hallucinations and a persecution complex. . . . Another sister of the grandmother (fifth family member) heard voices which predicted her death. This unhappy woman was also taken to a mental hospital. Upon a temporary improvement she was released, and at this point threw herself with her five and eight year old children down a cliff 125 feet high. All three of them were killed.

Her great grandfather had been a conjurer. He hanged himself. The grandfather continued in his father's tradition. He was one day crushed to death by a tipping hay-wagon. His brother was kicked by a horse and died. That man's son was a successful cattle charmer, who was always called in by the farmers. . . . He strangled his wife and then committed suicide. His sister jumped into the well in front of the house and drowned herself. Our young woman stood in the fourth generation, and she was now suffering from psychological disturbances and anxieties.[5]

Russ Parker is vicar of Christ Church in Coalville, England. He has had 20 years of experience in deliverance ministry. In *Battling the Occult*, he lists several physical and spiritual problems associated with one's *parents'* occult or other sins, including one actual case of blindness from birth that was healed immediately upon exorcism. This man had apparently been possessed by an evil spirit at birth as the result of the criminal activity of his parents.[6] (See p. 316.)

Many secular researchers have also noted there is a hereditary factor for psychic predisposition: Dr. Fodor, the psychoanalyst/ psychic researcher referred to earlier, observes: "In most cases mediumship can be traced as a hereditary gift. If the heredity is not direct it is to be found in ancestors or collaterals."[7]

The compilation by the editors of *Psychic* magazine—*Psychics: In Depth Interviews*—reveals a consistent pattern. Most psychics interviewed admitted familial involvement. Famous mediums Arthur Ford, Eileen Garrett, and Douglas Johnson all had aunts who were mediums or psychics; Irene Hughes and Peter Hurkos both had psychic mothers; and virtually all 19 members of witch Sybil Leek's nuclear and extended family were sympathetic to psychicism. [8]

As with Edgar Cayce, Olga Worrall, and other well-known occultists, the predisposition often surfaces during childhood, especially in experiences with spirits. In the book cited above, Jeane Dixon, Eileen Garrett, Irene Hughes, Douglas Johnson, and "Kreskin" (who denies he is a psychic even though he practices automatic writing) also encountered psychic events at a young age. [9]

Babies grow into young children, of course, and here the problems continue. Just as there are cases of child demonization recorded in the Bible (Luke 9:38,39) they are also recorded throughout history. Martin Ebon's book *Demon Children* documents several cases of child demonization (or what are thought to be) and the terrible suffering and tragedy they bring; this is confirmed also by Samuel H. Young's *Psychic Children*. [10]

Thus, Dr. Fodor indicates that even babies and small children of occultists may actually be possessed as a result of their parents' sorcery:

> Inherited mediumship usually appears sponta-neously and early in life, like artistic gifts. The five-month-old son of Mrs. Kate Fox-Jenken wrote auto-matically. Raps occurred on his pillow and on the iron railing of his bedstead almost everyday. The seven-month-old infant of Mrs. Margaret Cooper gave com-munications through raps. Aksakof in *Animisme et Epiritisme* records many instances of infantile medi-umship. The child Alward moved tables that were too heavy for her normal strength. The nephew of Sey-mour wrote automatically when nine days old.
>
> In Bonnemere's *Les Canisards* and in Figuier's *Histoire du Merveilleux* many cases are quoted of Canisard babies of 14-15 months of age and of infants who preached in French in the purest diction. [11]

Dr. Koch attempts to explain the mechanism by citing the illustration of magic:

> Magic conjuration, when applied intensively, leaves behind, in the middle level of the subconscious, engrams which enter the hereditary chain and constitute a latent breeding ground and efficient cause for psychological disorders in the next generation. This mental constitution will more certainly experience a development in the next generation when there enters, in addition to this latent efficient cause, a further psychological provocation through occult activity in the children, as an incidental cause. Engrams can, through suspension of occult activity in the following generations, fade rapidly and become recessive; on the other hand, in descendants who themselves practice magic, it can be intensified and appear as a dominant trait in the next generation. In this way the development of strong mediums can be explained. When three generations have all actively experimented and practiced magic, the fourth will reveal an intense mediumistic sensitivity. Two or three successive generations of charmers will, first of all, as already noted, develop clairvoyance, but then also somnambulance, psychic dissociation, and a generally increased sensitivity for paranormal phenomena. Magic conjuration thus has, according to our findings so far, a primary effect of psychological disturbances, and a secondary effect of the development of mediumistic abilities. The connecting link between these two effects is the process of "opening" the subconscious. The powers of the subconscious are unlocked and mobilized. Since this unlocking process is carried out by laymen who have no scientific training, psychological complications set in to say nothing, for the moment, of the religious factors. It often happens that in the third and fourth generations clairvoyance emerges, without the person concerned being aware of the occult roots in the first and second generations. The secondary effect still exists, even though its origin may have been forgotten in the course of the generations.[12]

Consider the case of a pastor who was apparently demon influenced without even knowing it—or the cause:

> At the end of one meeting, people were invited to come forward for prayer. When Bennett laid his hands on the head of a minister, there was a sharp reaction. The man slipped from his chair and appeared to go into a coma. Later he was encouraged to go aside to talk and receive further prayer. He agreed that he needed deliverance from this evil and agreed to further prayer. The moment the name of Jesus was mentioned there was another reaction.
>
> Taking authority over this evil in the name of Jesus those who were ministering to him cast out the spirit. Within a few moments, the man was on his feet, delivered and free. His family had been involved in the occult at some earlier time, and he had not known this.[13]

We stress that an experience of this nature does *not* necessarily mean that Christians are to have great concern over their family histories. First, for most people this information may be unavailable. Second, among Christians an experience of this type is probably rare. Third, when people are converted to Christ, they belong to Him alone. As God does for many other areas, we can expect that, if and when necessary, He will work accordingly to heal and deliver people from such things they know nothing about.

Why this does not happen in every case is unknown. Perhaps the best attitude to take is simply to note that such cases apparently exist—and also to realize that if something like this is a problem in a person's life, God will certainly work to take care of it on His own terms or through other means. We stress again that, generally speaking, Christians do not need to be concerned over the sins of their ancestors. Only when there are spiritual problems that seem to fit the phenomena of occult bondage should the possibility be explored.

But the heredity predisposition for psychic abilities or occult influences is not the only possibility to consider where the phenomenon of transference is concerned; the active occultist can also influence those around him.

Nonhereditary Transference

Psychic powers or effects may also be transmitted to individuals by virtue of direct transference. Before reading this material, be assured that committed Christians are protected from such influences. Indeed, occultists have often found they have no power over genuine Christians who are living for Christ. Former witch Doreen Irvine is one example. In *Freed From Witchcraft* she recalls on page 98:

> I tried to put curses on the preacher, but they did not work. There was a barrier between my power and the preacher, who was a man of great faith and courage. I was puzzled. My powers had never before failed. I had no idea that far greater power than that of Satan was protecting this man—the mighty power of the Lord Jesus Christ.

On the other hand, many of the gurus (e.g., siddha or power yogis), such as the late Rajneesh and Muktananda, or Sai Baba, Nityananda, and Da Free John, have induced the transmission of occult power into their disciples solely by touch, thought, or glance. Of course, Western occultists can do this as well. Nevertheless, the spiritual dynamics of this ability indicate it as a spiritistic phenomenon.[14] Transference often occurs during ritual occult initiation or standard initiation into Eastern sects where it is known as *shaktipat diksha*. Here the guru or leader transfers occult power into the initiate for purposes of occultic energizing. (This is also a common phenomenon of psychic healing, which is, in effect, a similar transference of occult power.[15]) In some cases, the effect is to spark interest in the psychic realm or to develop psychic abilities. But in many cases something more profound occurs: a complete religious conversion or a form of possession. Some of the gurus make regular

converts by this method, almost as if it were a spiritual counterfeit to biblical regeneration and/or laying on of hands. One
converted psychiatrist provides an illustration of the occult
power involved (cf. pp. 153-55):

> Suddenly I start shaking all over and experiencing
> inner reactions. . . . A glance and a wave of his hand,
> and I just fell apart . . . stunned . . . all I could do was
> sit on the floor for some time to regain my compo-
> sure. I'm still amazed to witness myself break up like
> this, although I have heard that many people have
> such reactions as they draw closer to Baba. . . . It
> seems the closer I get the less control I have.[16]

Johanna Michaelsen reports that when touched by the psychic
surgeon with whom she worked (who was then under the control
of the spirit guide), "A strange shock ran through my body as his
hands touched me."[17]

When Swami Muktananda initiated Albert Rudolph (Swami
Rudrananda) into his spiritual tradition (Vedanta), Rudrananda:

> Immediately felt within me a surge of great spiri-
> tual force which hurled me against the stone walls and
> allowed a great electric shock to send a spasm of
> contortions through my body. Movements similar to
> an epileptic fit controlled my body for almost an hour.
> Many strange visions appeared and I felt things open-
> ing within me that had never been opened before.[18]

Rudrananda observes the relationship of this energy transfer/
possession and later speaks of the normality of the student being
spiritually "possessed by his teacher."[19] He described his own
experience of this phenomenon when he felt his own guru enter
and possess him in a spirit form.

> Slowly Swami Nityananda came toward me and
> entered into my physical body. . . . It was a terrifying
> experience.[20]

Carole Carmichael describes a typical experience while under the tutelage of Swami Rama:

> The energy was shaking my being and filling my body.... The force was engulfing me; I felt as if I were caught in the violent wind of a tornado—it was surging through my head, heart, lungs and spine down through my legs, surrounding my entire body. The force was filling my body with air and moving my lungs rapidly. My heart beat faster than I thought possible. My breath was being drawn in and out so rapidly that I could hardly breathe; in fact, the force was breathing for me.[21]

But there is also the opposite phenomenon. Rather than an inputting of spiritistic power, the occultist draws energy from other people by some form of psychic vampirism. This typically occurs in mediumism to generate energy for spiritistic materializations, apported material, and other manifestations:

> As a rule, most mediums require assistance for the production of their phenomena. The sitters of the circle are often drained of power. According to Maxwell, Eusapia Paladino could quickly discern people from whom she could easily draw the force she needed. "In the course of my first experiments with this medium, I found out about his vampirism, to my cost. One evening, at the close of a sitting at L'Agnelas, she was raised from the floor and carried on to the table with her chair. I was not seated beside her, but without releasing her neighbors' hands she caught hold of mine while the phenomena was happening. I had cramps in the stomach—I cannot better define my sensation—and was almost overcome by exhaustion."
>
> Dr. Kerner states that the Seeress of Prevorst ate little and confessed that she was nourished by the substance of her visitors, especially of those related to her by the ties of blood, their constitution being more sympathetic with her

own. Visitors who passed some minutes near her often noticed upon retiring that they were weakened.

Some mediums draw more of the sitters' vitality than others. These mediums become less exhausted and consequently can sit more often. Mrs. Etta Wriedt, the direct voice medium, always left her sitters weak. Vice-Admiral Moore complained that he hardly could use his legs after a sitting.[22]

Then there is the strange phenomenon of mediumistic induction—the seemingly "innocent" transference of occult ability. This results merely from being in the proper environment, whether or not one intends to pursue occult practice.

> Another way of receiving mediumistic abilities is through occult transference. If someone with the ability to use a rod or pendulum holds the hands of a person without the ability, a transference can take place which surprisingly is permanent. Transferred powers, however, are never as strong as inherited ones.[23]

The prominent neuropsychiatrist and psychic researcher Shafica Karagulla recounts a personal illustration of this phenomenon:

> I tried to use the divining rod but got no effect. My young friend, the Princeton graduate, tried, but without results. At this point, [dowser] Reverend Stanley suggested another experiment which he said worked with most people. I stood beside him with one hand on his shoulder and with the other hand, I held one branch of the divining rod. He held the other branch. When we moved over the spot where he had detected water, the rod began to bend downward with such force that although I have strong wrists, I could not prevent it. The young man tried this with similar results. We were both mystified by the force with

which the rod bent downward to the floor[24] [cf. John Weldon, "Dowsing: Divine Gift, Human Ability, or Occult Power?" *Christian Research Journal*, 1992].

In another case, Martin Ebon, the well-known psychic investigator, mentions that the wives of W. B. Yeats and Sir Arthur Conan Doyle (of "Sherlock Holmes" fame) "both became mediumistic when their husbands developed a lively interest in spiritistic phenomena."[25]

Dr. Fodor observes:

> The spread of modern spiritualism discloses the phenomenon of mediumistic induction. Those who sat with the Fox sisters usually discovered mediumistic abilities in themselves. Mrs. Benefict and Mrs. Tamlink, the two best early mediums, were developed through the gift of Kate Fox. . . .
>
> The most famous early [psychic] investigators became mediums. Judge Edmonds, Prof. Hare, William Howitt, confessed to have received the gift. It is little known that in his last years Dr. Hodgson was in direct contact with the Imperator group. Conan Doyle developed automatic writing and direct voice in his family. H. Dennis Bradley received the power of direct voice after his sittings with George Valiantine. The Marquis Centurione Scotto developed through the same instrumentality. Eusapia Paladino could transfer her powers by holding the sitter's hand.[26]

But when this occult energy, whatever it is, is either transferred into a person or taken from them, how might this affect the person physiologically, psychologically, or spiritually?

In a related area, occultists often seek to transfer their powers to someone else at death. If they are unable to do so they often undergo an unbelievable death agony. Indeed, for committed occultists in general, Koch observes from his wide experience that "a very difficult and terrible death struggle [is] a symptom which has emerged in every case of occult practice within my knowledge."[27] Dr. Unger comments that such a situation may become "a nightmare of suffering [for the occultist] when children do not wish to receive the occult power."[28]

> However, it is not only the active engagement in occult sins like those we have just mentioned which leads to demonic subjection, but one frequently finds that people whose parents or ancestors have practiced sorcery also fall under the ban of the devil. In fact, powerful sorcerers and mediums often seek to transfer their occult powers over to some relative or friend, be it an adult or child, before they die. Later the people onto whom the powers have been transferred suddenly become aware of their strange inheritance.[29]

Another dangerous element of transference is common to all forms of psychic healing where the "healer" temporarily assumes the sickness or disease they are seeking to cure. This can be excruciatingly painful and may last for hours or even days or weeks. It may also account for a portion of the unsavory character development which can afflict occultists. Dr. Hereward Carrington, an early supporter of mediumism, argues:

> These influences . . . are contagious to a remarkable degree. All experienced spiritualists know that a medium is liable to "take on" the conditions of a spirit or of another person, when in a sensitive state, and this is true of his mental and spiritual life as well as his physical health. We can acquire the other's irritable disposition, his sourness and lack of balance, for the time being, just as easily as we can acquire other symptoms; and unless this is recognized and the medium takes care to throw off these influences, they are liable to remain with him more or less and influence him—just as we sometimes experience the after influence of a bad dream in the daytime.

The practical conclusion to be drawn from all this is that it is very dangerous to the mental and moral health of a psychic to develop under the guidance of a medium who is mentally, morally, physically or spiritually ill—for these conditions will possibly sooner or later be "taken on," and they are liable to influence the medium to his own detriment.[30]

The point is well-taken, because from a biblical perspective who knows the extent of spiritual illness an occultist endures? Further, their defective philosophy makes its mark on their lives, and this moral character may, as Carrington observes, be transferred. The mental health of many occultists must also be considered. If mental conditions are to some extent transferred, one can only say, "Let the buyer beware."

As an example, we mention one psychic who entered a trance state to help an emotionally disturbed woman whose brother had apparently been murdered. During the trance, the psychic actually "relived" the murder, including experiencing the sheer terror of the victim, and the hatred and revenge of the murderers and the murder itself. "It was all as if it were my own," she reported. Leaving the condition of the trance was difficult, plus all of the emotions were brought forth into the conscious state where they remained, causing serious mental problems.[31]

We provide one final example—this time of serious physical ailments—from the life of Indian miracle worker and spiritist Satha Sai Baba. Here, as mediums and psychic healers often do, he is allegedly taking upon himself the karma, diseases, etc. of other people. Considering the extent of his suffering, one could more reasonably assume he had come under the spell of sadistic spirits rather than healing energies.

Even as he fell, the left hand clenched its fist; the left leg stiffened; the toes became taut. Evidently, he had taken upon himself in his infinite mercy, the stroke of paralysis destined to incapacitate or perhaps kill some saintly person! Having seen him while taking on the typhoid fever, the gastric pain, the bleeding ear, the mumps, and even the stroke . . . [we waited]. The face twitched and muscles drew the mouth to the left . . . the tongue lolled. The left eye appeared to have lost its sight. . . .

Respiration was hissing, at times; the left side of the body the upper and lower limbs were rigidly held in a position of extensor tone. There were gross twitchings of the face occasionally on the right side. The head would be suddenly tossed to one side or the other, with a groan of anguish and the utterance of un-understandable syllables. . . .

The body perspired a great deal but he could be given only a few spoonfuls of water, the spoon being inserted, after pressing the jaw apart. He was apparently severely exhausted. Moreover he suffered from what Dr. Krishnamurthi names "angina pectoris," paroxyoms of intense pain, originating at the breast bone and radiating thence mainly to the left shoulder and arm. The physical frame groaned. . . .

It was a heart-rending experience—to catch those hazy sounds and interpret them, for the words emerged from a mouth gone awry and a tongue turned left. He warned us not to frighten the other devotees with our fear. . . .

Rumours circulated. . . . The wildest of these was that Baba was under the maleficent influence of black magic! Others surmised that he had gone into Samadhi. . . .

Two hours later, we had a tragic jolt. His breathing worsened; he gasped and rolled. His feet and palms became cold. . . . For 4 full hours, Baba broiled us thus, in mortal anguish.[32]

So far, we have examined a number of negative consequences of the occult: mental illness, social consequences, familial hazards, and others. In our next chapter we examine the potential for physical damage and disease arising from occult practice.

15

Physical Harm, Disease, and Torture by the Spirits

While it must be stressed that most illness is not demonically instituted, nevertheless, in the Bible, demons are collectively presented as inflicting a variety of physical and psychological ailments upon their victims. The array of symptoms suggest the possibility of a basic monopoly over the workings of the human mind and body, including skin disease (Job 2:7), destructive and irrational acts (Matthew 8:28; Luke 8:27), deafness and inability to speak (Mark 9:25; Luke 11:14), epileptic-like seizures (Matthew 17:15; Mark 9:18; Luke 9:39), blindness (Matthew 12:22), tormenting pain (Revelation 9:1-11), insanity (Luke 8:26-35), severe physical deformity (Luke 13:11-17), and other conditions. (See Appendix E for a complete list.) Demons can give a person supernatural strength (Luke 8:29) or attempt to murder them (Matthew 17:15).

There are a large number of accounts of mediums and occultists, or those who frequent them, suffering physically in a variety of ways from their practice (ill health, various diseases, alcoholism, poltergeist attacks, early deaths, etc.).[1] One article, "ESP and Drugs," noted: "There have been a few instances where one who had an out-of-body experience had such difficulty returning to his body that the symptoms have been described as similar to heart attacks."[2]

Medium Edgar Cayce, (6'2" in height), died in misery, weighing a mere 60 pounds, apparently physiologically burned out from giving too many psychic readings. The biography on Cayce by Joseph Millard reveals the extent of suffering Cayce's occultic involvement cost him: from psychic attacks to mysterious fires, the periodic loss of his voice, erratic personality changes and emotional torments, etc. His life had more than the normal share of misery, but of course the psychic readings were of little comfort; they only responded that a certain amount of "scourging" was necessary for the development of the soul.[3] Indeed, the biographies of most occultists reveal similar tragedies, such as Lutyen's biography on Krishnamurti or those of Aleister Crowley.[4]

Carrington refers to one cause of ill health among mediums:

> Mediums have found to their cost that the production of [e.g., ectoplasmic] phenomena (especially of the physical order) is at times a very exhausting process, and unless they keep themselves in good bodily health, they discover that they become run down and nervously exhausted, in which case they render themselves subject to insomnia, depressing mental emotions, and, if this gets worse, to obsession and even greater dangers and difficulties. It is very important, therefore, for all mediums to keep up their physical health.[5]

Fodor observes:

> The mediums who are conscious during the production of the phenomena suffer more than those in trance. The extrication of power from their organism is a veritable trial for nerve and flesh. The phenomena in themselves are often equivalent to putting the body on the rack. This was known from ancient days.[6]

The famous Russian medium Ninel Kulagina was the subject of repeated parapsychological experimentation. During the test she had unusual burn marks appear on her body and her clothes would spontaneously catch on fire—presumably the result of her trafficking in occult energy sources. She "endured pain, long periods of dizziness, loss of weight, lasting discomfort, sharp spinal pains, blurred vision, and a near fatal heart attack from her activities."[7] It was suggested that her occult practices had weakened her physically to the point where a heart attack could occur under conditions when it normally would not; nevertheless, the attack was a massive one and left Kulagina a permanent invalid until her resulting death in 1990.

At times the body is violently agitated or catatonically motionless. Sometimes it is wracked with unendurable pain. In the case of Krishnamurti, who endured this torment off and on for years: "I toss about, groan and moan and mutter strange things, in fact almost behave like one possessed. . . . All the time I have a violent pain in my head." A biographer describes him as enduring "agonizing pain" in the spine, "throbbing and burning" at the neck with "immensely concentrated" energy in his presence, as "just tortured," etc. "It is almost impossible to believe what his poor body endured each night." His heartrending cries and sobs "sound like some animal in awful pain."[8]

There are no rules which tell us when harmful effects will occur; they simply do, perhaps to the carnal delight of the infernal spirits who are thus able to provide at least some humans with a foretaste of the torment they know awaits them personally (Matthew 8:29).

Two researchers record the results of one experiment upon a skeptical psychiatrist eager to disprove the aforementioned powers of Kulagina:

> Within two minutes, serious changes were shown in the psychiatrist's heart condition. His ECG graph went far above normal, showing great emotional stress. Kulagina's heartbeat, too, was faster than normal, but the psychiatrist's heartbeat increased at such an alarming rate that the scientists feared for the safety of the psychiatrist's life! Sergeyev had to stop the experiment five minutes after it had begun. Sergeyev acknowledged to us that had the experiment continued, they were certain the psychiatrist would have been killed.

Several times during the telekinetic experiments with
Sergeyev, Kulagina became unconscious. Instruments mea-
suring the electrical field around her showed that when she
took electrical energy from around her and sent it to an
object, it apparently drained her completely of energy. On
several occasions, an electrical force from the surroundings
rushed back into her body, usually through the arm, and left
burn marks on the skin. . . . "I have witnessed this startling
phenomenon," Sergeyev said simply. "No object could have
caused the burn marks other than the reentry into her body
of some powerful energy. On one occasion she exclaimed,
'I am burning!' and collapsed unconscious. A burn mark
appeared on her hand. On several occasions, these burn
marks were four inches long. I have been with her during
this return of energy when her clothes caught fire. When
these incidents happened, Kulagina became unconscious
and very ill, and we had great difficulty in reviving her.

"Eventually it wore her down. One more jolt and her
heart would cave in. Possibly the scientists should have
known that, but they were too eager to experiment to think
about it."[9]

Perhaps it goes without saying that if people freely experiment
with a powerful energy of which they are ignorant as to its
source, functioning, and impact, it is not surprising there may be
these kinds of consequences. Whatever one believes about the
source of such energy (spiritistic, human, or some combination
thereof), one is playing with fire. No one in his right mind would
ignorantly tamper with live electrical circuitry, but psychics,
occultists, and parapsychologists seem eager to research "live
spiritual circuitry" in an area they know nothing about.

In a related concern, Dr. Fodor points out the tendency among
mediums and occultists to take artificial stimulants—ostensibly
a result of the psychic vampirism on the physical body:

After prolonged exercise of mediumship, intem-
perance often sets in. The reason is a craving for

stimulants following the exhaustion and depletion felt after the seance. Many mediums have been known who succumbed to the craving and died of delirium tremens.[10]

It was apparently this drain on Edgar Cayce—the demons using his energies to perform through him—which caused his weight to be reduced to a mere 60 pounds. In some rare cases at seances, mediums are reported to have had up to *half* their bodies temporarily "disappear," and their weight, as measured on scales, reduced by 10 to 118 pounds.[11]

Elsewhere Fodor refers to various cases of injury which resulted from a seance member attacking the medium's control spirit:

> We know from Mme. D'Esperance's mediumistic history, that in Helsingfors in 1893, Yolande, her beautiful materialized spirit control, was attacked and raped in the dark. The result was two years of illness on the part of the medium.[12]

In the *Encyclopedia of Psychic Science*, Dr. Fodor detailed the experience:

> A suspicious sitter seized Yolande while the medium was believed sitting inside the cabinet. "All I know," she writes, "was a horrible excruciating sensation of being doubled up and squeezed together, as I can imagine a hollow gutta-percha doll would feel, if it had sensation, when violently embraced by its baby owner. A sense of terror and agonizing pain came over me, as though I was losing hold of life and was falling into some fearful abyss, yet knowing nothing, hearing nothing, except the echo of a scream I heard as at a distance. I felt I was sinking down, I knew not where. I tried to save myself, to grasp at something, but missed it, and then came a blank from which I awakened with a shuddering horror and sense of being

bruised to death." The result of this experience was the outbreak of the earlier hemorrhage of her lungs and a prolonged illness. [13]

Former medium Gasson also warns of dangers of tampering with ectoplasm—the substance that exudes out of the medium's body during a seance:

> When touched (only permissible by the controlling guide) it will move back into the body and if suddenly seized the medium will scream out or be caused to be violently sick. Such sudden graspings of ectoplasm have very often caused great bodily harm to the medium and could even result in loss of life. The reason for this being so dangerous is that the ecto-plasm becomes solid through contact with the air and before it is able to return back into the medium's body in the normal way, it has to dematerialize to its origi-nal state. If touched suddenly, without warning or permission, or unexpectedly contacted with light, the solid ectoplasmic mass will rush straight back to the body of the medium before having a chance to dis-solve to its natural state. I have known of many mediums who have been crippled or blinded for life owing to the sudden impact of the solid ectoplasm which springs back with as much force as if it were connected to the medium by an excessively strong piece of elastic. I myself was blinded for nearly 24 hours after such an incident occurred. The force of the ectoplasm against the stomach caused a scar from side to side, which took many days to disappear. [14]

Aleister Crowley, who dedicated himself to a life of blatant wickedness, drugs, Satanism, and orgies, ended up in an insane asylum for six months after trying to conjure the devil. His children died, and his wives either went insane or drank them-selves to death. He knew the cost, but could never get free of what it was that controlled him: "Every human affection that he had in his heart—and that heart ached for love as few hearts can ever conceive—was torn and trampled with such infernal ingenuity in his intensifying torture that his endurance is beyond belief."[15]

As Dennis Wheatley points out, other authorities besides Crowley, like Montague Summers and Harry Price, also were affected. Wheatley, who studied witchcraft for over 50 years, is "thoroughly afraid of it." He personally knew the above three men, and even though they were experts, the cost was great. Wheatley concludes: "Even with their great knowledge, they weren't safe. So how can anyone else be?"[16] A good question, indeed. Even the occultists' own spirit guides cannot be trusted. Dr. Fodor explains:

> Harm may come to the medium through the careless disregard of the conditions by the sitters, but sometimes also from the part of the invisible operators. An evil operator may take possession of the medium's body or a well-meaning control may commit a mistake just as an experimenting scientist might. . . .
>
> Things often happen against the will of the medium, quite frequently against the will of the sitters. Mme. d'Esperance said that she always entered the seance room "with a feeling of anxiety mixed with wonder if I should ever come out again. As a rule I always felt that I was placing my life in the hands of the persons about to assist, and that they were even more ignorant of danger than myself." . . . In the seances of Eusapia Paladino the spirits often broke the promises of the medium.[17]

Not surprisingly, there is often an initial uneasiness experienced by mediums, channelers, and other spiritists regarding their spirit contacts, over just how much they can be trusted. This attitude is usually dismissed after continued contact and reassurance by the spirits, but it seems to have afflicted most spiritists at one time or another.

Even the well-known novelist and UFO contactee Whitley Strieber (*The Wolfen*; *Cat Magic*) suspected his alleged UFO contacts might actually be demons—and that he was in an actual life-and-death struggle for his eternal soul. Alone at night he "worried about the legendary cunning of demons. . . . There are worse things than death, I suspected. And I was beginning to get the distinct impression that one of them had taken an interest in me."[18] UFO close encounters frequently result in physical harm (see John Ankerberg and John Weldon, *The Facts on UFO's and Other Supernatural Phenomena* [Eugene, OR: Harvest House, 1992]).

Mohammad suspected his "angel" Gabriel who revealed the Koran was an evil *jinn* (Islamic demon);[19] Edgar Cayce suspected his trance states might be satanic,[20] Uri Geller and Dr. Andrija Puharich both doubted the motives and sincerity of their spiritistic contacts,[21] Penny Torres wondered if her spirit guide "Mafu" wasn't a demon,[22] and even Crowley himself had doubts—despite the "gods" having taught him "to trust them absolutely to provide me with everything I really need for my work."[23]

Nevertheless, even "friendly" spirit guides tend to extract a price for communion with them. The tally sheet of the psychic surgeon who prepared Johanna Michaelsen to replace her is typical of the pain occultists endure in this life (e.g., two years in a mental institution, two children dead, abandonment by her husband), all rationalized through the Eastern concept of karma: "It was for the sake of karma that I needed to suffer their [her children's] loss."[24]

Michaelsen herself commented:

> I couldn't understand why Hermanito [the spirit guide] . . . treated Pachita [the medium] so cruelly— never allowing her any new or pretty clothes, and refusing to treat her when she was sick, which was often now. Even "karma" seemed a poor excuse for that. And her family was falling apart around her.[25]

But unfortunately, the demonic entities who seek out humans for their own purposes do not easily surrender their plans. If they select a person, he obeys—or else. It seems the spirits would rather have the contact dead or insane than not following their plans.

Consider the following typical examples from the experience of shamans and/or those who encounter so-called kundalini awakening:

> He who is seized by the shaman sickness and does not begin to exercise shamanism, must suffer badly. He might lose his mind, he may even have to give up his life. Therefore he is advised, "you must take up shamanism so as to not suffer!" . . . The man chosen for shamandom is first recognized by the black spirits. The spirits of the dead shamans are called black spirits. They make the chosen one ill and then they force him to become a shaman.[26]

> Among the Siberian Tofa, too, shamans become sick before their initiation and are tormented by spirits. . . . Shaman Vassily Mikailovic . . . could not rise from his bed for a whole year. Only when he agreed to the demands of the spirits did his health improve.[27]

> The trances themselves ceased to "control" him as soon as he gave up his own resistance to them and the forces behind them. Similarly, another case had severe headaches, but these stopped as soon as she ceased trying to control the [kundalini] process and simply "went with it." The pain, in other words, resulted not from the process itself but from her resistance to it. We suspect that is true of all the negative effects of the physio-Kundalini process.[28]

But even family members may also suffer. In the case of Korean shamanism, up to 40 percent of families will actually suffer the death of a loved one rather than submit to the travails of shamanism upon the entire family.

> Often not only the shaman himself but his whole family are visited by misfortune. . . . The Koreans

talk about a "bridge of people" (*indari*) that comes into being when a member of the family is chosen to be a shaman and another member has to die as a result of this. . . . A God has "entered into" the shaman and, in return, demands another human life [If the chosen shaman is submitted to initiation, death is averted]. . . . But most families are unwilling to have a shaman in their circle, so the indari phenomenon occurs quite frequently. . . . On average seven or eight times in every twenty cases of shamanic vocation.[29]

Obviously, the spirits tend to get their way. Thus, with sufficient intimidation or torture, they are usually able to achieve their purposes. Edgar Cayce found his voice was repeatedly taken from him unless he agreed to go into the hypnotic trance state through which the spirits spoke. Despite serious reservations as to the nature of his spiritual contacts (he suspected the devil), he complied.[30] This is again reminiscent of shamanism:

The Yakut shaman Tusput who was critically ill for more than twenty years, could find relief from his suffering only when he conducted a seance during which he fell into a trance. In the end he fully regained his health by this method. However, if he held no seances over a long period of time he once again began to feel unwell, exhausted, and indecisive. In general, the symptoms of an illness subside when a candidate for shamanism enters a trance.[31]

As Dr. Fodor observes, mediumship is also never abandoned easily:

Curiously enough mediumship, if suppressed, will manifest in symptoms of disease. Dr. C. D. Isenberg of Hamburg writes of a case in *Light*, April 11, 1931, in which a patient of his suffered from sleeplessness and peculiar spasmodic attacks which generally occurred at night. The spasm seized the whole body;

even the tongue was affected, blocking the throat and nearly suffocating her. When the patient mentioned that in her youth she tried table tilting, the doctor thought of the possibility that the mediumistic energy might block his patient's organism. A sitting was tried. The lady fell into trance and afterwards slept well for a few days. When the sleeplessness became worse again the sitting was repeated and the results proved to be so beneficial that the chloral hydrate treatment previously employed was discontinued.[32]

Another area of physical dangers includes the tragic "accidents" that happen to stalk the psychically involved. In *Occult ABC*, Dr. Kurt Koch has observed that people under occult subjection and/or demonization "frequently are in fatal accidents. I have many examples of this in my files."[33] Elsewhere he reiterates that "frequent accidents and suicides are a familiar phenomenon in the realm of the occult."[34]

In the authors' own readings, we have observed many similar events. The famous medium Eileen Garrett's parents both committed suicide.[35] Well-known parapsychologist Edmund Gurney (author of *Phantasms of the Living*) died a tragic death either by suicide or accident.[36] The Russian occultist Gurdjieff died in a car wreck; famous Brazilian psychic surgeon Arigo also died in a car crash; "Christian" spiritist William Branham, likewise.[37] Krishnamurti's brother Nityananda died at 25 and Krishnamurti himself (who experienced possession) has suffered strange and incredibly agonizing torments throughout his life.[38] "Mad Guru" Rudrananda died at the age of 45 in an airplane crash.[39] James Ingall Wedgewood, a Theosophy convert and leader of the Theosophic-born Liberal Catholic Church went mad for the last 20 years of his life.[40] One of Scientology founder L. Ron Hubbard's sons was mysteriously found dead in the desert—and we could go on and on.

In *The Transcendental Explosion*, John Weldon documented some of the Transcendental Meditation-related casualties, including suicide, heart attacks, mental illness, possession, epileptic seizures, hallucinations, blackouts of up to 20 hours, eyesight problems, extreme stomach cramps, mental confusion, sexual licentiousness, severe nightmares, the reoccurrence of serious psychosomatic symptoms previously under control (i.e., bleeding ulcer and depression requiring psychiatric care and medication), etc.[41]

As noted in the last chapter, when mediumism is openly practiced, the medium herself can experience the actual diseased condition of other people during psychic healing, for "in all probability you may sympathetically 'take on' and be affected by, the symptoms of the disease from which the patient suffers."[42]

Spontaneous Human Combustion

We even find rare incidents of spontaneous human combustion (SHC): people who simply burst into flame with their clothing and surroundings usually left untouched. Vincent Gaddis in *Mysterious Fires and Lights* refers to several cases, as do Mitchell and Rickard in *Phenomena: A Book of Wonders*.[43] There are over a hundred well-documented cases like this, where the victims are unable to escape, as if in a kind of trance. The fire burns primarily human flesh—which is usually the least combustible of materials. While an occult association is at this point conjecture (no studies have been done), SHC may also be related to poltergeist phenomena, or we just might be seeing rare examples of simple demonic revenge upon humans for whatever reason.

The following three documented cases, reported by Dr. Gary North, are typical:

1) On September 20, 1938, a woman was dancing on a crowded dance floor in Chelmsford, England. Without warning she burst into flames. Not her clothing—her body. Her flesh emitted blue flames, indicating tremendous heat, as she crumpled to the floor. Her escort and others tried to put out the flames, but it was hopeless. Within a few minutes, there was nothing left of her except a few ashes. There was no longer any trace of a human being. Coroner

Leslie Beccles announced: "In all my experience, I've never come across any case as mysterious as this."

2) In December 1956, in Honolulu, Mrs. Virginia Caget dashed into the room next to hers in an apartment house that was occupied by a seventy-eight-year-old invalid man, Young Sik Kim. He was on fire in an overstuffed chair. Blue flames shot out of his body, making it impossible for her to approach him. When firemen arrived fifteen minutes later, the victim and his chair no longer existed, except for his undamaged feet, still propped on his wheelchair, unmoved. Had he felt no pain? There are numerous cases in the literature that indicate precisely this.

3) July 1, 1952, St. Petersburg, Florida: Mrs. Mary Reeser, a sixty-seven-year-old widow, was visiting in her room with her neighbor, Mrs. P. M. Carpenter. When she left her that evening, Mrs. Reeser was seated in her armchair by the window, dressed in a rayon nightgown, slippers, and a housecoat, and was smoking a cigarette. The next morning, a Western Union messenger failed to raise her by knocking at her door to deliver a telegram. Concerned about her normally light sleeping neighbor, Mrs. Carpenter started to open the door. The brass doorknob was hot. She cried out, and two house painters ran to see what was wrong. Together they broke into the house. Although both windows were open, the room was hot. In front of an open window were some ashes: a chair, an end table, and Mrs. Reeser. All that remained of her were a few pieces of charred backbone, a shrunken skull the size of an orange, and a wholly untouched left foot, still in its slipper. Her room was generally unaffected, except for some melted wax candles and melted plastic fixtures. From four feet above the floor was the soot. The clock had stopped at 4:20 a.m., but when plugged into an unmelted wall outlet, it started running again. There were no embers and no smell of smoke. Mrs. Reeser had weighed 175 pounds the night before; now only ten pounds remained.

The FBI was called in. The case received lots of publicity locally. Result: No explanation. Professor Korgman happened to be visiting friends nearby and volunteered to study the case. His conclusion: spontaneous human combustion. But he had never seen a head shrunken by fire. The skull should have exploded, not shrunk. Said Korgman, "Never have I seen a skull so shrunken, or a body so completely consumed by heat. This is contrary to normal experience and I regard it as the most amazing thing I've ever seen. As I review it, the short hairs on my neck bristle with vague fear. Were I living in the Middle Ages, I'd mutter something like 'black magic!' "

Not living in the Middle Ages, he can only mutter "spontaneous human combustion." But what comfort is that? The phenomenon exists. It exists in the twentieth century.[44]

Gaddis, while reporting on numerous SHC cases, also records some physically harmful incidents relating to seances. In one case:

> At a seance two months before his death there was a sudden brilliant flash from a levitated trumpet, followed by a shout for lights. The medium was found unconscious and bleeding from the nose and fingernails. A Mr. Herbert Wright, who was in charge of the light switch in the room, received a terrific blow in his solar plexus when the flash occurred. As he staggered he managed to turn the switch, then fell to the floor unconscious.
>
> During the ten minutes that Mr. Wright was unconscious, clouds of steam rose from his body, and his clothing was saturated with perspiration. Later a "psychic burn" was found encircling his body, red in color, three-fourths of an inch wide, commencing at the solar plexus and returning to it. He stated that this burn was painful, but that he felt greater pain in the nerve centers of his body.[45]

Finally, there are seemingly thousands of cases of various kinds of attacks by spirit beings on mediumistic and occultic practitioners. We will mention only one example, chosen for the message it provides.

Things had thus gone on for many months, when M. at least awakened to the fact that a great transformation was passing over his moral and intellectual nature, and that some other mind had permeated his entire being, and he was now conscious that he was ceasing to think his own thoughts; in short, there could not be any doubt that fetters were being woven around him, which he was growing daily more incapable of breaking. The condition of servility and submission which the [spirit] control at first effected, was now thrown off and the latter showed signs of absolute power. No treatment, either hypnotic or medical, had the slightest influence upon the strange phenomenon, and M. had now given up all hope from this quarter. Some of the authorities, whom he had consulted, did not believe in obsession or possession. Other ascribed it to hysteria and fixed ideas—help there was none. Dr. Raupert goes on: I tried to argue with the personality and prove to him that he was merely a subconscious product on the part of M. When I persisted in denying the presence of a personality other than and different from that of M., a very frenzy seemed to shake the frame of M. and words of the most abusive kind were levelled at me: "What fools you are," it exclaimed, "to tamper with things you do not understand, to facilitate the invasion of spirits and then deny that they exist, to play with hell-fire and then be surprised that it hurts and burns! I challenge you to propose any kind of experiment to test my utter and entire independence of the person of this idiot, with whom I can do absolutely as I please. See, how I can handle him and ill-treat him. I am now beating and hurting him and he can do nothing to defend himself." With this there appeared red spots in different parts of M's face and he groaned as if in physical pain.

Many similar cases can be found in this author's works, particularly *Modern Spiritualism* and *The Supreme Problem.* . . .

There are other Spiritualists who have written much on this subject of spirit-obsession, as for instance, Dr. J. M. Peebles, whose work *The Demonism of the Ages or Spirit Obsessions* should be read by all interested in Spiritualism. Many cases are given in this work.[46]

This is why Dr. Fodor, referring to the phenomenon of obsession, observes the person "may be driven to criminal, insane acts" if an "evil personality gets into control."[47]

So far, we have been examining the hazards of genuine occult involvement, but there are also equal if dissimilar hazards in fraudulent occult activity. Many people have sacrificed large sums of money, not to mention their own peace of mind, physical health, or even their life because they naively trusted in a fraudulent practitioner who promised them physical healing, gave erroneous financial advice, or wrongly predicted their future. In the following chapter we explore this tragic kind of deception.

16

Fraud

Previous chapters have indicated the reality of occult powers and their consequences. But in the world of the occult, incidents of fraud are almost as pervasive as the tragedies. In this chapter we will show how deception may be employed in this area. Fraud may result from a number of factors: e.g., the simplicity of fraud and human gullibility or the lessened moral responsibility occultism brings. Fraud may also result from the mercurial nature of occult powers themselves. Since these unreliable powers often fail even in genuine occultism, the practitioner may be tempted to resort to legerdemain to retain credibility, or when monetary recompense is involved.

Dr. Fodor calls fraud "the greatest element of danger in psychic research."[1] He notes that "many mediums are hysterics and when they feel their mediumistic power ebbing they cannot resist the temptation of supplanting it by artifice."[2] Psychic surgeons, who as a group constitute exceptionally powerful mediums, are among the worst offenders.[3]

On the other hand, fraudulent techniques can be employed as a principal means of livelihood (i.e., the occult practitioner is simply a charlatan). Finally, fraud may also result from the lies and deceptions of the spirits themselves, such as the widely publicized falsehoods of "Mafu" or the spirits speaking through Edgar Cayce, as noted by his biographers Joseph Millard and Thomas Sugrue.

With millions of people seeking the advice of spirits today, there is no lack for tales of woe and deception. When Jesus spoke of Satan as a liar and murderer from the beginning (John 8:44), He certainly told us the truth. Why occultists themselves are usually the last to realize this is a mystery left perhaps to their own pondering.

For example, the dangers to life and limb in an area such as psychic diagnosis and healing should be obvious. Many cases of false diagnosis complicate the physical condition by delaying proper treatment. There are many incidents of wasted time and money spent seeking out useless psychic healers or "surgeons," not to mention the fact that even genuine psychic healing often erects a worse problem on a spiritual level.[4]

Whatever the situation, it is the pocketbook of the believer which is often the first casualty. The *New York Times* reported on a case where a wealthy woman was instructed by "the spirits" to give her friend, the operator of a Ouija board, nearly $60,000.[5] Kent Jordan observes, "The history of Spiritualism is, unfortunately, cluttered with similar cases: Spirit voices urging the often bereaved, elderly and lonely sitters to give or will their money to the medium, the 'blessed instrument of this communication,' to buy them houses, finance vacation trips, or be otherwise lavish with gifts."[6] Margaret Gaddis, a writer with a 50-year interest in psychic research, remarks, "At best, mediumship is a dubious blessing, usually deteriorating the health, and severely straining integrity when [psychic] powers fluctuate in financial crises."[7]

For example, Dr. Fodor refers to the nineteenth-century medium Eusapia Paladino who, when the power was weak or absent, deliberately cheated even though she knew she would have recourse to great power when it was available.[8] "Practically every scientific committee detected her in attempted fraud, but every one of these committees emerged from their investigations quite convinced of the reality of these phenomena, except the Cambridge and American investigation which ended in exposure."[9]

The noted psychic investigator Dr. Hereward Carrington went so far as to confess that unless spiritism can be ethically justified, it is better left alone:

But it is not good developing something which leads one ultimately only into a mire of harmful results and a false philosophy.... It is very important, therefore, for the Spiritualist to have his belief founded in correct ethical principles, for, as I have before pointed out, the reproach has been raised against Spiritualists that "they are everything but spiritual."[10]

This is precisely the problem. Mediumism and all forms of occultism are *known* for being unethical; their reputation justly precedes them wherever these are found.

Regardless, those who result to deliberate imposture suffer no lack of variety in the methods available to them. Fodor discusses the methodology of fraud:

The ways and means of fraudulent production of phenomena has a literature of its own. Carrington aptly states "the ingenuity of some of these methods is simply amazing, and in some respects the race between fraudulent mediums and psychical investigators has resembled that between burglars and police —to see which could outwit the other. It may be said, however, that these trick methods are now well known. To take one simple example, it may be pointed out that Mr. David O. Abbot's book *Behind the Scenes with the Mediums* and my own *Psychical Phenomena of Spiritualism* have between them explained more that a hundred different methods of fraudulent slate-writing.[11]

Of course, a good stage magician can duplicate much mediumistic phenomena. There are currently several professional magicians, such as James Randi, who are following the tradition of Houdini in attempting to debunk most or all occultism as fraudulent. The fraudulent methods can be truly impressive as seen in, for example, the books of journalist and stage magician

Danny Korem,[12] but by no means can they account for the production of the genuine supernatural phenomena found in the occult.

In *Powers* Korem reveals how he exposed the famous psychic James Hydrick. He also reveals, "I have encountered very few verifiable cases of real supernatural powers in relation to the number of reports I received." Further, after 15 years of research into supernatural claims, he is convinced that human psychic abilities don't exist at all and that "God is the author of good supernatural powers and Satan is the perpetrator of evil supernatural powers."[13]

M. Lamar Keene was, at one time, one of the world's highest-paid mediums. He was also considered one of the most proficient and would routinely produce alleged spirit messages, materializations, psychic healings, clairvoyance, trumpet mediumship, apports, etc. But he was a fraud. For over 13 years he practiced his wares before his conscience got the best of him and he decided to confess his unethical methods. In *The Psychic Mafia* he tells his story. "The average person is exceedingly easy to fool," he says.

In Chapter 5, "Secrets of the Seance," Keene reveals many of the tricks of the trade. Nevertheless, even after he publicly confessed his fraudulent practices, the will to believe persisted. Most of his sitters and even the church board of directors either refused to accept his confession or kept attending the faked seances of Keene's associate!

Not surprisingly, Keene's reaction was one of shock. After telling them the "spirits" did not exist, that they were fakes, people continued to respond to him on the basis of what they *learned* from the "spirits"! He recalls, "I was crushed. I knew how easy it was to make people believe a lie, but I didn't expect that the same people, confronted with the lie, would choose it over the truth."[14]

Why did these people continue to believe? Because they wanted to. Belief was more comfortable than unbelief; this is precisely why so many cults and spiritual cons flourish everywhere in America today. David Koresh and the Waco, Texas, tragedy is only one of many recent examples.

Nevertheless, Keene knows firsthand that there is rampant fraud at spiritists' retreats, although he asserts there may also be genuine mediumism. He refers to what he calls a "network of organized mediumistic espionage" taking in millions of dollars per year.[15] He himself collected 18 thousand dollars one Sunday in his church and knew another fake medium who made 40 thousand dollars a year "extra income" merely selling "blessed healing" cloths "magnetized" with spirit power.[16]

On the other side, both Gasson (a former medium) and Carrington (who exposed false mediums) believe that while fraud cases are probably in the relative minority, it is also probably true that most cases are never detected.[17]

Near the end of his book, Keene mentions some relevant facts as to why he made his dramatic public confession. Virtually all of the mediums he knew had ended their lives in miserable fashion:

> Looking ahead, if I stayed in mediumship, I saw only deepening gloom. All the mediums I've known or known about have had tragic endings.
>
> The Fox sisters, who had started it all, wound up as alcoholic derelicts. William Slade, famed for his slate-writing tricks, died insane in a Michigan sanitarium. Margery the Medium lay on her deathbed a hopeless drunk. The celebrated Arthur Ford fought the battle of the bottle to the very end and lost. And the inimitable Mable Riffle, boss of Camp Chesterfield—well, when she died it was winter and freezing cold, and her body had to be held until a thaw for burial; the service was in the Cathedral at Chesterfield. Very few attended.
>
> Wherever I looked, it was the same: Mediums, at the end of a tawdry life, dying a tawdry death.[18]

He reflected, "I was sick and tired of the whole business—the fraud bit, the drug bit, the drinking bit. The entire thing." He

went on to point out that his conscience would never let him
entirely abandon his more noble instincts:

> With all the money flowing in—with the glamor,
> excitement, and adulation of being a successful me-
> dium—was I happy? No. For one thing, I was always
> aware, like all mediums, that most people looked
> down on us, that we weren't really respectable. . . .
>
> Then there was the little matter of conscience.
> Most mediums probably are what psychiatrists call
> sociopathic. They have a moral block, a defective
> conscience. Things that other people consider wrong,
> they consider legitimate. Cheating, lying, stealing,
> conning—these are sanctified in the ethics of medi-
> umship as I knew it.
>
> Though most mediums apparently manage to anes-
> thetize their consciences (if they have any), I couldn't.
> Not completely. Looking in the mirror, I'd feel a pang
> of something I recognized as shame (it has been so
> long since I've acknowledged the feeling that it was
> unfamiliar).[19]

But what was perhaps most discouraging for him was that after
telling his story to the IRS, FBI, and state attorney general, "No
police investigation of any medium was launched as a result of
my action nor, to my knowledge, did the Internal Revenue Service look into the matter of mediumistic bookkeeping. As a
matter of fact, my former partner is doing better than ever."[20]

Keene's story also provides an inside look into the heartless
cruelty of much mediumship and the morality accompanying it:

> The mentality that is capable of such heartless
> manipulation of people's most wounded feelings is in
> my judgement capable of even more. I am not being
> melodramatic, but factual when I report that since
> renouncing mediumship I have received threatening
> phone calls. "Lay off the mediums, or else," muffled
> voices warned.[21]

On one occasion, he was the victim of an apparent attempted murder.[22] Nevertheless, he concludes by asking the following question:

> Who can measure the human misery that spiritualism and its false claims and broken hopes leaves in its murky wake? I know of one elderly woman who gave thousands to our church, now shut away friendless and penniless in a nursing home. Another woman—and how many more like her?—suffered a stroke induced at least in part, I'm sure, by the conflicts and upheavals caused by preying mediums. I know scores of people, professionals such as doctors and teachers, who were so enamored of the fantasies of spiritualism that they tore up roots and relocated half-way across the country to be near a favorite medium. (Many did this because of me.) The personal and family dislocations, the emotional pain, the career setbacks and financial losses, are incalculable.[23]

But seance mediums are hardly the only class of occultists who prey on the gullible. If we include the collective toll taken by fake astrologers, channelers, gurus, healers, dowsers, psychics, and many others, the resulting misery would make the mediums' collective deception seem mild by comparison.

17

Spiritual Deception, Destruction, and Deliverance

> *Within the Church today—and I include many evangelical churches—there are many who have experienced direct or indirect involvement with the occult. For us to turn a blind eye to their plight is to disregard a particularly needy segment of our society. Outside the organized churches the number of occult-oriented people is astronomical.*
>
> —W. Elwyn Davies
> in Montgomery,
> *Demon Possession*

We now turn to the most severe damage offered by intransigent occult practice. Here the consequences are not only physical, emotional, and social—they are eternal and quite personal.

We have seen that psychic and occult activity lead a person into various dangers, but these are by comparison shadowy hazards. It is the spiritual dangers which carry eternal consequences.

The real battle is a spiritual conflict (Ephesians 6:10-18). Satan and his hosts have declared war against God. They fight not for territory, but for souls. And like it or not, we are the battlefield. Men and women are the target, and the weapons of warfare can be cunning or brutal. For the more people who are converted to the occult, the less are converted to Christ. But the victory belongs to Christ and to all those who trust in Him. In this spiritual battle there is only one source men may turn to for deliverance: Jesus Christ (1 John 3:8).

Unfortunately, psychic practitioners of all stripes tend to become hardened against God and Christ, sometimes obsessionally so. Of course, sometimes the reverse is true: Hostility toward Christianity leads to occult involvement.

For example, medium Jane Roberts initially had no interest in psychic matters. What she did have was dislike for the biblical God, and this seems to have opened her to spiritism all the more readily. As a result, upon Ouija board experimentation, she became a medium, and before her death published a score of books that have probably led hundreds of thousands of people away from Christ. All these books came under the guidance or inspiration of "Seth," her spirit guide.

Seth's consuming hostility toward Christianity leaves no room for doubt as to his nature. But Mrs. Roberts was already prepared for Seth before meeting him. What was her attitude toward God before using the Ouija board? In her own words, "I would not tolerate Him as a friend." She confesses:

> I was brought up a Catholic, but as I grew older I found it more and more difficult to accept the God of my ancestors. Irony whispered that He was as dead as they were. The heaven that had sustained me as a child seemed in my teens to be a shallow mockery of meaningful existence. Who wanted to sit around singing hymns to a father-God, even if He did exist, and what sort of intelligent God would require such constant adoration? A very insecure, appallingly human kind of God indeed.
>
> The alternative, that of hellfire, was equally unbelievable. . . . That God, I decided, was out. I would not tolerate Him as a friend. For that matter He didn't treat His son too well either, as the story goes. . . .
>
> Before I was twenty, then, I'd left behind me that archaic God, the Virgin, and communion of saints. Heaven, hell, angels and devils, were dismissed.[1]

But in the end, what did the late Jane Roberts gain by her spiritism? Only eternity will reveal the true cost.

But the fact that occult involvement inevitably brings a world-view opposed to biblical revelation and a predisposition against the things of Christ should warn us now. Psychic healer Gordon Turner says, "You see, I don't believe, I can't believe in a personal God."[2] Psychic surgeon Edivaldo says, "If the devil can relieve pain . . . then I prefer the devil. . . . Don't give me one [a Bible] because I won't read it. I want to believe in Christ my own way."[3] Ritual magician David Conway states, "We must at once discount the idea that at a certain point in prehistory God breathed into man a soul which gave him his humanity and a special place in the natural (and 'supernatural') scheme of things."[4] Robert Monroe, as a direct result of his thousands of experiences with spiritistically induced astral projections, concludes: "To date, in twelve years of nonphysical activities, I find no evidence to substantiate the biblical notions of God and afterlife in a place called heaven."[5] Initially, this brought him sobs of deep grief, because he now knows "without any qualification or future hope of change that the God of my childhood, of the churches" was not as he once thought Him to be.[6]

Such are the consequences of allowing one's experience to define one's theology in a world of spiritual warfare. Psychic Wanda Parrott says,

> But I no longer have time to spare in getting my soul saved. If I have learned one lesson only in all these years, it is this. . . . We are all part of that vast Union known as God, and therefore we have our beginnings, middles and endings in God's spirit-energy body. Therefore, what is there to be saved from if we are already where we were and where we are going? So relax and enjoy life while we have it. I do not fear God.[7]

In *The Dangers of Spiritualism*, John Godfrey Raupert pointed out long ago how consistently the spirits predispose their contacts against Christian faith:

> A spirit, starving to gain the confidence of his victim, will be Catholic with a Catholic, Unitarian

with a Unitarian, even a Nihilist and Anarchist, where such learnings are seen to prevail. It will defend and declare the reasonableness of any absurd fad or belief that may be characteristic of the inquirer.

When trust and confidence have been secured, the spirit will slowly begin to undermine any true Christian foundation that may exist, deny the divinity of Christ, the authority of conscience, the responsibility of human life, and the reality of judgment to come. It will feed the mind on empty platitudes, very acceptable to the natural man, but ultimately contradictory of the very fundamental truths of the Christian religion. The very circumstances, known to all the world, that those who embrace Spiritism always cease to profess historic Christianity in any form is in itself ample proof.[8]

Professor Edmond Gruss of Los Angeles Baptist College also explains:

Both Christian and non-Christian writers mention that communications from the "other side," whether through mediums, automatic writing, pendulum, Ouija board, or other means, present a denial of the cardinal doctrines of the Christian faith. . . . Orthodox theology has no place, in spite of the fact that all who received them have been brought up in that tradition.[9]

The research of the authors into scores of spirit-written books bears out a common fact: Without exception, they all deny basic Christian doctrine.

Yes, people can tap into genuine powers. Yes, they can feel joy and love, and at first these powers and experiences appear benevolent and benign. But the tip of the iceberg masks a deeper and much more consuming reality. These powers have a hidden agenda which explains why these powers eventually turn destructive. Only Christ, the Creator, has power over these forces. It is to Him and Him alone someone can turn for deliverance.

So how do people find deliverance from occult practices and the misery they bring? Practicing occultists are wrong when they claim they can deliver someone by magical techniques, psychic counseling, or emotional appeals to supposedly more evolved spirits for assistance. As Dr. Koch and others have pointed out, victory comes only through the power of Christ—not through magic and charming rituals of the occultist or shaman, not through holy water, not through the prayers of mediums for their spirit guide's "rescue work," etc. Apart from the power of Christ, demons have no respect for the attempts of men to control them, and so use such procedures only to further their own ends.

Former mediums have shown the elaborate methods demons will go through to deceive people. If the demon is thought to be cast out, this encourages trust in the false exorcism and simply allows the demon free rein. And the spirits will permit mediums a certain control for strategic purposes: to perpetuate the spirits' own control and people's commitment to false methods.

Thus, the deliverance is rarely actual, and sometimes the person ends up in a worse condition, while the demons retain their influence.

If exorcism is not done properly, it is perhaps better not done at all. If the person does not give his life to Christ (which is typically the case in non-Christian methods), he may be worse off, and even the exorcist may suffer dramatically (cf. Matthew 12:43-45; Acts 19:13-16). And as we have shown earlier, to seek "psychic counseling" for one's difficulty is only to compound the problem.

Counseling the Occultly Oppressed

The following material is intended as a brief, general guide to help pastors and concerned Christians assist those who are suffering from occult involvement. Because most of our research has primarily been from the literature, the authors have had comparatively little personal counseling experience with the occultly oppressed. We are by no means authorities in the area of occult counseling. Further, we think the church needs to take a hard look at this entire field in order to provide appropriate research, sound guidelines, and further recommendations. It would seem to be an area the church will be dealing with for a long time to come. Until then, we can only offer the insights of those personally involved. If not everyone agrees with the following material, we would hope that they would become involved in addressing issues that are of particular concern to them.

Dr. Kurt Koch had 40 years of counseling the occultly oppressed, and his book *Occult Bondage and Deliverance* is recommended. The first portion of the following material is adapted from pages 85-131 of his book. For a complete treatment, the reader should consult the full text and other relevant literature (such as Kurt Koch, *Christian Counseling and Occultism*; John W. Montgomery, ed., *Demon Possession*; Russ Parker, *Battling the Occult*). We should emphasize here that we are primarily dealing with occult oppression; further, we are listing steps that have proven effective, not absolute rules that must be followed. Finally, it is important to realize that in many cases, deliverance from problems related to the occult will occur through a simple confession of sin and prayer for the person to be delivered. If this is not sufficient, then the following information should prove helpful. (See Appendix H for additional helps.)

First and foremost, a correct diagnosis is essential; for example, mental illness must not be mistaken for occult bondage.[10] A person must truly be experiencing demonic oppression from real occult activities; otherwise, misdiagnosis can cause serious problems. How does one determine if a person is suffering from occult oppression? Obviously, the counselor must be aware of the causes and symptoms of this malady and also be involved in some type of counseling of the person in question. Accurate information is essential to accurate diagnosis (see pp. 308-10).

Second, it must be recognized that a genuine battle is in progress. A very real enemy has been encountered, and this enemy is dangerous. But it must also be realized that Christ has obtained victory. Because a real battle has been engaged, Dr. Koch cautions that people are not to rush into the area of occult counseling. Rather, they should seriously look to God for leading in this area. Spiritual maturity and spiritual insight are vital:

> Without a commission from God, a Christian should not venture too far into the area of the demonic and the occult. There are certain rules that have to be obeyed. . . . People with a sensitive nervous system or maybe with an occult oppression of their own should never attempt to do any work in this field. Recent converts and young women should also refrain from this type of work.[11]

Third, we need to recognize God's sovereignty. Christ and Christ alone is the source of deliverance. The usual non-Christian procedures—secular psychology, psychic rituals, hypnosis, meditation, etc.—are useless and may compound the problem. Further, God does not require our "often complicated counseling procedures"; however, deliverance without any counseling at all is rare. Also, full deliverance may take weeks, months, or sometimes years; or, by God's sovereignty, it may require only a few hours.

Fourth, all paraphernalia of occultism must be destroyed (cf. Acts 19:19). "Magical books and occult objects carry with them a hidden ban. Anyone not prepared to rid himself of this ban will be unable to free himself from the influence of the powers of darkness."[12] "Yet even the little figures made out of precious stones which often originate from heathen temples have to be destroyed if the owner finds he cannot free himself from his occult oppression."[13]

In addition, all occult contacts and friendship must be broken, and not even gifts from occultists should be accepted. In the difficult case of a saved person living with parents who are occultists, it may even be necessary for the person to secure other living arrangements. If saved persons are attacked by demons and/or their spiritual life declines while they are praying for their parents, Dr. Koch advises "the children of spiritistic families not to pray for their parents at all if they are still engaged in occult practices."[14] "Inexperienced counselors, however, will be unable to appreciate decisions of this nature, for they will have little knowledge of the terrible attacks which can be leveled by the powers of darkness."[15]

Perhaps prayer could resume after a person's Christian life has been sufficiently strengthened or the conditions change. Apparently, because the powers of darkness may attempt to strike back without mercy, such advice is more heedful than one would expect. Battles should be undertaken only when the participant is fully equipped (Ephesians 6:10-18).

Fifth, deliverance from the power of the occult requires complete surrender to Christ on the part of both counselor and counselee. Our first responsibility must be to Christ and our relationship to Him. We cannot help others in so difficult an area until we ourselves are securely grounded as Christians. Every person who really wants to be delivered from the occult's hold must be prepared to commit his life entirely to Christ. Further, "When a person is delivered from a state of occult subjection, he must withhold nothing in his life from the Lord. These areas which are not surrendered to his Lord will soon be occupied again by the enemy."[16] In other words, if Jesus Christ Himself is truly our Lord, then He will protect us from the lordship of others; but if our commitment is halfhearted, we may be asking for unnecessary problems.

Sixth, the occultly oppressed person must acknowledge and confess his participation in occult activity as sin, because such practices are sinful before God and require confession (Deuteronomy 18:9-12; 1 John 1:9). In addition, confession must be voluntary, or it is worthless. The purpose of confession is to bring into the light that which is occult (hidden, secret). Dr. Koch advises that confession be made in the presence of a mature Christian counselor. "Occultly oppressed people should, in fact, make an open confession of every single hidden thing in their lives in order to remove the very last foothold of the enemy."[17] Further, "The confession of a subjected person should not only cover the occult, but also every other department of his life."[18] In other words, nothing should be allowed to build up or develop which may give the devil an opportunity (Ephesians 4:27).

In addition, a prayer of renouncing everything occult is important:

In the normal way the thing that follows confession is absolution—the promise of the forgiveness of sins. In my counseling work among the occultly oppressed, however, I have found that I have had to abandon this sequence since the subjected person usually finds it impossible to grasp the fact that his sins have been forgiven. He is simply unable to believe. A barrier seems to lie in his way. I, therefore, always encourage the victim of occultism to pray a prayer of renunciation first of all. [19]

Thus:

In counseling the occultly oppressed, a prayer of renunciation is, however, of great significance. The question is "why?" Every sin connected with sorcery is basically a contract with the powers of darkness. By means of sorcery, the arch enemy of mankind gains the right of ownership over a person's life. The same is true even if it is only the sins of a person's parents or grandparents that are involved. The devil is well acquainted with the second commandment which ends, "for I the Lord your God am a jealous God, visiting the iniquity of the fathers upon the children to the third and the fourth generation of those who hate me." [20]

The powers of darkness may continue to claim their right of ownership, although quite often the descendants of occult practitioners remain completely unaware of the fact, perhaps since they have had no contact with sorcery themselves. Nevertheless, immediately after a person in this situation is converted, Satan soon makes his claim felt.

In praying a prayer of renunciation, a person cancels Satan's right both officially and judicially. The counselor and any other Christian brothers present act as witnesses to this annulment of ownership. Although many modern theologians ridicule the whole idea, the devil is in earnest. Hundreds of examples could be quoted to show just how seriously he takes the matter. When the occult oppression is minimal, the person who has made his confession will have little difficulty in repeating a prayer of renunciation after the counselor. The prayer can take the form "In the name of Jesus I renounce all the works of the devil together with the occult practices of my forefathers, and I subscribe myself to the Lord Jesus Christ, my Lord and Savior, both now and forever. In the name of the Father, and of the Son, and of the Holy Spirit. Amen."

The prayer is not a formula. Every time it is prayed it can take a different form. In severe cases of oppression, on the other hand, a number of complications can arise when it comes to praying a prayer of renunciation.[21]

For example, the person may be unable to bring his hands together to pray, or his lips or vocal cords may be unusable. He may fall into a trance when it comes to renouncing the devil: "What can we do in circumstances like this? One can either command the evil powers in the name of Jesus, or else call some other Christian brothers to join in praying for the subjected person."[22] Renunciation may be followed by a remarkable change for the better. Nevertheless, "Not everyone experiences such elated feeling after deliverance but the change of ownership is still valid no matter how one feels. . . . Renunciation is particularly important in cases where natives are converted out of a heathen background."[23]

Seventh, it is vital to assure the individual that in Christ his sins have been forgiven, and that he now possesses an eternal salvation that cannot be taken from him. No matter how bad a person's sins may have been, they have been forgiven. Appropriate Scripture passages may be read, such as John 5:24; 6:47;

20:31; Romans 5:20; Galatians 1:4; Ephesians 1:7,13,14; Colossians 1:14; 1 Peter 1:3-5,18,19; Hebrews 1:3; Isaiah 53:4-7; 1 Peter 2:24; 1 John 1:7-9; etc.

Eighth, prayer is another critical aspect of counseling. People who are delivered from the occult are still vulnerable even after being delivered. It is thus vital that a small group of Christians take it upon themselves to continue to pray for these people and care for them after their conversion. Sometimes Christians do not recognize how important this is. Many converted occultists have been through a living hell because they could find no one in the church to help them. Doreen Irvine's story is a particularly poignant illustration.[24]

> If necessary, the group need only consist of two Christians. They should meet together at least twice or three times a week for perhaps a quarter of an hour at a time in order to pray for the oppressed person. The best thing is for the subjected person to be present as well, yet this is not absolutely necessary. Neither is it essential for the oppressed person to have made an open confession before all the members of the group. This need only have been made before the counselor at the very start.[25]

It is also to be recognized that counseling should involve teamwork. The support of other Christians, church elders, etc., is important. As Koch explains, "Counseling the occultly oppressed is really a matter of teamwork. The individual counselor is far too weak to take upon his own shoulders all the problems he meets."[26] For example, people with occult subjection will often suffer their first attacks after they seek to follow Christ and serve Him. In other words, the battle often does not begin until a person receives Christ. Further, "There is a possibility that if a person puts too much of his own effort into trying to help the demonically oppressed that a transference will take place."[27]

When a person is delivered from occult oppression, it is also crucial that he grow as a Christian. He must really lay hold of the four basic spiritual elements comprising Christian discipleship: study in the Word of God, Christian fellowship, continuous prayer, and communion. Further, the new Christian must be grounded in the study of basic Christian doctrine and Christian evidences.

Dr. Koch observed from his own ministry that sometimes those counseling the occultly oppressed will discover that the demons have returned into a person's life. And at this point, it seems the battle is fiercer than before.

> Very often one finds that the powers of darkness return when a person is liberated in a Christian atmosphere, and then has to return and live in an atmosphere of occultism and sorcery. This is frequently what happens in the case of young people from spiritistic families who are converted when away from home and later have to return and live in the demonically affected house of their parents.[28]
>
> People who have been delivered from occult oppression and yet have to return again and live in an occult or spiritistic atmosphere never find real and lasting peace. I usually find that I have to advise young people stemming from such environments, "Stay away from your parents—or from your uncle, aunt, or relation—if they are not prepared to forsake their occult practices and interests." This advice is not always appreciated, however. In fact, on occasions I have been actually rebuked for having given a person advice of this nature. Finally, repeating what we have just been saying, anyone who fails to act on all that the Bible says for our protection will live in continuous danger of falling victim once more to the influence of the exorcised spirits.[29]

No matter how difficult or how wearying the counseling of occultly oppressed people may be, the truth remains that the victory is won because of what Christ has accomplished.[30] Counselors need to believe God's promises and act in faith even in what seem to be hopeless situations. No situation is finally hopeless, for with God all things are possible. Furthermore, the mere fact that a battle continues to rage is not evidence that the battle will be lost. Many times in biblical history and throughout church history, spiritual battles have been undertaken which have required great endurance, perseverance, patience, and faith. In the area of counseling those with occult oppression, and in the area of biblical demonology in general, there is much that is not known. Therefore, our reliance on Christ is all the more important. Finally:

> It is also very important to remember when counseling and caring for the occultly oppressed that this kind of counsel will only thrive in the right spiritual atmosphere. One must never look upon a person and his needs as just another "case," or as some new "sensation" or "object of investigation." True deliverance will never be forthcoming in an unscriptural atmosphere—even if the battle for the oppressed person appears to be very dramatic. We must be on our guard against every kind of excess, and above all against exhibitionism. Let us therefore be: Sound in our faith, sober in our thoughts, honest and scriptural in our attitude.[31]

In conclusion, Satan offers us power, but God offers us love. It is much more fulfilling to live with love than to live with power. The lust for power can really never be fulfilled, whereas God offers us an eternal relationship which is truly fulfilling.

The deadness of soul felt by millions of people who have had their life sucked out is testimony to the devil's gifts. The "freedom" Satan offers is a naked autonomy leading to license and bondage. But the freedom Christ offers is a loving dependence leading to inner strength and unspeakable joy.

We repeat: The real danger of psychic involvement is its denial of Christ and the eternal torment it brings. You may either accept Christ as personal Savior and Lord, or reject Him.

In all eternity no single decision will be more consequential.

For those individuals who would like to receive Jesus Christ as their personal Lord and Savior, we suggest the following prayer (if you have been involved in the occult, this participation should also be renounced and forsaken):

> Dear God, these spirits are not of You and I ask for Your protection from them. I confess my sin of seeking what You have forbidden and I renounce these spirits and all involvement with them. I ask Jesus Christ to enter my life and to be my Lord and Savior. I recognize this is a solemn decision that You take very seriously. I believe that on the cross Jesus Christ died for my sin and I receive Him into my life now. My commitment to You is that I will follow Him and not the spirits. I ask for Your help in doing this. Amen.

If you prayed this prayer, there are several things you need to do to grow in the Christian life. Start to read a modern translation Bible and find a good church that honors Christ. Tell someone you have just become a Christian so they may pray for you and encourage you in your new life with Christ.

Appendixes

Recommended Reading

Notes

Index

Appendix A
(see Chapter 2)

Biblical Warnings Against Occult Involvement

Whether or not practitioners accept the categories, the data point unmistakably to the conclusion that the essence of occult practice constitutes a trafficking with demons. From this reality flow a number of other concerns: idolatry, spiritual deception, the likelihood of possession, psychological and physical harm, and the immoral, ethically consequential teachings that inevitably accompany demonic involvement or revelations. Our purpose is to simply document that God does indeed warn against the occult.

God teaches that spiritual warfare is a reality (Ephesians 6:10-18; 2 Corinthians 2:11; 1 Peter 5:8) and that supernatural manifestations are not to be accepted uncritically but to be tested by the Word of God (1 John 4:1; Revelation 2:2; Acts 17:10-12; Deuteronomy 18:20-22; Matthew 24:24, etc.). Scripture also speaks of the reality of a personal devil and myriads of demons who should be regarded as cunning enemies of both the believer in Christ and the nonbeliever (John 8:44; 13:27; Matthew 6:13; 9:34; 12:24; Luke 8:12; 13:16; 2 Corinthians 4:4; Colossians 1:13; 2 Thessalonians 2:9; Acts 16:16-18; 2 Corinthians 2:11; 11:3; 2 Timothy 2:26). Indeed, one of the devil's tactics is to masquerade as an "angel of light" and a servant of righteousness (2 Corinthians 11:13-15).

The Scripture also warns that false prophets are linked to evil spirits and that there are "doctrines of demons" (1 John 4:1; 1 Timothy 4:1); that there is great power in the occult (Isaiah 47:9); that Satan is the god of this world (2 Corinthians 4:4); that the whole world lies in the power of this evil one (1 John 5:19); that demons work through people by giving them psychic abilities (Acts 16:16-19; Exodus 7:11,22; 8:7); and that Satan and his hordes are active in the affairs of the planet (Ephesians 2:2; Daniel 10:12,13,20).

In many instances, Scripture explicitly cites Satan or his demons as the reality behind occult involvement, idolatry, and false religion (Deuteronomy 32:16,17; 1 Corinthians 10:19-21; Psalm 106:35-40; 1 Timothy 4:1; 2 Thessalonians 2:9,10; Acts 16:16-19, etc.). This is one reason why God considers occult activity in virtually all its forms as an abomination (Deuteronomy 18:9-12)—because it links those for whom Christ died to evil spirits who are His enemies. Thus, occult involvement will eventually lead to judgment for those who refuse to forsake it (Revelation 22:15; 2 Chronicles 33:6).

Scripture condemns by name spiritism, mediumism and necromancy (Deuteronomy 18:9-12; 2 Chronicles 33:2,3,6); various forms of sorcery and divination (Deuteronomy 18:9-12; Hosea 4:12; Exodus 22:18; Isaiah 44:25; 29:8,9; Ezekiel 21: 21; e.g., astrology, Deuteronomy 17:2-5; 2 Kings 17:15-17; Isaiah 47:9-14); and magic (Acts 13:8; 19:16-19; Isaiah 47:9,12).

In their numerous forms these basic categories (magic, spiritism, divination, and sorcery) cover almost the entire gamut of occult activity. But the irreducible reality of all occultism is spiritism.

Thus:

> [Spiritism] . . . is one of the oldest known forms of religious expression. It is also one of the deadliest where the certainty of divine judgment is concerned. . . . It is terminal error, since it demonstrates not only an active rejection of God, but an active embrace of his replacement. It is, as the prophets put it, "spiritual adultery," carried to completion. It is faithlessness fulfilled.
>
> The extent to which a society endorses or indulges in widespread spiritism, therefore, is something of a spiritual thermometer. It can give us a rough estimate of our collective state of spiritual health. . . . The Bible levies its judgment against spiritism at two levels. It treats spiritism as a symptom of social decline as well as an act of personal culpability.
>
> All sin provokes God's judgment. Advanced or developed sin provokes it more directly and immediately. As a social symptom, spiritism represents the final stage of a long process of spiritual decay. It is the terminal phase of our flight from God. It is terminal because God's judgment on spiritism is not meant to admonish or correct, but to cleanse and extirpate.
>
> On an individual scale, the practice of spiritism is terminal because it represents an ultimate confusion of values. It trades humanity's privilege of intimacy with God for sheer

> fascination with a liar who secretly hates all that is human
> and all that humans hold dear. [1]

In 20 years of studying spiritistic contacts and literature and the effects on the lives of spiritists, we can confirm this view wholeheartedly.

Clearly, the Scripture warns against the occult. And just as clearly, those who practice it disobey what God's Word commands. In essence, occult activity courts deception and betrayal from the demonic realm as well as judgment from God for engaging in it, and thereby promotes spiritual evil under the guise of legitimate religious practice.

Appendix B
(see Chapter 4)

The Teachings of the Spirits

First, we will present a brief summary in which we compare the spirits' views from channeled literature with Bible teaching. Then we will quote the spirits in more detail to further document their beliefs.

God

The spirits teach that God is ultimately an impersonal force (an "it"), like electricity or a "personalized" universal energy that constitutes everything. God is "infinite power," "all life," "universal consciousness," etc. The consensus of "most channeled material" is that "God is all that is" and that "the universe is a multi-dimensional living Being," i.e., God.[1] Thus "Seth" teaches, "There is no personal God... in Christian terms."[2]

But the Bible teaches that God is a personal, holy, and loving Being who created the universe distinct from Himself (Genesis 1:1; John 3:16).

Jesus

The spirits teach that Jesus is an evolved spirit or a man just like us. Jesus was the person who highly emulated the Christ spirit which is also part of us all. The spirits say that Jesus has died and has now evolved to a higher state of existence just like other people have. Thus, one spirit confesses that Jesus was only a representative of the impersonal divine force living in all men (the Christ spirit) and that Christians who believe in the biblical Jesus "worship a dead Christ."[3]

But the Bible teaches that Christians worship a living Christ, that Jesus *is* the Christ, and that He is fully Man and fully God in one Person. He is the only unique Son of God (Luke 2:11; John 1:1; Romans 1:4; Philippians 2:1-9; Titus 2:13).

Man

The spirits teach that man in his true nature is perfect and one essence with God. "White Eagle" says to all men, "You too are part of God."[4] Another spirit teaches it is a "vicious abomination" to teach men that they are evil or sinful.[5]

On the other hand, the Bible teaches that man is a created being and not part of God (Genesis 1:27). Man sinned by disobeying God, resulting in his being separated from God's fellowship (Genesis 3:3-8).

Sin

The spirits teach that sin is merely "mistakes," "an illusion," or ignorance of one's own deity, and that sin in a biblical sense is nothing God is concerned with. As one spirit teaches, it is "talk of sin and guilt" that is the true evil, even though it "may be camouflaged by the use of religious buzz words such as 'Jesus loves you' or 'praise the Lord.' . . . If the minister or priest happens to be one who loves to rant and rave about sin and guilt, the forces he draws in will be dark and ugly."[6]

But the Bible teaches that sin and guilt are real. Sin is disobedience to God's law (1 John 3:4; 5:17), which, apart from repentance and faith in Christ, will result in God's judgment (John 3:16,36; Matthew 25:46).

Salvation

The spirits teach that "salvation" involves realizing that one is already part of God. Each man must accomplish this for himself by practicing various occult techniques. According to the universal teachings of the spirits, salvation does not occur by the atoning death of Christ—which one spirit characteristically claims is "a tragic distortion of the real nature of God's love."[7] The spirits speaking through medium Carl Japikse teach that the Christian view of the atonement is a great social and spiritual evil. Being "born again" for salvation is a "hysterical belief" and an "escape from responsibility."[8] Believing in Jesus "does not serve the plan of God."[9] Accepting Christ as one's Savior at a religious gathering is like "a circus sideshow."[10] Thus, man's "struggle is not between salvation and damnation," and Christians who believe so are "ignorant fanatics" who prefer "spiritual darkness."[11]

But the Bible teaches that salvation involves receiving the gift of forgiveness of sins from a loving God. Salvation has been provided for man by God's grace and is received by man through faith in Christ's death for us (Ephesians 1:7; 2:8,9).

Death

The spirits teach that at death there is no final judgment. It is merely transition into the wonderful spirit world. "All 'spirit teaching' [agrees]. ... There is no hell, no punishment."[12]

But the Bible emphasizes again and again that death brings judgment and entrance either into an eternal heaven or hell (Matthew 25:46; Hebrews 9:27).

Satan

The spirits teach there is no devil. As one spirit argues, "There is no devil. ... It is utterly absurd to believe [in] a 'prince of darkness.' "[13]

But the Bible teaches that Satan and his demons are real as Jesus Himself taught (Matthew 4:1-10; 8:16; 17:18).

Now we will cite the words of some of the most popular spirits in America concerning their religious teachings. This is necessary because so many millions of people today believe that *these* spirits offer teachings that are consistent with the Bible and Christian faith. As you read the words of the spirits carefully, ask yourself some questions. Are these teachings good or evil? Are they true or false? Are they what we would expect from lying spirits or truly good spirits?

1. "Ramtha"—the spirit speaking through medium J. Z. Knight in Douglas Mahr's, *Ramtha, Voyage to the New World*, Ballantine, 1987; citations are listed by pages.

"Ramtha's" teaching on God: Ramtha teaches the Christian God is an "idiotic deity" (p. 219); "God, the principal, is all things" (p. 250).

"Ramtha's" teaching on man: "You are God" (p. 61); "God the Father is you" (p. 136); "Everyone is what you call a psychic" (p. 139); "Love yourself . . . live in the moment, to exalt all that you are" (p. 149).

"Ramtha's" teaching on sin: "There is no such thing as evil" (p. 60); "For 2,000 years we have been called sinful creatures . . . [but] we are equal with God or Christ" (pp. 180-81).

"Ramtha's" teaching on salvation: "Do not preach to this world. . . . The world doesn't need saving—leave it alone" (p. 130); "Relinquish guilt . . . do not live by rules, live by feelings. . . . You are the Lord of Hosts, you are the Prince of Peace"

(p. 149); "Now to become enlightened is to make the priority of enlightenment first—the priority of love of Self first" (p. 227).

"Ramtha's" teaching on death: "God has never judged you or anyone" (p. 62); "No, there is no Hell and there is no devil" (p. 252).

"Ramtha's" teaching on Satan and demons: "Devil? I looked far and wide for the creature. . . . I found him nowhere [but] I found him thriving in the hearts of frenzied entities in a fervor of madness to save the world from its sins. . . . That is where he is. [Do] you understand?" (pp. 252-53); "The devil is not really evil . . . because he's really God. . . . Who else would he be?" (p. 251).

2. "Jesus"—the spirit who worked through medium Helen Schucman in *A Course in Miracles*, 1977; citations are listed by volume and page.

"Jesus' " teaching on God: "The recognition of God is the recognition of yourself. There is no separation of God and His creation" (1:136).

"Jesus' " teaching on Jesus: "There is nothing about me [Jesus] that you cannot attain" (1:5); "Christ waits for your acceptance of Him as yourself" (1:187); "Is [Jesus] the Christ? O yes, along with you" (1:83).

"Jesus' " teaching on man: "God's Name is holy, but no holier than yours. To call upon His Name is but to call upon your own" (2:334); "You are the Holy Son of God Himself" (2:353-54).

"Jesus' " teaching on sin: "Sin does not exist" (3:81); "Sin is the grand illusion . . . joyously [release] one another from the belief in sin" (1:375, 377-78); "See no one, then, as guilty . . . [within all men] there is perfect innocence"; "No one is punished for sins [and you] are not sinners" (1:88).

"Jesus' " teaching on salvation: "[Divine] forgiveness, then, is an illusion" (3:79); "[It is] a terrible misconception that God Himself [judged] His own Son on behalf of salvation. . . . It is so essential that all such thinking be dispelled that we must be sure

that nothing of this kind remains in your mind. I was not 'punished' because you were bad" (1:32-33, 87); "A sense of separation from God is the only lack you really need to correct"; "Salvation is nothing more than 'right-mindedness' "; "You are one with God" (1:11, 53; 2:125); "Do not make the pathetic error of 'clinging to the old rugged cross.' . . . This is not the gospel I . . . intended to offer you" (1:47).

"Jesus' " teaching on death: "There is no death, but there is a belief in death" (1:46); "Death is the central dream from which all illusions stem" (3:63).

3. "Seth"—the spirit speaking through Jane Roberts and written down by her husband in *Seth Speaks*, Prentice Hall, 1972; citations are listed by pages.

"Seth's" teaching on God: God is "All That Is" (p. 405).

"Seth's" teaching on Jesus: "He [Jesus] will not come to reward the righteous and send evildoers to eternal doom" (p. 389).

"Seth's" teaching on sin: "A strong belief in such [concepts of good and evil] is highly detrimental" (p. 191).

"Seth's" teaching on salvation: "The soul . . . is not something you must save or redeem, and it is also something you cannot lose" (p. 89).

"Seth's" teaching on Satan and demons: "The devil is a projection of your own psyche" (p. 7); "There are no devils or demons" (p. 405).

4. "Lilly" and other spirits channeled through medium Ruth Montgomery. (Note: Some of the following statements are Montgomery's, although they reflect the teachings of the spirits which she has adopted as her own beliefs.)

The spirits' teaching on God: "God is the name of What Is." (Ruth Montgomery, *Here and Hereafter*, Fawcett Crest, 1968, p. 74).

The spirits' teaching on man: "God wishes that it [psychic ability] be utilized and developed to the fullest potential" (Ruth

Montgomery, *A Search for Truth*, Bantam, 1968, p. 160); "We are God" (Ruth Montgomery, *A World Beyond*, Fawcett Crest, 1972, p. 12).

The spirits' teaching on death: "There is no such thing as death" (Ibid., 66); "God punishes no man" (Ruth Montgomery, *Here and Hereafter*, Fawcett Crest, 1968, p. 174).

The spirits' teaching on Satan and demons: "I have seen no signs of a devil on this side of the veil ['veil' here means death]" (Ruth Montgomery, *A World Beyond*, Fawcett Crest, 1972, p. 64); "The devil was not a person ever" (Ibid., p. 65).

5. Various spirits who allegedly knew Jesus on earth, written through medium Kahlil Gibran in *Jesus, the Son of Man* (New York, A. A. Knopf, 1959); citations are listed by pages.

The spirits' views on God: "Israel should have another God" (p. 32).

The spirits' views on Jesus: "Jesus the Nazarene was born and reared like ourselves. . . . He was [only] a man"; "Jesus was a man and not a god. . . . It's a pity his followers seek to make a god of such a sage" (Ibid., pp. 43, 109, 113).

6. A spirit calling itself "The Christ" claims to be the biblical Jesus who, after 2000 years in the spirit world, has now "acquired new ideas and experiences" and thus he castigates Christians who believe in biblical salvation; further, he endorses occultism, teaches all men will become God, and encourages his listeners to reject Christian teachings and accept spirit contact. [14]

Now consider again the content of what you have just read. Do the spirits endorse the occult when God forbids it (Deuteronomy 18:9-12)? Do these spirits deny there is a devil when Jesus taught that Satan was a real, personal being (Matthew 4:1-10)? Why do you think the spirits claim men are not sinners when all men know in their hearts they are? Why do the spirits teach that God is impersonal when God has revealed Himself in the Bible as a personal Being? Why do the spirits teach man to be selfish when such behavior is universally condemned? Why do the spirits deny that Christ died to forgive men's sins when Christ Himself taught this was the very reason He came (Matthew 20:28)? Why do the spirits claim Jesus was simply a man when all the evidence proves He was God-Incarnate, the only begotten Son of God as He Himself taught (John 3:16; 5:18; 10:30; 14:6)? Why do the spirits say men are God, when all men know they are not God? Why do the spirits deny the existence of evil, when its reality is obvious to all?

Not Who They Claim to Be

Do people intuitively sense the spirits are not who they claim to be? Many do. Modern channeler J. Z. Knight who channels "Ramtha" went through a period where she felt Ramtha might be a demon but was eventually persuaded to trust him (*Holistic Life Magazine*, Summer 1985, p. 30). When unbiblical revelations began coming from Edgar Cayce's unconscious trance sessions, the famous medium openly wondered if "the devil might be tempting me to do his work by operating through me when I was conceited enough to think God had given me special power" and "if ever the devil was going to play a trick on me, this would be it" (Thomas Sugrue, *Stranger in the Earth*, 1971, p. 210). The famous psychic Uri Geller and parapsychologist Andrija Puharich, M.D., were also uneasy over their spirit contacts. They felt something was "funny" or "wrong" and suspected they were being "played with," wondering whether or not the entities themselves were unstable (Puharich, *Uri*, 1975, pp. 173, 188-89).

Gurdjieffian J. G. Bennett discusses the *latihan* experience in the religion of Subud. This experience has a number of similarities to spirit possession and some people seem to sense something evil:

> In the latihan, we are gradually pervaded and permeated with the life force that flows into us from our own awakened soul. . . . The latihan itself lasts for half an hour or more. . . . Some trainees are convinced that there is indeed a force, but an evil one. Others are simply afraid. . . . Indeed, the sense of being alone in the presence of a great Power is the strongest and clearest element of the whole experience. It is that Power that gives new life to the soul, and not ourselves, not anything that we do (Bennett, *Concerning Subud*, 1959, 95, 103-07).

The point is this: The religious teachings of the spirits are exactly what one might expect from demons. The irony is that the very theory that is most probably true, that Satan and demons do exist, is the one most rarely considered by those involved in these very practices.

Appendix C
(see Chapter 5)

Occult Criminality

A number of problems surround the relationship between occult activity and homicide. (Larry Kahaner's *Cults That Kill: Probing the Underworld of Occult Crime* is essential reading here.)

- *Disbelief.* Evidence may never be heard or reported because of skepticism. It is true that more police departments are becoming aware of the problem (a few have units devoted solely to investigating criminal occult activity), but often there is a denial that, where present in significant proportions, occultism may have been a contributing factor in serious crimes.
- *Absent or conflicting evidence.* Those who are serious about occult murder are secretive and dispose of evidence methodologically. Conflicting evidence can be interpreted in various ways when the motives are multiple, and investigators downplay the occult factor for less bizarre answers.
- *Impotence.* Police may find it almost impossible to infiltrate satanic or related groups. Often someone cannot join such groups without an initiation that involves criminal acts.
- *Fear of repercussions.* Most people instinctively avoid that which is overtly evil. Investigators may be concerned that reprisal is more likely in groups with a satanic philosophy and where trial and conviction are unlikely.

In several cases where alleged Satanism, ritual killing, and other crimes were involved, the *Chicago Tribune* (July 29, 1985) illustrated a number of the problems discussed above:

> "It's something I don't want to be identified as knowing that much about," said a psychiatrist who has interviewed the children in one of the cases. "I think anybody who works in this area ought to carry a badge and wear a gun. And not have a family."

"Good luck with your life," said another child therapist, one of whose patients is among the children making such accusations. "My car was blown up ten days ago."

"People," one psychiatrist says, "just aren't ready for this."

A mistrial was declared in the case when the jury announced that it was deadlocked 6-6, and Jewett said several jurors told him later that it had been their disbelief of the girl's testimony about Satanic rituals, and not about being abused, that prompted them to vote for acquittal.

"There's no doubt in my mind that she was a participant in Satanic worship," Jewett said, "But she also described incidents of human sacrifice, bestiality and cannibalism. . . ."

His dilemma is shared by Rick Lewkowitz, a deputy district attorney in Sacramento who is prepared for a preliminary hearing in the case of five men, many of them waiters in the same restaurant, who are charged with 77 counts of sexually abusing nine children.

"There've been descriptions of Satanic rituals," Lewkowitz said in a telephone interview. . . . "Four of the children have described one specific incident where three children were killed by the sexually abused victims."

Lewkowitz is convinced that the children are telling the truth. "I don't see where these kids would be able to come up with the consistent detail they come up with, if not from their own experience," he said.

The principal obstacle confronting them, say those investigating the various cases, is the almost total lack of physical evidence, including bodies, to confirm the children's allegations.

Of course, it is a big world with lots of places to hide bodies. Perhaps the estimated 25,000 to 50,000 children who disappear off the face of the earth each year might account for some of them.

Most of the one-and-a-half to two million children who disappear are found. But many are kidnapped by child molesters and Satanists who use them in pornographic films, occult rituals, and/or "snuff" films. Robert Simandl is a 20-year veteran of the Chicago police department and a leading authority on crime and Satanism. He is one of many who thinks there is an international network of Satanists responsible for selling drugs, child pornography, and other crimes.[1]

Up to 50,000 children are never found and never accounted for— children who, presumably, never wanted to be lost in the first place. One

can only wonder what may have happened to them. We know for a fact
what happened to some: "Each year between 2,500 and 5,000 *uniden-
tified* children are found slain, and many are thought to be the victims of
child abductors."[2]

Appendix D
(see Chapter 5)

Magical Implements

Inanimate objects can also become vehicles for satanic power. For example, pagan idols are not merely artistic pieces of dead wood. They often have a power behind them, as idol worshipers know only too well. Indeed, many objects used in occult practices carry spiritual potency. Ouija boards, tarot cards, I Ching, rune dice, crystals and gems, astrology charts, talismans, dowsing rods, and many other physical implements used in occult, idolatrous practices may become channels for demonic powers. Koch warns of the dangers of even possessing the magic book known as *The 6th and 7th Book of Moses*, let alone of using it. The use of the name Moses here is a camouflage, occultists apparently attempting to make him a "patron saint":

> The book has already caused untold harm in the world and people who read it suffer in the process. A house in which the book is kept is also a place where misfortunes often occur.[1]

Dr. G. W. Peters, professor and chairman of the Department of World Missions at Dallas Theological Seminary, has some pertinent observations:

> Yet I cannot help but believe that there is such a thing as demonic focalization in certain objects and operating uniquely through certain formulas. These objects (including words) become special embodiments and vehicles of demonic powers and convey supra-human and supra-natural potency. Strange phenomena proceed from them. Sounds and voices are heard, flames are seen shooting forth from rocks and trees as lightning or bright flashes, and strange and destructive influences are emanating from them. Dr. John S. Mbiti reports several rather peculiar experiences in *African Religions and Philosophy* (pp. 194-197).

Trustworthy eye-witnesses have informed me that they have seen flames shooting up from rocks repeatedly in Timor, Indonesia, and trees have been seen burning without being destroyed. Experiences as described by Dr. Mbiti and the reports from Timor are quite common in Southeast Asia and the South Pacific. . . .

It has been experienced that the transportation of an idol has actually brought serious physical disturbances, destruction, and death to the new locality and community. In some instances, nothing but the return to the former place would restore peace and tranquility to the new locality. . . .

It is my impression that the focalization of demonic powers in objects and practices is the secret of "magical" powers of charms and fetishes. Here also is the secret of the potency of the "curse" in witchcraft, sorcery, the evil eye, etc. Let no one imagine that words do not carry power, that they cannot become embodiments of dynamics. It is so with the Word of God. His Word is power-bearing. It is a living and powerful Word. . . .

In clearest words does the New Testament exclude the idolators from the kingdom of God. Why? Because idolatry is the most serious form of human and demonic confrontation of God and the sharpest and deepest focalization of evil under the cloak of a religious object. . . .

Two things, however, are clear. First, the Bible realizes the reality of evil in these practices. It does so not because they are superstitions and pagan cultural and religious "hang-overs," but because they are embodiments of evil. Second, the Bible condemns such practices without compromise and apology.[2]

As if to confirm Dr. Peters' conclusion, in Dr. Koch's experience there has been no possessor of *The 6th and 7th Book of Moses* without psychological harm:

But it is a remarkable observation of pastoral experience, that in all homes and families in which *The 6th and 7th Book of Moses* is kept, or even used, psychological disturbances of various kinds appear.[3]

Appendix E
(see Chapter 5)

The Atlanta Child Murders—
The Ultimate Hazard of Pagan Religion:
Child Sacrifice and Societal Collapse
Dr. Sondra A. O'Neale, Ph.D.

When people speak of an occult revival in America, others may want to believe that the phenomenon is relatively harmless to themselves and to the nation—that it is just another unchristian religious occurrence. In actuality this "revival" is *the* most insidious challenge to the body of Christ as the supreme sphere of moral (or from their vantage point, immoral) influence in national life. What occultists want is a world of insecurity, perverseness, and evil, such as the Babylonians, Egyptians, Canaanites, and other pagan cultures practiced before our Lord and the early church transformed civilizations, bringing men and nations hope, peace, and security from the ravishments of capricious gods. Before the advent of the Christian faith, the sole philosophical underpinning of world religions (except that of the Hebrews) was the occult and the overt worship of Satan as the ultimate god of the universe, regardless of the pagan aliases with which he was identified.

Whenever the father of evil is revered, he insists upon the deepest of sins for "adoration": sodomy (Leviticus 20:5-16); homosexuality (Romans 1:26,27; Leviticus 20:13); animal worship (Romans 1:22-25; Exodus 32:7-35); necrophilia (cf. Psalm 106:34-39); lewd pagan ritual (Ezekiel 22:9; 23:48,49; Galatians 5:21); astrology (2 Kings 17:16; 2 Chronicles 33:3); drug-induced ecstasy (Isaiah 29:9) as in the root Greek word for "sorcery," i.e., *pharmekia*: enchantment with drugs (Revelation 9:21; 18:23; 21:8; 22:15; Galatians 5:20); exploitation of the stranger, the poor, the widows, and fatherless (Psalm 94:6; Jeremiah 2:34; Job 24:1-12); slavery (Revelation 18:3 NASB); psychic oppression and direction (Psalm 55:3 NASB); spirit worship (Leviticus 19:31; 20:6,27; Deuteronomy 18:10-12); kidnapping (Revelation 18:13; Exodus 21:16; 1 Timothy 1:10); murder for blood sacrifice (Ezekiel 22:3,4); and child sacrifice (Isaiah 57:5; Jeremiah 7:31; Ezekiel 23:39; Leviticus 20:1-5; Psalm 106:37,38).

All of these elements were present in the Atlanta murders.

What we uncovered during the questioning of one witness led to the unmistakable conclusion that a mongrel occult organization had killed the 29 children and young adults in Atlanta and at least 30 of the 37 women and female teenagers (who were unexplainably not placed on the children's list), both white and black. Those were killed during the same time period as other murders attendant to the children's cases, of which police would not admit connection in order to ameliorate public hysteria. This occult group combined "rules" of astrology, witchcraft, and numerology, and financed its hierarchy through 1) pornographic film of the ritual slayings, 2) an extensive drug network which blanketed Atlanta's poorer communities (and through which they employed some of the children), and 3) through the sale of illicit sex, including bestiality but predominantly homosexual en masse.

Claiming to be just a guard at the clan's nightly orgiastic mystical ceremonies, the witness revealed that identification in the drug order (i.e., pushers, drop locations, dollar values, administrators, etc.) merely reflected the twin echelon of spiritual responsibility in the group. Her descriptions of 1) the occult symbolism, 2) the manner of the children's deaths, and 3) of the lewd rites over which a high priest presided, masked in a Pan-like goat's head and directing potential victims to ascending analogous ritual circles, are authenticated by other witnesses interviewed and by texts of occult mysticism and ritual sacrifice.

Corroborating textual evidence includes the dates of the children's deaths (as can be verified from the time of disappearance and/or from medical examiners' reports). These feast days and ancient sabbaths (i.e., February 2, June 22, August 1, October 31, etc.), which are antithetical to traditional Judeo-Christian observances, are deemed by occult communicants to be the best times to tap into the old pagan cycles of nature and astrology. The death dates in the Atlanta cases can be traced back to what scholars such as Sir James George Frazer (*The Golden Bough*), Dr. Montague Summers (*The History of Witchcraft and Demonology*), Dr. Margaret A. Murray (*The God of the Witches*), et. al, attest are equinoxes, solstices, or sabbaths of astrological change.

Additionally, parents and other informed parties report that crosses and other witchcraft carvings and ritual markings were placed on several bodies. Several of the young boys were partially castrated, and large hypodermic needles had been used to extract virgin semen to be used for magical potions. Some of the young girls were raped, strangled, and tied to trees (again after vital hormones had been extracted) as part of an annual nature ritual.

All but three of the 29 children and young adults were fatherless, some were even orphaned and left to fend for themselves. According to Dr. Leo L. Martello and magician Aleister Crowley, both master Satanists, these are the victims which Satan wants: rejected, neglected, powerless children—the cast-offs of an indifferent society.

Witchcraft literature (*The Atlantians* and *The Georgians*) claims that Atlanta is unique in occult reconstructions of ancient Europe and American Indian myth and as such has been designated as one of America's occult centers. In short, the city is supposed to be the lost Atlantis.

While the central sociopolitical power base of this child-killing cult has been in Atlanta for years, in 1978 they began to attract several political, homosexual, and racially centered subcults around the city. They also sponsored a witches' convention which in effect brought the occult out of the city's closet. Astrologers and psychics from all over the country and the world came to Atlanta. The ensuing newspaper coverage of the convention enabled recruitment of many curious onlookers who later became dedicated cult followers.

Until further arrests are made in the Atlanta cases (if ever), I cannot be more specific about the four subgroups than as follows:

1. A mainly black American subcult formulated to bring forth the advent of a "Messiah" in the Far East. The group uses excessive mind control and race-baiting to inspire blind loyalty among its followers. Much of its recruitment effort is among marginal mental patients with a history of mental illness and among young men and women with a criminal background who have no consciousness of commitment to society. Indigent children are recruited under the guise of benevolent assistance.

2. A racially integrated drug/prostitution/pornography/occult ring similar to that which Mike Warnke discloses in *The Satan Seller*.

3. An all-white group known for historical, political involvement based on the hatred of black people. This met with other subgroups in outlying natural settings to exchange the children

from ritual group to ritual group. While the nation knows of this organization's political activity, few people take seriously the religious trappings that the adherents flaunt so openly.

4. An old, established (and unfortunately accepted) cult in America which has infiltrated and gained control of law enforcement agencies throughout the country, but especially so in Atlanta. Some of those men which society trusts to protect and uphold the law used their authority to recruit children, to sexually abuse them, and to initiate them into the sado/sexual cult world.

Members of this faction further use their position to protect the other subcults and to thwart attempts to expose the cults' involvement in the cases and the conviction of cult members.

Some occultists are visited by Satan in the form of a dark and twisted personage. Yet Scripture also says that Satan transforms himself into an angel of light. This is the dichotomy which the Atlanta cult structure seeks to imitate. Just as Charles Manson directed his followers to commit carnage in Sharon Tate's home and leave evidence indicating that black militants were responsible so that a race war, "Helter Skelter," would ensue, so the political motive in the Atlanta cases was to terrorize America and further polarize the nation into armed racial camps.

Race, sex, and skin color were precisely the determiners for the city, the victims, and even for the selected perpetrators. Never before the kidnappings and murders in Atlanta has the twentieth century seen the multiplying horror of the racial myth in its most urgent religious sense. Listen to the words of a neo-pagan Satanist: "Whatever is white is good, pure. Whatever is black is bad, evil. . . . And we renounce all that is good, Christian, pure. . . . We give our souls to Satan and to a blood pact *to sacrifice a child to him*" (Doreen Valiente, *ABC of Witchcraft*).

Another Satanist, Leo Martello (*The Wicked Ways of Witchcraft*) states:

What the Church has chosen to call Devil Worship or Satanism is merely the worship of those deities that existed before Christianity. . . . There were Black Magicians who made pacts with the devil, who truly believed in the power of evil. The 17th century Italian chronicler of demonology,

Francesco-Maria Guazzo, describes eleven steps that the initiate Satanist must go through.

Among those steps which Martello includes in "The Satanic Oath" are:

- Initiate's name is included in the "Book of Death."
- A promise to sacrifice children to the devil.
- A promise to pay annual tribute to the devil (black-colored gifts, etc.).

Two of several private detectives who investigated the Atlanta murders and who shared their findings with me report that spirit slavery in the afterlife is one of the spin-off motives for the child sacrifices. Their informants (both men in their mid-twenties, now dead through mysterious circumstances) said that the spirit-soul is induced to stay on earth after death to serve at the behest of the "godfather"/master as his obedient slave. Said one detective,

> These children were chosen because they had no father or authority figure in the home. The child was indoctrinated through the use of drugs, hypnosis and mind control to believe that the uniformed executioner was his eternally-destined master and that the child's "karma" could only be fulfilled if he served in total subjection both in life and in death.

That such racial and color consideration is a resurrection of ancient demonology is seen in Canaan's book *Studies in Palestinian Customs and Folklore, II. Haunted Springs and Water Demons in Palestine*:

> They now think that En Fawwar is inhabited by two spirits, a *hurr*, "free man" (master) and an "abd," "servant." The first is a white person, the second a negro (also slave-born) as the Arabic words themselves indicate. These two powerful spirits are continually fighting each other. When the *hurr* gains the victory he allows the water to flow for the benefit of thirsty mankind. But soon the "abd" rises and resumes the battle. As soon as he overpowers the *hurr*

he shuts off the blessing to avenge himself on the human race.

> This representation of
> good against evil,
> white against black,
> angels against devils,
> light against darkness,
> upper against lower world and
> God against Satan...
>
> is a very old idea in Semitic religions. . . . It is not necessary to have two anthropoid spirits inhabiting a spring. The importance lies in the colors white and black.

In another instructional occult book, *The Greater Key of Solomon*, S. Liddell MacGregor Mathers says that in order for Satanists to summon forth demons to do their bidding, they must sacrifice "animals":

> In many operations it is necessary to make some sort of sacrifice unto the Demons, and in various ways. Sometimes white animals are sacrificed to the good Spirits and black to the evil. Such sacrifices consist of the blood and sometimes of the flesh. They who sacrifice animals, of whatsoever kind they may be, should select those which are virgin, as being more agreeable unto the Spirits, and rendering them more obedient.

Mathers is, of course, speaking of humans, not animals, although animalism and the animalization of humans is a major tenet in occult philosophy. Two years after the murders supposedly stopped in Atlanta, parents, hospital workers, and others who have seen the bodies were finally able to get testimony public that many of the bodies had been drained of blood, that the skin was in many cases extremely hardened to a rocklike stage (even within hours of death) and that the vestige had aged and shriveled so much so as to be an old, old man or woman rather than a teenage or younger youth.

To date, no one has been on trial in Atlanta for the murder of a *child*, and to date we in America have done little about the unexplained soar to over 50,000 children (among 250,000 children in America who are missing every year, but the remainder are found) who annually disappear off the face of the earth, never accounted for in life or in death.

The real tragedy of the Atlanta murders is not only that forces of evil can twist the truth of God's love for all peoples of every race, nationality, and color into a damnable lie; *it is the inability and/or unwillingness of responsible leadership in government, law enforcement, and the press to recognize the spiritual, occult motives behind the murders and the portending implication that America is more than ever a spiritual battleground for active, visible, overt occult worship and all the criminality involved therein.* Neo-paganists are no longer willing to be secretive, underground practitioners of what they call "the ancient arts."

Christians must first of all recognize that we are indeed in such a warfare. We cannot assume that America is such a Christian nation that pagan worship, including spiritual fornication and human sacrifice, cannot happen here. Through Christian involvement in the political process, we have entered a warfare against moral disintegration in America. But we cannot allow that same political machinery to "protect" us from the truth about conditions like Atlanta.

Prayer is urgently needed. According to Ephesians 6 we cannot battle a spiritual onslaught with nonspiritual equipment. Further, we must heed the warnings of men and women whom God has raised up to begin an explanation of the religious philosophy behind criminal occult activity. We must claim God's promise in Mark 4:22, "For nothing is hidden, except to be revealed; nor has anything been secret, but that it should come to light," to the end that the public will know the full truth about what happened to Atlanta's children. With God's grace a nation with an understanding of where witchcraft, astrology, and occult worship can lead will forsake these wicked ways and turn to God through His victorious and everlasting Son, Jesus Christ.

The political system in this country desperately resists such exposure for fear of the public panic that would result. But without public awareness, political figures do not seem willing to move aggressively against the horrendous wave of criminal activity. Underworld traffic in drugs, pornography, and prostitution (especially that which involves children) must be given a higher priority in the distribution of public funds. The public must insist that police stop relying on psychics, parapsychologists, and other diviners who promise to find missing bodies and other clues, but who are usually occult workers themselves.

The police need to begin a serious investigation of occult criminality, beginning in Atlanta.

Appendix F
(see Chapter 10)

Biblical Demonology

Demons are not the spirits of dead men as some suppose, for the dead are not free to roam (Luke 16:19-31; 2 Peter 2:9). Nor are they primitive mythic personifications of natural forces (the "gods" of nature). They are neither the personifications of evil nor the mere inventions of religious imagination.

According to Scripture, demons are fallen angels: angelic beings in rebellion against God. Their rebellion under the headship of Satan (Jude 6; 1 John 3:8; Matthew 25:41; Ezekiel 28:12-17) has resulted in their fall (Luke 10:18) such that they become evil, self-centered beings who seek to thwart the purposes of God (Revelation 2:10; 1 Peter 5:8; Ephesians 6:11; Matthew 13:39; Luke 22:31; 1 Thessalonians 2:18; Mark 4:15). Their principal concern is to deceive men through false religion and to blind them to spiritual truth (2 Corinthians 4:4; Acts 26:18; 2 Corinthians 11:14; 2 Thessalonians 2:9,10; Revelation 20:10).

Biblically speaking, if we were to catalog the powers and abilities of angels, we would thereby provide a glimpse into their capacities and hence discern the abilities and limits of demons, who are merely corrupted angels. However, it must never be forgotten that demons are only creatures who are ultimately constrained by the sovereign power and purpose of God. When needed, the Christian has power over them (1 John 4:4; James 4:7). We know that Christ was victorious over Satan at the cross (Hebrews 2:14; Colossians 2:15; John 12:31), that this victory will be brought to completion at the Second Coming, and that Satan's eternal interment will occur at the end of the millennium (Revelation 20:2,3,7-10).

The following list (slightly revised from an earlier published work) indicates the capacities and methods of angels in general, biblically defined, which would include the fallen angels:

1. Revelation 9:1-11; Matthew 12:22—power to torment (see Luke

8:31 regarding demons from the abyss); blindness and dumbness.

2. Revelation 9:14,15—immense power; four angels released to kill one-third of mankind.

3. 2 Corinthians 4:4; 1 John 5:19—extent of influence; the world is said to be greatly influenced by Satan's authority. (In Matthew 4 Jesus did not question Satan's right to grant Him the world's kingdoms.)

4. Genesis 3:1-3—purposeful deception.

5. 2 Corinthians 11:14,15—evil spirits imitating good spirits.

6. Genesis 6:1-4—apparent sexual involvement and cohabitation.

7. Luke 8:26-35—producing insanity and having great physical strength.

8. Luke 13:10-17—inducing sickness for 18 years; producing suffering and deformities.

9. Job 1:16-18; Revelation 13:13—Satan produces whirlwinds, fire from heaven, and great miracles in the presence of men (cf. Hebrews 1:7, Psalm 104:4).

10. Job 2:7—Satan produces painful boils or welts over the body.

11. Matthew 9:32,33; 12:22; 17:15,18—dumbness, blindness, and epilepsy; attempted murder by fire and water.

12. Luke 8:30; 11:24-26—multiple possession. They apparently seek "rest" by possessing humans (Matthew 12:43-45).

13. Luke 9:39—convulsions, child possession, mauling.

14. Matthew 8:30-32—animal possession.

15. Acts 16:16—predicting the future, fortune-telling.

16. 2 Thessalonians 2:7; 2 Peter 2:11; Acts 19:16—anger, great strength, and power.

17. Ephesians 6:10-16; Judges 9:23—treacherous natures; scheme wickedly; attack humans.

18. Hebrews 2:2; Acts 7:53; Galatians 3:19—provide supernatural revelations.

19. Numbers 22:23-27—animals can recognize them.

20. Genesis 3:1-5—ability to speak through an animal (a "serpent").

21. Job 1:7—supernatural power to travel.

22. Matthew 4:8—instantaneous projection of a false reality.

23. John 13:2; Matthew 13:19,39—apparent ability to remove thoughts, to implant thoughts, and manipulate the mind.

24. John 8:44—morally corrupt; a liar and murderer.

25. Matthew 8:28; John 13:27—possession of humans.
26. Revelation 12:12—great wrath.
27. Luke 22:3—ability to incite a man to betrayal.
28. 2 Corinthians 12:7—physical ailments.
29. 2 Corinthians 4:4—deception; blinding minds.
30. Revelation 12:9; 20:8—deceives the nations and the world.
31. Job 4:15—invisibility, but give awareness of their presence.
32. 1 Samuel 16:14,15—ability to terrorize.
33. Genesis 19:1-10; John 20:12; Acts 12:9; Hebrews 13:2—can assume human form.
34. Exodus 7:10-12,20-22; 8:7—to an extent, duplication of God's miracles: Men having demonic powers changed sticks to snakes, water to blood (control over matter/energy), and had control over the animal kingdom (frogs).
35. Deuteronomy 18:9-13—defile with occult practices and human sacrifice.
36. Matthew 24:31; Luke 16:22—can transport human beings.
37. Revelation 9:15; 1 Chronicles 21:1; Daniel 10:13; 1 Thessalonians 2:18—limited ability to control events and human actions.
38. 2 Samuel 24:17; 1 Corinthians 5:5; Hebrews 2:14; Acts 12:23—can destroy the flesh; have the power of death.
39. 1 Corinthians 7:5—can influence a person toward evil.
40. Deuteronomy 32:17; Colossians 2:18—objects of worship.
41. Psalm 106:37—child sacrifice and murder.
42. Acts 10:38—oppression.
43. Revelation 2:10—can control humans to secure their own ends.
44. Acts 13:10—seek to pervert the ways of God.
45. Genesis 19:13,24—fire and brimstone rained down upon a city (destruction of Sodom and Gomorrah).
46. Genesis 31:11—influence upon the dream state.
47. 2 Samuel 24:15,16—send pestilence, have power to destroy a city.
48. 1 Kings 13:18; Acts 23:9—can communicate by speech to humans.
49. Genesis 19:1-2,12—can assume physical form and interact with humans.
50. Genesis 19:11—to strike with blindness.
51. Luke 2:9,13,15—can materialize and dematerialize at will.
52. Hebrews 12:22; Matthew 26:53—vast in number.
53. Luke 1:19,20—speak to men; control of vocal cords (paralysis and possession).

54. 1 Corinthians 13:1—different languages, speech.
55. 1 Kings 22:19-23; Galatians 1:8; 1 Timothy 4:1; 1 John 4:1—preach a false gospel and deception about God.
56. Jeremiah 23:16; Ezekiel 13:1-9; Colossians 2:18; Galatians 1:8; Matthew 24:24—false visions and experiences.
57. Revelation 16:14—can work miracles.

Appendix G
(see Chapter 16)

Where Do We Find a Scorecard?

The medium believes that her "control spirit" is a "good" spirit, but that "evil" spirits can on occasion filter in. This contrast of "good" versus "evil" focuses trust upon the "good" spirits. Often the "evil" spirits are caused to "repent" by the "good" spirits, and all the sitters glow with the satisfaction of having helped another "earthbound" spirit see "higher spiritual truth." In fact, as Gasson and other former mediums have shown, the "good" spirits are simply wicked ones impersonating benevolent entities to foster trust on the part of their human contacts.[1]

Of course, since it is virtually impossible for any occultist to determine if a "good" spirit is really what it claims, there are no safeguards to begin with. The only standards are biblical and these have been rejected by definition. The spirits are free to act as they wish because there are always believable rationalizations to explain all their actions. Thus, there are degrees of evil displayed by the "evil" spirits, but not all of them "repent." And even the "good" spirits do not always do their job. Dr. Fodor discusses some who did not:

> Evil spirits, according to spiritualistic philosophy, do exist. . . . The controls, as a rule, are able to keep evil spirits away. But sometimes, for unknown reasons, their power fails. . . . If an evil spirit has already taken possession of the medium, it is considered of the utmost importance to maintain the circle unbroken until the invader can be ousted. Possession by evil spirits is usually manifested by fits, violent convulsions and uncouth mouthings. It may cause serious harm to the medium. . . .
>
> A case of control by an evil entity is recorded by Bozzano from the mediumship of L.D. . . . It was with difficulty that the sitter's life was saved.

Willie Reichel, in his *Occult Experiences*, describes the sudden intrusion of a black female spirit who went around the circle of 14 persons striking and spitting on nearly all of them and using horrible language.

Besides injuring the medium or the sitters, the danger of an enduring possession may have to be faced. Such possession, or obsession, would be called demoniacal.[2]

The spirits are trusted, nonetheless—even though the subtlety of the spirits' imitating capacities is well-known. Satprem observes what every long-standing spiritist knows: "The spirits can take all the forms they wish."[3]

As occultist Conway confesses:

The shapes assumed by demons are far from horrendous—at least to begin with. . . . Little children, gentle old folk and beautiful young people of either sex are some of their favorite human disguises. . . . They will frequently display as much resourcefulness as the most cunning human being.[4]

For example, consider the evil spirits who impersonated Robert Monroe's daughters as part of their attack strategy while he was out of the body:

Then, as I was trying to hold off the first, a second climbed on my back! Holding the first off with one hand, I reached back and yanked the second off me, and floated over into the center of the office, holding one in each hand, screaming for help. I got a good look at each, and as I looked, each turned into a good facsimile of one of my two daughters. . . . I seemed to know immediately that this was a deliberate camouflage on their parts to create emotional confusion in me and call upon my love for my daughters to prevent my doing anything more to them.

The moment I realized the trick the two no longer appeared to be my daughters. . . . However, I got the impression that they were both amused, as if there was nothing I could to to harm them. By this time, I was sobbing for help.[5]

In a similar fashion, Johanna Michaelsen had two spirit guides (one was a "gentle and loving" Jesus). In *The Beautiful Side of Evil* she reports how at one point "they now had werewolf faces. They just stood there watching me, growling softly."[6]

They told her they had changed shape to show her that what seems *evil* on the surface is not necessarily evil at all.

> Then suddenly it was clear; however frightening these beings appeared, they were not evil. I decided to learn to trust and accept them regardless of the discrepant images they might present.[7]

Indeed, often demons will attack their host, only to deliver the person later as their "faithful spirit guide"—at least sometimes. Medium Jane Roberts recalls one incident of being attacked by a terrible black thing, but this time "Seth" was nowhere to be found:

> I found myself in our bedroom, out of my body, and suddenly I realized that someone or something was directly above me.... It sounds ridiculous, but I knew that this thing was "out to get me." ... Although I'd read of people being attacked by demons or the like while they were [astral] "projecting," I just didn't believe in demons. So what was it? I didn't have time to wonder, because it bit me several times on the hand. It was amazingly oppressive.... And where was Seth? Where were all those "guides" who were supposed to come running to your aid when you got in predicaments like this? All these thoughts went scurrying through my mind as I tried to fight this thing off. I was very conscious of the creature's weight, which was really amazing, and its intent—which was to maul me up as much as possible, if not to kill me outright.[8]

In this case, Roberts got no help. But obviously, those who think they are delivered from an evil spirit can only conclude that what delivered them was a good spirit. This was the experience of Johanna Michaelsen. She had experienced plenty of visits from evil spirits, so when "good" spirits appeared she trusted them.

For years I had experienced the workings of those [spirits] tied to Satan. Now I was experiencing the workings of God. The *feeling* between the two was so totally different. I could tell the difference.[9]

This spiritistic duplicity has even founded major religions. Consider the experience of Joseph Smith, founder of the occult Mormon religion.[10] In "Writings of Joseph Smith" in the *Pearl of Great Price*, 2:15-19, we find the following account:

I kneeled down and began to offer up the desire of my heart to God. I had scarcely done so, when immediately I was seized upon by some power which entirely overcame me, and had such an astonishing influence over me as to bind my tongue so that I could not speak. Thick darkness gathered around me, and it seemed to me for a time as if I were doomed to sudden destruction.

But, exerting all my powers to call upon God to deliver me out of the power of this enemy which had seized upon me, and at the very moment when I was ready to sink into despair and abandon myself to destruction...just at this moment of great alarm, I saw a pillar of light exactly over my head, above the brightness of the sun, which descended gradually until it fell upon me.

It no sooner appeared than I found myself delivered from the enemy which held me bound. When the light rested upon me I saw two Personages, whose brightness and glory defy all description, standing above me in the air. One of them spake unto me, calling me by name and said, pointing to other—"This is My Beloved Son. Hear Him!"

My object in going to inquire of the Lord was to know which of all the [Christian] sects was right, that I might know which to join....

I was answered that I must join none of these, for they were all wrong; and the Personage who addressed me said that all their creeds were an abomination in his sight.

Obviously, the entity that delivered Smith from destruction was not the biblical Jesus Christ but a demon impersonating Him to start a false religion.[11]

By a similar ploy Paramahansa Yogananda, founder of the Self Realization Fellowship and author of the widely read *Autobiography of a Yogi*, was persuaded as to the legitimacy of a spirit impersonating his dead master (and with the legitimacy of his master's occult philosophy).

> When I was in Bombay just before returning to America, I realized that the satanic power was trying to destroy my life, to prevent me from fulfilling the mission given to me by God and my guru. I wasn't afraid; I knew God was with me and I remembered Master's promise of protection. I put a little light on in my room, because the evil forces do not like light. For a little while I sat meditating, watchful of my spirit. And then I felt sleepy. As I opened my eyes and looked toward the right wall of the room, I saw the black form of Satan, horrible, with a catlike face and tail. It leaped on my chest, and my heart stopped beating. Mentally, I said, "I am not afraid of you. I am Spirit." But still my heart wouldn't work. Suddenly I glimpsed an ocher robe, and there stood Master. He commanded Satan to leave; and as soon as he spoke, the evil figure vanished and my breath started to flow again. I cried out: "My Master!" He said, "Satan was trying to destroy you. But fear not. I am with you ever more." I could even smell the familiar, gentle fragrance that emanated from Master's form, just as when he was incarnate on earth.[12]

Yogananda went on to become instrumental in two key events which helped spread occultism in America. First, he persuaded the famous trance medium Arthur Ford to become a medium rather than a Christian minister. In the long run, this led to thousands of persons accepting mediumism as a divine gift.[13] Ford himself went on to start the Spiritual Frontiers Fellowship which seeks to integrate Christianity and the occult. Second, Yogananda founded the Self Realization Fellowship which seeks to integrate Christian faith with Hinduism and the occult.

For those instructed in the biblical category of spiritual warfare, it goes without saying that the phenomenon of "good" and "evil" spirits in mediumism, spiritism, and the occult in general is simply a clever ploy on the part of demons. These "good" spirits of the occult perform their part well.

Former 20-year medium Raphael Gasson points out the reality behind these deceptions. As an example, he discusses a typical "rescue

seance" which, in this case, was held to get rid of a poltergeist distur-
bance. We quote him at length:

> A small seance was held in the house and the medium imme-
> diately went into a trance, becoming possessed instantly by a
> spirit who flung himself (in the body of the medium) at the feet of
> the medium's husband present in the circle and also himself a
> medium. The spirit sobbed with apparent terror and asked to be
> saved because he didn't know what he was doing and "they" were
> after him ("they" were defined later). The man answered the
> spirit assuring it that there was no need for fear and attempted to
> solicit details. The spirit claimed to be that of an old enemy of the
> owner of the house who had died and been in the spirit world
> about a year, and had continued from that exalted sphere to
> attempt to harm his old enemy, the houseowner, in any way
> possible. In following out his attempts he had automatically
> attracted a whole group of very unpleasant spirits who came to
> help him turn the house upside down and generally make it so
> uncomfortable for the owner and his wife that they would be
> driven to leave the house, thus losing a considerable amount of
> money as well as experiencing distress of mind and a certain
> amount of physical upset. Now the poor spirit, who had this petty
> motive in sight at the beginning of his operations, was alarmed at
> the presence of his unwanted spirit helpers and begged to be saved
> from them! The medium's husband soothed the distraught spirit,
> made it apologize for the evil of its past behavior and pray for help
> to put it right, and the spirit then withdrew from the medium's
> body. Its place was taken by an African Witch Doctor. This spirit
> was harder to dispose of, but eventually it accepted defeat and
> withdrew. Thereupon followed six or seven more devils, all of
> which had to come through separately, admit their fault and
> promise amendment. After this the medium considered her work
> was done, the seance finished, and there were no more demon-
> strations of an unwanted kind in the house after that. The owners
> settled down presumably to a much-earned rest. It is queer how
> these Rescue cases, differing in detail and circumstances, have all
> the same essentials and follow the same procedure.

Can the Devil really cast out demons? What are these spirits
which are referred to as "evil" spirits? What are these "good"
spirits which show the evil ones the "Light?" How is it done? The

answer is very simple. The Devil is most certainly not casting out demons, neither is his house divided, neither are those spirits which show the others the light good spirits. In fact they are all demons! Demons have to use some method of deception in their attempt to prove the counterfeit is of God and so they play a game of make-believe. Although they are literally evil spirits, one pretends to be the "good" spirit while the other proclaims his "evil"-ness. The "evil" spirit starts first, finding no difficulty in cursing and swearing and taking great care that he does not overcome the team of workers too often, occasionally pretending to be mastered by them. The act is well-planned. On the other hand, the demon is acting as a "good" spirit, professing to be highly evolved and able to deal with "bad" spirits for their own good. The so-called "good" spirit speaks to the "evil" spirit who at first appears to be antagonistic, but eventually obeys orders and they both trot off together to laugh at the credulity of human nature that makes it possible for such a hoax to be played out.

Certainly Satan has not cast out demons because they still remain in control of the seance, but Spiritualists, blindly believing they are doing God's work, cannot see that the Devil has managed to produce a double counterfeit of the casting out of demons. They will argue from the Scripture that if Spiritualism is of the Devil, it would not be possible for them to cast out evil spirits. Satan has managed to establish another lie in the heart of man, which is his ultimate aim in using such a long drawn out farce. This rescue work achieves a very pleasing result to Satan since few people will suspect that a demon would appear to cast out another demon. Consequently many can be deceived in this direction into believing that Spiritualism must be of God.[14]

Here we have "an encounter of the divine" without God, dramatic spiritual experiences without salvation, the conviction of truth in the presence of error, the use of Scripture without its power, and the conclusion of spiritual legitimacy in the midst of spiritual peril.

How do we know the "good" spirits are liars? Because occultists who are converted to faith in Jesus Christ, be they witches, mediums, psychics, gurus, spiritists of all stripes, UFO "contactees," etc., always seem to discover that their once-friendly "familiars," "spirit helpers," "ascended masters," "devas and gods," "space contacts," etc., now turn against them. We saw this earlier with former psychic Johanna

Michaelsen, whose spirits displayed a "murderous demonic rage" in reaction to her movement toward faith in the biblical Jesus Christ.[15] Ex-medium Raphael Gasson remarks:

> In time almost evey medium gets to know his guides. There may be several guides for different purposes: for instance, I had a spirit guide who claimed to be an African Witch Doctor, stating that he had been in the spirit world for 600 years and declaring himself to be my "door-keeper" to keep out evil spirits from my body. (I realize just how much of a door-keeper he was when this familiar spirit attempted to kill me when it became obvious that I was out to denounce Spiritualism.)[16]

For example:

> Evidently he had no intention of letting go his hold upon me as easily as I had thought. Each time I testified, attacks came in some way or another. Beforehand, dizzy spells made me so weak that I had to clutch something to remain standing up, let alone speak. After I had testified and had returned home, sleepy spells made me almost unconscious and my once familiar spirits attempted to get me into deep trance again, against my will—a thing they did not reckon to do, normally speaking. Several times they succeeded in using my own hands to attempt to strangle me.[17]

Another converted medium, Victor Ernest, tells a similar story in his *I Talked With Spirits*:

> But when other churches had me speak on demonism in special meetings, the demons I had once welcomed into my body in seances attacked my mind and vocal cords.
> Sometimes my memory would go blank, other times my throat would constrict and I couldn't speak. As soon as I prayed for help through the power of Jesus' blood, the attack ceased and I continued. These assaults continued sporadically for thirteen years before my spiritual defenses were built up to keep demons from penetrating my body. As my spiritual armor became strong, I was able to help others assailed by spirits.[18]

Former Satanists and witches have also documented some of the horrors of the occult in their various books. As we saw, Satanism combines sex, drugs, occult ritual, demon contact, a thirst for power, and even hexes against enemies and their families. But witchcraft is not much different, despite witches' claims to merely practice a benign form of nature religion.

A former leading European witch, Doreen Irvine, explains:

> Witchcraft of the black kind is not far removed from Satanism. The main difference between the two is that Satanists worship the Devil in the Satanist temple, whereas witches attend a coven of the thirteen witches, one of whom is the head. They require no temple to worship Satan.[19]

She points out other similarities to Satanism and its powers:

> Black witches have great power and are not to be taken lightly. They are able to call up, or call down, powers of darkness to aid them. Very often they exhume fresh graves and offer the bodies in sacrifice to Satan. They break into churches, burn Bibles and prayer books. Whenever holy ground is desecrated, an emblem of witchcraft is left behind: Goat's blood is splashed on headstones of graves and walls. They hold nothing sacred and will stop at nothing to pursue their goals. Nothing! Black witches have power to put curses on people, and the curses work. People have been known to die because of the curse or spell of a black witch.[20]

But as we saw earlier, even so-called "white" witches may also use their powers for overt evil. Satanists and witches, of course, do not tolerate a member turning to Christ. Irvine experienced the same treatment Satanists receive—from her own witch "friends." When she turned to Christ and renounced witchcraft:

> Their answer to me was a severe beating. They dragged me half-conscious to a car and drove me to a lonely spot, where I was dumped. They believed, I'm quite sure, that I was dead or would die within a short while. But someone found me and rushed me to a hospital, where I stayed for

four days—such was the extent of the beating I received. It was only by a miracle that my life was spared and Satan's plans for me were smashed.[21]

The black witches sent me letters, threatening my life if I didn't keep quiet about witchcraft. They were awful letters, saying: "You will die if you don't stop running down witchcraft." Some of the letters were written in blood. It really frightened me at first, for I knew that black witches carry out their threats. . . . Would I stop warning people of the evil and dangers of the occult because my life was in danger? No, most certainly not. People should be warned.[22]

Irvine also mentions the missionary activity of witches which seeks to gain converts to the cause (a theme repeated in Satanist proselytizing):

Many people, especially the young, were taking a fresh interest in the occult. It was important to give witchcraft a new look, and these guidelines were laid down: Never frighten anyone. Offer new realms of mystery and excitement. Make witchcraft less sinister. Make it look like natural, innocent adventure. (Everyone is attracted by adventure and mystery). Cover up evil with appealing wrappings. New recruits were needed if evil was to conquer. Time was short. Now was the time to trap people. Once people were involved in witchcraft, it would be too late to get out. Fear would hold many back from retreating. There would be no way out.[23]

Appendix H
(see Chapter 17)

Demonization of Christians: Pros and Cons

What about actual demon possession? And can Christians as well as non-Christians be demon-possessed? This is one of those issues that would be nice to avoid, but pastoral concerns make this difficult. First, everyone agrees that Christians can be influenced by demons; the debate is whether or not a genuine Christian can be indwelt by a demon. Second, although the term "demon possession" is more or less accurate as a descriptive phrase, it may also imply theological inaccuracies such as the "ownership" of a person. No demon ever "owns" a Christian, nor can a demon ever cause a genuine Christian to lose his or her salvation, which is forever secure. [1]

The biblical term used is not "demon possession" but "demonization." What is demonization?

> When we look at the word for demonization, improperly translated "demon possession," it is highly instructive to notice its root and structure. The verb *daimonizomai* means "to be possessed by a demon."
>
> The participle from the same root, *daimonizomenos*, is used twelve times in the Greek New Testament. It is used only in the present tense, indicating the continued state of one inhabited by a demon, or demonized. This participle has components to its structure. First there is the root, *daimon*, which indicates the involvement of demons. Second is the causative stem, *iz*, which shows that there is an active cause in this verb. Third is the passive ending, *omenos*. This conveys the passivity of the person described as demonized.
>
> Putting it all together the participle in its root form means "a demon caused passivity." This indicates a control other than that of the person who is demonized; he is regarded as the recipient of the demon's action. In other

words, demonization pictures a demon controlling a somewhat passive human.[2]

The arguments on both sides of this issue can be found in, for
example, C. Fred Dickason, *Demon Possession and the Christian* (argument that Christian demonization is possible) and Tommy Ice, *A Holy
Rebellion* (argument against Christian demonization).

The argument against Christian demonization can be summarized
as follows: First, Christians cannot be demonized because Scripture
gives genuine Christians strong reassurance to that effect.

Examples include: "You have overcome the evil one" (1 John 2:14);
"But the Lord is faithful and he will strengthen and protect you from the
evil one" (2 Thessalonians 3:3); "We know that anyone born of God
does not continue to sin; the one who was born of God keeps him safe,
and the evil one does not touch him" (1 John 5:18); "Greater is He who
is in you [the Holy Spirit] than he who is in the world [Satan]" (1 John
4:4 NASB).

Second, Scripture gives no proof of a Christian ever being indwelt by
a demon, nor do we find experiences in Scripture suggestive of the fact.
As Tommy Ice argues:

> Another reason believers cannot be demonized is that
> the New Testament nowhere says they can! Nor does the
> New Testament ever use language, referring to a believer,
> that describes demon possession. Looking at the same issue
> from the perspective of what the New Testament does
> command a believer to do when Satan and his demons
> attack him we find sobering instructions. Every time a
> response is commanded by the believer to Satan or demons
> it is always "to stand" or "resist" him (Ephesians 6:10-14;
> James 4:7; 1 Peter 5:9). Whenever a person who is demon
> possessed is dealt with the Bible indicates that they are
> "cast out" (for example Matthew 8:16; Mark 1:34). The
> Greek term *ekballo* means to "drive out," "expel," or
> literally "to throw out" forcibly. . . . Never are believers
> said to respond to Satan or demons by casting them out,
> which is always the remedy in the New Testament for a
> demon possessed person. Instead, for the believer the
> command is always to stand or resist, which is the counter
> to an external temptation by Satan and the demonic. This

supports the idea that Christians cannot be demon possessed since they are never commanded or told how to deliver believers (or anyone) from demonic possession.[3]

Further, 1) the integrity of those claiming demon inhabitation of a Christian, 2) the alleged experiences themselves, and 3) the weight of the extra scriptural arguments cannot prove what Scripture itself never clearly teaches.

No one denies there are responsible, mature Christians with wide experience in this field who say that, to the best of their knowledge, genuine Christians have, on occasion, been indwelt by demons. But that doesn't prove it so.

Thus, those who argue a Christian can never be demonized say that if we make people think they are demonized when, in fact, they cannot be, we are only causing their self-deception and a great deal of unnecessary and difficult or impossible counseling. Why put people through the anxiety of thinking they are or may be demonized if this is impossible?

On the other hand, the argument for Christian demonization can be summarized as follows:

Can Christians be demonized? The evidence is weighty. The symptoms, causes, and tests of which we have read argue to the internal type of control that comes with inhabiting spirits. The control of bodily actions and voice by spirits, speaking in unlearned languages, the difference in reaction between the counselee and the demon, the fact that the invader referred to the invaded in the third person (he, she, etc.), and the relief produced through biblical counseling and confrontation of demons are evidence that a separate spirit-person was expressing himself through the human by operating the control center of the brain. . . . It would be difficult to dismiss this type of evidence and witness or even to argue against it effectively. Alternate theories might be suggested to explain some of the phenomena. However, most of those arguments stem from those who deny any demonization at all, not to mention the demonization of Christians. Even those who recognize the reality of demonization often seek to explain away the evidence on the grounds of secularly learned and practiced psychology. Further, the objector cannot stand at a distance instead of on the scene to discount the evidence. Again, it is those who have little or no experience in this area who are the most vocal objectors. We must allow the distinct probability that biblically guided investigation and counsel has shown in experience that some Christians have been demonized. The evidence is heavily weighted toward that conclusion.[4]

In the material below we will briefly look at some of the major arguments pro and con, topic by topic.

The Promises of Scripture

Those who say a Christian can never be demonized argue that the Scriptures offer many promises of divine protection for the believer.

Why don't the passages on the defeat of Satan and the authority the believer has over Satan (e.g., "resist the devil, and he will flee from you") convince advocates of Christian demonization that a Christian cannot be demonized? After a careful examination of the relevant verses, they reply that these Scriptures cannot be universally applied to all Christians at all times in every circumstance. For example, they say such promises are legitimate for those who walk in obedience to Christ, but not necessarily for those who do not. Further, advocates present arguments showing why these Scriptures are not necessarily directly applicable to the issue of Christian demonization at all. Properly interpreted, no Scripture rules out Christian demonization, they claim.

Consider 1 John 5:18: "We know that anyone born of God does not continue to sin; the one who was born of God keeps him safe, and the evil one does not touch him." Certainly this passage cannot be interpreted to mean that believers are kept safe from every danger in life because Christians may encounter the same tragedies as all men. Further, the phrase "does not touch him" can only be restricted to demonization if it is proven this is its true interpretation, advocates insist.

For example, Dickason comments as follows,

> The word translated "touch" (hapto) means to take hold of, to grasp, and carries the idea of injury in this case. Some could take it to mean that Satan could not seriously affect the life of a believer. That has been shown not to be the case

in our previous treatment of other passages. It could mean that Christ keeps the believer secure in salvation, and the believer can never be returned to the kingdom of Satan. Or, as we pointed out, John could mean that Christ keeps us from coming under the devastating influence of Satan lest we become completely defeated and brought in the sphere of his control.[5]

However, only one meaning is allowably the intent of John. . . . But in neither case does this verse say that no believer can be seriously affected by demons or demonized. Certainly, the believer will not *become* demonized if he avoids habitual sin and guards himself by walking in obedience to the Word, avoiding the wiles of the devil. But what happens if the believer does not take these safeguards?[6]

Thus, Dickason argues: "None of the passages we have studied can, with any fair treatment, be construed to eliminate the possibility of a genuine believer's being inhabited by wicked spirits."[7] He proceeds to discuss several Scriptures which he feels indicate a Christian can be demonized. For example, the case of King Saul seems to indicate Saul was a believer, but because the evil spirit "came upon him" he *may* have been demonized (1 Samuel 16:14,23). Matthew 8:16 and similar passages stress the widespread activity of Jesus in casting out demons. But how reasonable is it to conclude that none of the people to whom Jesus did this were ever true believers? Because Jesus did not minister exclusively to unbelievers, it seems reasonable to conclude that at least some of those from whom He cast out demons were true believers (see Mark 1:23). There is also the case of the woman described as "a daughter of Abraham" whom Satan had kept crippled and bound for 18 years (Luke 13:10-16). Whether or not this involved a demonic indwelling, it seems to have constituted some form of demonization.

In essence, those who argue that a Christian can be demonized do not believe that their opponents' interpretation of the believer's protection passages is that convincing. In their exegeses of the relevant passages they attempt to show that 1) no Scripture can be given to prove a Christian can never be demonized under any circumstances; 2) several Scriptures at least *suggest* the possibility; and 3) because there is no scriptural *proof* either way, the issue must be decided by recourse to clinical counseling. Dr. Dickason, in particular, provides some good arguments about the acceptability of an experiential approach to this particular issue.[8]

For example, consider the disease of cancer. Just as there is no clear evidence for the demonization of a Christian in Scripture, this is also true of cancer: Scripture offers no evidence of the disease called cancer. Nevertheless, we now know what cancer is by its identifying characteristics. In a similar manner, if a Christian gives the identifying characteristics of demonization, then it is logical to conclude that he or she is demonized.

Spatial and Moral Considerations

Those who argue that a Christian can never be demonized offer additional reasons for their conviction. Perhaps the strongest and/or most common are those of spatial and moral considerations. Here people argue that it is impossible for both the Holy Spirit and a demon to simultaneously indwell a believer's spirit. They further argue that because of the absolute holiness of the Holy Spirit, it is impossible for a wicked spirit to coexist with Him in the same place. Because the Holy Spirit is greater than Satan, He will protect His children from being entered by a demon.

Those people on the other side of the issue respond by pointing out that in the believer the human spirit already coexists with the Holy Spirit, so in principle, spatial considerations are irrelevant. The Holy Spirit already dwells with the human spirit, so it should be possible for him to dwell with another spirit—or any number of spirits—because spatial considerations are irrelevant in the spiritual realm. For example, dozens or scores of demons apparently indwelt the Gerasenes demoniac (Mark 5:9). The very fact that many spirits can indwell one body proves that spatial considerations by themselves cannot be offered as proof that a Christian can never be demonized. Also, the mere fact that God is greater than Satan is not proof a Christian can never be demonized because power considerations alone fail to answer all the issues that can be raised. God often does not do what He has power to do.

Further, advocates of Christian demonization argue that the Holy Spirit already resides with moral evil in the sense that He indwells a believer who, though regenerate to be sure, still has a sinful nature. Therefore, if the Holy Spirit resides with evil in a believer (regardless of where that evil is located) it would not appear to be impossible that the Holy Spirit could reside with another spirit that is evil.

Finally, it is argued that no one really knows where or how any spirit resides within a person—whether it is a generalized or localized indwelling. For example, is a spirit's indwelling pervasive throughout the body/mind/spirit, or restricted to just the mind or to some part of the body? How can anyone know whether it is a believer's spirit that is indwelt in demonization? Thus, even granting that a believer's regenerated spirit is pure by virtue of its creation by God, how do we know that a demon cannot indwell a person while it yet exists outside the human spirit?

The Issue of Logical Expectation

One the strongest arguments against the demonization of a Christian is that it is extremely difficult to understand why, if it is true, that God would not have made the issue clearer and given us more specific instructions on how to deal with such an eventuality. After all, God Himself tells us through the apostle Peter that "His divine power has given us everything we need for life and godliness" (2 Peter 1:3).

Critics reply that it would be impossible for Scripture to literally discuss everything of spiritual importance. Therefore there are some things important to life and godliness which Scripture does not always comment upon directly such as Bible school/seminary, Sunday school, etc. Further, critics of Christian demonization argue that Scripture *does* give us the principles for both identifying and dealing with demonization. Because Scripture does not specifically teach Christian demonization is not proof it can never occur, they claim. Scripture is silent on many things that are both true and important. Why God did not emphasize this particular issue "more" clearly is unknown.

The Perception of Faith

Those who say a Christian cannot be demonized argue it is possible for the appearance of belief in Christ to be sufficiently convincing to fool any counselor. The counselor would wrongly conclude that such a person is a genuine Christian because he *seems* to be one. In fact, while he may certainly be along the road and close to true faith, he only *thinks* he is a genuine Christian and lacks true saving faith. In other words, it is possible for a person to truly believe he has faith, give evidence of it, and yet not really have saving faith. Since he is not really a believer to begin with, he may indeed be demonized. Thus, the counselor mistakes the demonization of an unbeliever for that of a believer.

On the other hand, those people who claim to counsel Christians who are demonized say that these individuals exhibit *all* the marks of a genuine believer—so much so that if they are not genuine believers, then the counselors cannot know whether or not *any* person is a true believer. Two of the people we talked with on this subject claimed that in the last decade they had counseled a total of 700 to 800 genuine believers who were demonized.

The Assumption of Silent Exorcism

A final argument of those who accept the demonization of Christians relates to the issue of whether or not demons are automatically exorcised by God's sovereignty at the point of a person's conversion. In other words, consider a non-Christian who became demonized as a result of his or her occult involvement or serious sin. He or she then becomes a Christian. Are the demons automatically forced to leave that person simply by the fact of his regeneration and conversion?

Those who say this is not the case point out there are many reasonable testimonies of people who were converted out of strong occult backgrounds who were not delivered from demons. The European witch and Satanist Doreen Irvine is one example. In *Freed From Witchcraft*, she points out she was not delivered from the demons indwelling her as a result of her activities and practices. She claims to have had 47 demons driven out of her almost a year after her genuine conversion.[9]

Those who counsel the demonized report that conversion simply does not always drive out the demons. It may—but it may not. Nor is this surprising, they say. They point out that God usually doesn't heal people supernaturally from all the consequences of their sins simply because they have become Christians. For example, individuals with previous drug or sexual addictions may continue to suffer the normal consequences of their activities or continue to struggle with an addiction for years. But as new believers grow in the faith and become strong Christians, these problems are successfully dealt with. And this is exactly the case with demonization. In particular, when individuals have become demonized as a result of their pagan religion and are then converted, there can be months and even years of struggle from things such as ancestor worship, strong familial ties to the occult, and indwelling spirits.

This is one reason why proponents argue that if Christians can be demonized and yet the church adopts the contrary position, then these people may never get the help they need for deliverance.

So what are our personal conclusions? In talking with many responsible individuals who counsel in this area and from reading on both sides of this issue, we conclude from our own limited perspective that it is possible for a Christian to be demonized. But we would stress this is a rare occurrence. And further, no Christian who is living for Christ need be concerned about the possibility.

Regardless, if this issue is so controversial, why do many people argue adamantly that Christians can *never* be demonized? There are several reasons, including the fact that the very idea can be emotionally upsetting. Many people fear the thought that they might have to deal with family, friends, or people in their church who could be demonized. Also, the popular view is that Christians cannot be demonized, and comfortable or cherished beliefs die hard. Further, in the West we simply do not have the kind of experience that Christians have in countries where there are extensive pagan practices and demonization. As a result, we are unprepared to deal with what we have never encountered. Finally, there is the issue of personal pride and/or professional reputation which, in an environment where the very idea may be ridiculed, can make it difficult for someone to seriously consider the possibility.

Let's try and put all this into perspective. No one can deny that many nations today are undergoing a major revival of the occult. As more and more people turn to occult practice, they are becoming demonized in the process. (In talking with one reliable source who had personally talked with knowledgeable Africans, they told him they knew of very few African heads of state who had not sold themselves to the occult for its power. In addition, even our own Washington, D.C., is fast becoming a hotbed of demonism.) This is something the church simply must prepare to deal with because many occultists are turning to Christ. These people need our help. If, in fact, some of them remain demonized, we think we need to at least be open to the possibility.

Having given a brief overview of the pros and cons of this subject, we will continue our discussion by looking at some of the general symptoms of demon possession.

The following are conceded to be characteristic signs:

1. Dramatic personality changes involving alterations in intelligence, demeanor, moral character, violent swings of mood, unexplainable depressions, hallucinations, suicidal or homicidal urges, irrational fears, changes in consciousness such as passing in and out of trance states, etc.

2. Dramatic physical changes involving superhuman strength, convulsions, falling down, catatonic symptoms, insensitivity to pain, changes in the voice, including changing to the opposite sex, foaming at the mouth, etc.
3. Dramatic spiritual changes including development of psychic abilities, occult speaking in tongues, hostility to Christ, fear of Christ, negative reactions to prayer, etc.

Mark Bubeck offers the following extended information:

Some folks have questions about how they can determine if their problem is symptomatic of demonic affliction. Through experience and examples from the Word, I submit some symptoms which may indicate severe demonic affliction. These are not meant to be conclusive evidence of demonic affliction but are merely indicative of the enemy's work.

1. A compulsive desire to curse the Father, the Lord Jesus Christ, or the Holy Spirit.
2. A revulsion against the Bible, including a desire to tear it up or to destroy copies of the Word.
3. Compulsive suicidal or murderous thoughts.
4. Deep feelings of bitterness and hatred toward those for whom one has no reason to feel that way (e.g., the Jews, the Church, strong Christian leaders).
5. Any compulsive temptation which seeks to force you to thoughts or behavior which you truly do not want to think or do.
6. Compulsive desires to tear other people down even if it means lying to do so. The vicious cutting use of the tongue may well be demonic. Satan will try to get you to attack anyone who is a threat to a problem area in your life.
7. Terrifying feelings of guilt and worthlessness even after honest confession of sin and failure is made to the Lord.
8. Certain physical symptoms which may appear suddenly or pass quickly for which there can be found no medical or physiological reason.
   a. Choking sensations.
   b. Pains which seem to move around and for which there is no medical cause.
   c. Feelings of tightness about the head or eyes.

    d. Dizziness, blackouts, or fainting seizures.

9. Deep depression and despondency.

10. Terrifying seizures of panic and other abnormal fears.

11. Dreams and nightmares that are of a horrific, recurring nature. Clairvoyant dreams—dreams that later come true—may well be demonic. One can usually eliminate this problem by remembering to say a prayer like this before he goes to sleep each night: "In the name of the Lord Jesus Christ, I submit my mind and my dream activities only to the work of the Holy Spirit. I bind up all powers of darkness and forbid them to work in my dream abilities or any part of my subconscious while I sleep."

12. Sudden surges of violent rage, uncontrollable anger, or seething feelings of hostility.

13. Terrifying doubt of one's salvation even though one once knew the joy of this salvation.[10]

In John L. Nevius' book *Demon Possession*, he recounts how ancestor worship in China seems to have made many Chinese readily subject to demonization. The characteristic indication is noted as the persistent acting out of a new personality which may use personal pronouns (first person for the demon, third person for the possessed), and which has knowledge and intellectual/physical power not possessed by the subject. In addition, the demon has its own sentiments, physical manifestations, and facial expressions. Finally, there is a complete change of moral character, including aversion to and hatred of God, especially Christ.[11]

Again, it is essential that a proper diagnosis be given and that all non-occult explanations be exhausted before a diagnosis of demonization is offered. This will require counseling involving the person's past history, current problems, etc. A medical and/or psychological history and examination are important to rule out an organic or emotional cause of the symptoms. Space does not permit an extended discussion of specific counseling procedures, but these may be found in Mark Bubeck, *The Adversary* (Moody); C. Fred Dickason, *Demon Possession and the Christian* (Moody); Merrill Unger, *What Demons Can Do to Saints* (Moody); Neil Anderson, *The Bondage Breaker* (Harvest House); Ed Murphy, *The Handbook for Spiritual Warfare* (Nelson); and Timothy M. Warner, *Spiritual Warfare* (Crossway).

The fact that serious psychological problems can coexist along with demonization underscores the importance of careful evaluation. But things such as very strong fearful or hateful reactions to God and Jesus would certainly seem to be indicators of the presence of an evil spirit. For example, Kurt Koch points out that when he has prayed with the mentally ill, there was a stillness and passivity when the name of Jesus was mentioned. But if the illness was demonic, there was a noticeable reaction.[12]

Again, once all other possible causes have been examined and ruled out, and the additional evidences of demonization are present (such as a person going to a trance state at the mention of the name of Jesus), only then may we assume that we are dealing with a demon.

For example, Russ Parker, who has been involved in deliverance ministry for approximately 20 years, observes that of all people he has been asked to pray with for release from evil spirits, only about one-third were actually involved with demonic oppression.[13] He also points out, "Far too many people have been hurt by [deliverance] ministry which has been too hastily and lazily begun."[14]

Most of the people he has counseled with did not need a "full-scale exorcism." What they needed was deliverance from demonic oppression. He says that five steps for deliverance involve: 1) recognition of the problem (proper counseling and diagnosis to be sure the problem is demonic), 2) repentance (inviting people to say a prayer of repentance for whatever sins have led to their condition), 3) renunciation (renouncing the things of the occult and destroying all occult paraphernalia), 4) release (commanding the spirit to loose its influence or hold of the person, commanding it to leave, and forbidding it to return), and 5) renewal of spiritual life (spiritual follow-up involving Christian fellowship, prayer, communion, worship, etc.).

It should be stressed that even if a Christian is demonized, demonic spirits may be exorcised by nonritualistic methods without direct confrontation. In other words, such simple things as repentance and commitment to spiritual growth in Christ alone are in many (and perhaps most) cases enough to get rid of evil spirits.

People who counsel in this area say that, unless necessary, the normal method is not usually dramatic confrontation but working toward the principles of strong Christian commitment and growth in the life of the demonized person. It seems that once the spirits recognize they are going to have little, if any, influence over a person, they leave willingly.

Counselors point out that it is not always necessary or even possible to know if a particular problem is something of the flesh or something demonic. The point is that the solution is the same in either case: repentance, acceptance of Christ's Lordship, commitment to growth, etc.

Another important consideration is for the individuals involved to have a clear and strong understanding of the triumph of Christ over Satan. This battle cannot be *our* triumph over Satan because we do not have the power. But Christ, the infinite God, does have the power, has defeated Satan at the cross, and thus can and will provide victory in any skirmishes that remain.

Also, it is important that an individual truly want to cooperate in his or her deliverance and that he or she be submitted to Christ. Otherwise, it may be difficult or even impossible to help the person. We may certainly pray for the demonized person who does not want deliverance, but a confrontation may be fruitless.

Parker also points out that it is important that the individual's faith be activated and that he becomes involved in his own deliverance. It is especially crucial that he be desirous of being set free and be honest and frank about his condition, because it is difficult for many people to admit the need for deliverance.

As noted earlier, prayer is essential. Let us give a more specific example. Mark Bubeck's book *The Adversary* contains a wonderful "warfare prayer" which has proved invaluable in helping to deliver people from severe demonic affliction.

Here we reproduce an extended segment from Bubeck's book.

> Another doctrinal tool that has proved of great benefit to me and to many others is the "Warfare Prayer" composed by Dr. Matthews. As a theologian, his unique and thorough way of including sound doctrine in this prayer is most helpful. I would urge anyone facing obvious spiritual warfare to use this prayer daily. It is good to read it aloud as a prayer unto the Lord. Eventually one will be able to incorporate the doctrinal truths expressed into his own prayer life without reading it.
>
> The devil hates this prayer. Usually before working with anyone who has deep demonic affliction, I will request that we read this prayer in unison. Many times the oppressed one can read only with great difficulty. Sometimes sight problems, voice problems, or mind confusion become so intense that the afflicted person can continue only with great effort. It is the truth of God that Satan cannot resist, and he vigorously fights it being applied

against him. Those serious about warfare should daily use a prayer of this type along with other prayer examples shared in this book.

Warfare Prayer

Heavenly Father, I bow in worship and praise before You. I cover myself with the blood of the Lord Jesus Christ as my protection during this time of prayer. I surrender myself completely and unreservedly in every area of my life to Yourself. I do take a stand against all the workings of Satan that would hinder me in this time of prayer, and I address myself only to the true and living God and refuse any involvement of Satan in my prayer.

Satan, I command you, in the name of the Lord Jesus Christ, to leave my presence with all your demons, and I bring the blood of the Lord Jesus Christ between us.

Heavenly Father, I worship You, and I give You praise. I recognize that You are worthy to receive all glory and honor and praise. I renew my allegiance to You and pray that the blessed Holy Spirit would enable me in this time of prayer. I am thankful, heavenly Father, that You have loved me from past eternity, that You sent the Lord Jesus Christ into the world to die as my substitute that I would be redeemed. I am thankful that the Lord Jesus Christ came as my representative, and that through Him You have completely forgiven me; You have given me eternal life; You have given me the perfect righteousness of the Lord Jesus Christ so I am now justified. I am thankful that in Him You have made me complete, and that You have offered Yourself to me to be my daily help and strength.

Heavenly Father, come and open my eyes that I might see how great You are and how complete Your provision is for this new day. I do, in the name of the Lord Jesus Christ, take my place with Christ in the heavenlies with all principalities and powers (powers of darkness and wicked spirits) under my feet. I am thankful that the victory the Lord Jesus Christ won for me on the cross and in His resurrection has been given to me and that I am seated with the Lord Jesus Christ in the heavenlies; therefore, I declare that all principalities and powers and all wicked spirits are subject to me in the name of the Lord Jesus Christ.

I am thankful for the armor You have provided, and I put on the girdle of truth, the breastplate of righteousness, the sandals of peace, the helmet of salvation. I lift up the shield of faith against all the fiery darts of the enemy, and take in my hand the sword of the Spirit, the Word of God, and use Your Word against all the forces of evil in my life; and I put on this armor and live and pray in complete dependence upon You, blessed Holy Spirit.

I am grateful, heavenly Father, that the Lord Jesus Christ spoiled all principalities and powers and made a show of them openly and triumphed over them in Himself. I claim all that victory for my life today. I reject out of my life all the insinuations, the accusations, and the temptations of Satan. I affirm that the Word of God is true, and I choose to live today in the light of God's Word. I choose, heavenly Father, to live in obedience to You and in fellowship with Yourself. Open my eyes and show me the areas of my life that would not please You. Work in my life that there be no ground to give Satan a foothold against me. Show me any area of weakness. Show me any area of my life that I must deal with so that I would please You. I do in every way today stand for You and the ministry of the Holy Spirit in my life.

By faith and in dependence upon You, I put off the old man and stand in all victory of the crucifixion where the Lord Jesus Christ provided cleansing from the old nature. I put on the new man and stand in all the victory of the resurrection and the provision He has made for me there to live above sin. Therefore, in this day, I put off the old nature with its selfishness, and I put on the new nature with its love. I put off the old nature with its fear and I put on the new nature with its courage. I put off the old nature with its weakness and I put on the new nature with its strength. I put off today the old nature with all its deceitful lusts and I put on the new nature with all its righteousness and purity.

I do in every way stand in the victory of the ascension and the glorification of the Son of God where all principalities and powers were made subject to Him, and I claim my place in Christ victorious with Him over all the enemies of my soul. Blessed Holy Spirit, I pray that You would fill me. Come into my life, break down every idol and cast out every foe.

I am thankful, heavenly Father, for the expression of Your will for my daily life as You have shown me in Your Word. I therefore claim all the will of God for today. I am thankful that You have blessed me with all spiritual blessings in heavenly places in Christ Jesus. I am thankful that You have begotten me unto a living hope by the resurrection of Jesus Christ from the dead. I am thankful that You have made a provision so that today I can live filled with the Spirit of God with love and joy and self-control in my life. And I recognize that this is Your will for me, and I therefore reject and resist all the endeavors of Satan and of his demons to rob me of the will of God. I refuse in this day to believe my feelings, and I hold up the shield of faith against all the accusations and against all the insinuations that Satan would put in my mind. I claim the fullness of the will of God for today.

I do, in the name of the Lord Jesus Christ, completely surrender myself to You, heavenly Father, as a living sacrifice. I choose not to be conformed to this world. I choose to be transformed by the renewing of my mind, and I pray that You would show me Your will and enable me to walk in all the fullness of the will of God today.

I am thankful, heavenly Father, that the weapons of our warfare are not carnal, but mighty through God to the pulling down of strongholds, to the casting down of imaginations and every high thing that exalted itself against the knowledge of God, and to bring every thought into obedience to the Lord Jesus Christ. Therefore in my own life today I tear down the strongholds of Satan, and I smash the plans of Satan that have been formed against me. I tear down the strongholds of Satan against my mind, and I surrender my mind to You, blessed Holy Spirit. I affirm, heavenly Father, that You have not given us the spirit of fear, but of power and of love and of a sound mind. I break and smash the strongholds of Satan formed against my emotions today, and I give my emotions to You. I smash the strongholds of Satan formed against my will today, and I give my will to You, and choose to make the right decisions of faith. I smash the strongholds of Satan formed against my body today, and I give my body to You, recognizing that I am Your temple; and I rejoice in Your mercy and Your goodness.

Heavenly Father, I pray that now through this day You would quicken me; show me the way that Satan is hindering and tempting and lying and counterfeiting and distorting the truth in my life. Enable me to be the kind of person that would please You. Enable me to be aggressive in prayer. Enable me to be aggressive mentally and to think Your thoughts after You, and to give You Your rightful place in my life.

Again, I now cover myself with the blood of the Lord Jesus Christ and pray that You, blessed Holy Spirit, would bring all the work of the crucifixion, all the work of the resurrection, all the work of the glorification, and all the work of Pentecost into my life today. I surrender myself to You. I refuse to be discouraged. You are the God of all hope. You have proven Your power by resurrecting Jesus Christ from the dead, and I claim in every way Your victory over all satanic forces active in my life, and I reject these forces; and I pray in the name of the Lord Jesus Christ with thanksgiving. Amen.[15]

Another area to mention is that possession may also occur as the result of serious sins unrelated to the occult.[16] In other words, although occult involvement (personal or ancestral) may be an important indicator for demonization, demonization may occur apart from it:

Michael Harper tells the story of a Salvation Army officer who had been born blind and who was brought to a meeting at which Jean Darnall was ministering. A charismatic word of knowledge declared that the man's blindness was due to an evil spirit which had entered him at birth. He had been born in prison. His father was a criminal and his mother had conspired with him. Criminal or immoral activity can become a vehicle for demonic intrusion, and this was the case for this officer. Following a deliverance prayer by which a spirit was cast out of him, the man saw perfectly for the first time in his life.[17]

We do not mention an incident of this nature to unnecessarily concern Christians. We only note that such experiences are found. Their extent and interpretation may be subject to debate, but the church at least needs to take a look at them.

In addition, our basic pattern for action in this entire realm must be that of Jesus Christ. First, Jesus was not preoccupied with demonic activity; it was only a portion of a much larger ministry. Second, Jesus cast out demons authoritatively and with few words. He did not engage in lengthy discussions with the spirits. Third, there was clear evidence that the person had been delivered from an evil spirit.

Then there is the problem if the demon resists the command to depart. At this point, those involved must simply stand on the fact of

Christ's authority, persevere in faith, and continue to command that the spirit leave in the name of Jesus.

Parker points out that sometimes there are signs of deliverance which are biblical such as convulsions, falling to the ground, or violent shaking. But sometimes nothing happens. "The real evidence that the work has been done will be in the consequent freedom and development of spiritual life" in the person who was truly delivered. [18] Thus, despite her faith in Christ, the former witch Doreen Irvine was tormented constantly until the demons were exorcised from her. Once this was done, her spiritual life grew by leaps and bounds, her emotional life was healed, and the ordeal was finally over. Remember, if it is difficult to be rid of the consequences of sins such as alcoholism or sexual addiction, we should not expect it would be any easier with the consequences of occult sins.

Sometimes there is no deliverance, as we find was true in Mark 9:29 where the disciples could not cast the demons out of the young boy. This exorcism apparently required additional consecration to prayer and/or fasting for deliverance.

A final word of caution. In so-called deliverance ministries there is both legitimacy and illegitimacy. For example, deliverance ministries that concentrate on demons of specific sins or other normal problems are obviously suspect. Over the years we have read of some 100 "demons" supposedly identified as demons of daydreaming, anger, postnasal drip, fingernail biting, headache, adultery, caffeine, legalism, eternal security, arthritis, etc. These kinds of deliverances often are rather hysterical and don't in the long run solve the basic problem because the basic problem is of human origin, not from an oppressing spirit.

> No demon of lust was expelled from the adulterous woman (John 8) or from the woman of ill repute mentioned by Luke (Chapter 7), or from the incestuous people of Corinth (1 Corinthians 5). No demon of avarice was expelled from Zacchaeus, no demon of incredulity from Peter after his triple betrayal. No demon of rivalry was expelled from the Corinthians whom Paul had to call to order. [19]

Thus, many people who are involved in questionable or false deliverance ministries can do more harm than good. Their effectiveness is explained in psychological terms alone because they are attempting to exorcise nonexistent demons. For example, psychologist Gary Collins comments,

> There is abundant evidence from studies in perceptual psychology that people see and act in accordance with the expectation of those around them. If someone convinces me I am demon possessed, unconsciously I might begin to experience the symptoms and show the behavior which fit the diagnosis. In like manner, if I assume someone else is possessed, I may begin looking for symptoms to prove my hypothesis. It is easy to develop a demonology mind-set in which almost everything we see or do is attributed to the devil. . . . One can also see how much damage can be done by well-meaning exorcists who, by the very act of exorcism, suggest to the counselee that demons are present. If the "exorcism" fails, the counselee is left not only with his original symptoms but with hopelessness and despair because he thinks his body is possessed by stubborn demons who refuse to leave.[20]

Some of the indications of genuine deliverance include praising God, feelings of having been delivered, the loss of psychic powers, relief from the problems that had beset the person (such as hearing voices, mental or moral disturbances, suicidal tendencies, physical problems, etc.), and new feelings of peace and love.

In general, true exorcism (whether it occurs in a dramatic ritual or through the process of Christian growth) produces a genuine healing involving a restoration of personal soundness and spiritual freedom. In addition, those specific attributes given by the demons such as psychic abilities or healings may be removed. As Dr. Dickason comments, "Supernatural powers supplied by demonic residents and connections suddenly disappear with expulsion of the demons"[21] (cf., Acts 16: 16-19). In the case of occult healings, this may result in the return of the maladies that had been removed by demonic power. It is as if God has rejected the demonic healing and freed the person to be healed through divine power—or at least the freedom of knowing they are now subject to God's will and wisdom.

In conclusion, we emphasize two things: 1) Only those who are spiritually prepared for this ministry and called of God should engage in a ministry of deliverance, and 2) It is important to realize that Christ has already won the victory. Those people who are called to deliverance ministry can have full confidence in the power and victory of Jesus Christ because:

> Christians are working between two victories: calvary and the return of Jesus Christ. Our enemy is a defeated foe, thanks to the triumph of the cross and the resurrection. Our victory is like the Normandy landings in World War II: it was the beginning of the end of the enemy's rule; it was only a matter of time before the war would be over. For us in Christ, the beachhead was established at calvary when a massive deathblow was dealt to the enemy, and now we are engaged in the final skirmishes. The outcome is already determined and will be fully displayed when Christ returns for His own. Our God reigns! We must focus on what Christ has done.[22]

Recommended Reading

William Menzies Alexander, *Demonic Possession in the New Testament* (Grand Rapids, MI: Baker, 1980).

Mark I. Bubeck, *The Adversary* (Chicago: Moody Press, 1974).

Mark I. Bubeck, *Satanic Revival* (San Bernardino, CA: Here's Life, 1991).

C. Fred Dickason, *Demon Possession and the Christian* (Chicago: Moody Press, 1987).

Richard Gilpin, *Biblical Demonology* (Minneapolis, MN: Klock, 1982 rpt.).

Thomas Ice and Robert Dean, Jr., *A Holy Rebellion: Strategy for Spiritual Warfare* (Eugene, OR: Harvest House, 1990).

Doreen Irvine, *Freed From Witchcraft* (Nashville, TN: Nelson, 1973).

Jerry Johnson, *The Edge of Evil: The Rise of Satanism in North America* (Dallas, TX: Word, 1989).

Larry Kahaner, *Cults That Kill: Probing the Underworld of Occult Crime* (New York: Warner, 1988).

Kurt Koch, *Between Christ and Satan* (Grand Rapids, MI: Kregel, n.d.).

Kurt Koch, *Demonology Past and Present* (Grand Rapids, MI: Kregel, 1970).

Kurt Koch, *Occult Bondage and Deliverance* (Grand Rapids, MI: Kregel, 1970).

Bob Larson, *Satanism: The Seduction of America's Youth* (Nashville, TN: Thomas Nelson, 1989).

C. S. Lewis, *Screwtape Letters* (New York: Macmillan, 1971).

John L. Nevius, *Demon Possession* (Grand Rapids, MI: Kregel, 1970).

Carl A. Raschke, *The Interruption of Eternity* (Chicago: Nelson-Hall, 1980).

Merrill Unger, *Biblical Demonology* (Wheaton, IL: Scripture Press, 1971).

Merrill Unger, *Demons in the World Today* (Wheaton, IL Tyndale, 1972).

Merrill Unger, *What Demons Can Do to Saints* (Chicago: Moody Press, 1977).

Notes

Preface
1. "Occultism," *Encyclopedia Britannica Micropaedia* (Chicago: University of Chicago, 1978), 15th edition, Vol. 7, 469.
2. Ronald Enroth, "The Occult," Walter A. Elwell, ed., *Evangelical Dictionary of Theology* (Grand Rapids, MI: Baker, 1984), 787.
3. See John Ankerberg and John Weldon, *The Facts on the Occult; The Facts on the New Age Movement; The Facts on Spirit Guides; The Facts on Hinduism in America; The Facts on UFO's and Other Supernatural Phenomena; Astrology: Do the Heavens Rule Our Destiny?; Cult Watch: What You Need to Know About Spiritual Deception* (all published by Harvest House); *Can You Trust Your Doctor? A Complete Guide to New Age Medicine and Its Threat to Your Family* (Chattanooga, TN: Ankerberg Theological Research Institute); cf., John Weldon and Zola Levitt, *Psychic Healing: An Exposé of an Occult Phenomenon* (Dallas, TX: Zola Levitt Ministries, 1991), and John Weldon and Clifford Wilson, *Psychic Forces*, section on parapsychology.

Chapter 1—The Modern Search for Enlightenment and Transcendence
1. Personal conversation, Jun. 1974.
2. EX-TM, P.O. Box 7565, Arlington, VA 22207, (202) 728-7580.
3. Taken from Malachi Martin, *Hostage to the Devil: The Possession and Exorcism of Five Living Americans* (New York: Bantam, 1977), 385-488.
4. Ibid., 419.
5. Ibid., 418.
6. Ibid., 485.
7. From a statement given to the authors on Jan. 15, 1984.
8. E.g., the 24-volume "From Heaven to Earth" series with medium D. Kendrick Johnson (Columbus, OH: Ariel Press).
9. Condensed and edited from material sent May 28, 1981.
10. Taken from Johanna Michaelsen, *The Beautiful Side of Evil* (Eugene, OR: Harvest House, 1982), 83, 85, 92-93, 98-101, 107-13, 126, 139-40, 146-49, 154, 209.
11. In Russ Parker, *Battling the Occult* (Downers Grove, IL: InterVarsity, 1990), 15.
12. Personal correspondence, Jan. 25, 1985.

Chapter 2—The Worldview and Practices of the Occult
1. William D. Halsey, ed. director, *MacMillan Dictionary for Students* (New York: Macmillan, 1984), 57.
2. "Monism," in Paul Edwards, ed., *The Encyclopedia of Philosophy*, Vol. 5 (New York: Macmillan Publishing Co. and The Free Press, 1972), 363.
3. David Conway, *Magic: An Occult Primer* (New York: Bantam, 1973), 35.
4. Gary North, *Unholy Spirits: Occultism and New Age Humanism* (Fort Worth, TX: Dominion Press, 1986), 59-61.
5. Conway, *Magic: An Occult Primer*, 29-30.
6. Charles Manson, letter to the editor, *Radix* Magazine, Nov.-Dec. 1976, 2.
7. Richard Cavendish, *The Black Arts* (New York: G. P. Putnam's Sons, 1967), 229.
8. Ibid.
9. Bhagwan Shree Rajneesh, "God Is a Christ in a Christ," *Sannyas*, No. 3 (May/Jun. 1978), 11.

10. Ibid.
11. Bubba Free John, *Garbage and the Goddess* (Lower Lake, CA: The Dawn Horse Press, 1974), 310-11.
12. Rajneesh quoted in the editorial, *Sannyas*, No. 5, (Sep.-Oct. 1978), 3.
13. Holger Kalweit, "When Insanity Is a Blessing: The Message of Shamanism," in Stanislav Grof and Christina Grof, eds., *Spiritual Emergency: When Personal Transformation Becomes a Crisis* (Los Angeles: Jeremy P. Tarcher, 1989), 85.
14. Keith Thompson, "The UFO Encounter Experience As a Crisis of Transformation" in Grof and Grof, *Spiritual Emergency*, 131.
15. Bhagwan Shree Rajneesh, *The Discipline of Transcendence: Discoveries on the Forty-Two Sutras of the Buddha*, Vol. 2 (Poona, India: Rajneesh Foundation International, 1978), 313-14.
16. It can be argued that the basic principles for Jung's analytical psychology originated from his encounters with the spirit world and that Jungian psychology is a form of psychologized occult cosmology. This makes its infiltration into the church all the more unfortunate. See Charles Strohmer, "Jung: Man of Mystic Proportions" in *SCP Journal*, Vol. 9, No. 219, 90; Carl Jung, *Memories, Dreams, Reflections* (New York: Vintage, 1965), 4, 183, 189-92; Colin Wilson, *Lord of the Underworld: Jung in the 20th Century* (Wellingborough, North Hamptonshire: Aquarian Press, 1984), especially Chapter 4; Stephen A. Hoeller, *The Gnostic Jung and the Seven Sermons to the Dead* (Wheaton, IL: Theosophical, 1982), 2-8; cf. Nandor Fodor, *Freud, Jung and Occultism* (New Hyde Park, NY: University Books, 1971); Alta J. La Dage, *Occult Psychology: A Comparison of Jungian Psychology and the Modern Qabalah* (St. Paul, MN: Ewellyn Publications, 1978); Carl Jung, *Psychology and the Occult* (Princeton, NJ: Princeton University Press, 1977).
17. La Dage, *Occult Psychology*, 162.
18. For Hinduism see Tal Brooke, *Riders of the Cosmic Circuit* (Batavia, IL: Lion, 1986). (Available from Spiritual Counterfeits Project, P. O. Box 4308, Berkeley, CA 94702; John Ankerberg and John Weldon, *The Facts on Hinduism in America* (Eugene, OR: Harvest House, 1992). For Buddhism see John Weldon, *Buddhism in America*, manuscript in partial form submitted as master's thesis to Simon Greenleaf University, Anaheim, CA, 1987.
19. La Dage, *Occult Psychology*, 162.
20. Ibid., 161.
21. Ibid., 163-64.
22. Ibid., 164.
23. John Warwick Montgomery, "The Apologists of Eucatastrophe" in John Warwick Montgomery, ed., *Myth Allegory and Gospel* (Minneapolis, MN: Bethany, 1974), 20; cf., Arthur Koestler, *The Lotus and the Robot* (New York: Macmillan, 1961), esp. 236-41, 268-75.
24. Conway, *Magic: An Occult Primer*, 70, 78, 120.
25. Ibid., Chapter 5.
26. North, *Unholy Spirits*, 75, 79.
27. Conway, *Magic: An Occult Primer*, 197.
28. Ibid., 70, 81.
29. Os Guinness, *The Dust of Death* (Downers Grove, IL: InterVarsity, 1973), 298, 300.
30. Ibid., 307.
31. R. K. McAll, "Taste and See," in John Warwick Montgomery, ed., *Demon Possession* (Minneapolis, MN: Bethany, 1976), 274.
32. Conway, *Magic: An Occult Primer*, 129-32.

Chapter 3—Reasons for the Modern Occult Revival

1. Slater Brown, *The Heyday of Spiritualism* (New York: Pocket Books, 1972), 159-60.
2. Nandor Fodor cites the *North American Review*, April 1855, as accurate in giving the figure of nearly two million spiritists in 1855 (Nandor Fodor, *An Encyclopdedia of Psychic Science* (Secaucus, NJ: Citadel, 1974), 362; G. H. Pember cites a figure of eight to eleven million followers in *Earth's Earliest Ages*, Revell edition, nd., 318; Alfred Douglas, *Extrasensory Powers: A Century of Psychical Research* (Woodstock, NY: Overlook Press, 1977), 54; on the authority of the editor of the *Home Journal* he cites 40,000 spiritualists in New York in 1853; cf., Alan Gauld, *The Founders of Psychical Research* (New York: Schocken, 1968), 15.
3. E.g., Clifford Wilson and John Weldon, *Psychic Forces*, Chapter 22, "The Occult History of Parapsychology" (Chattanooga, TN: Global, 1987), 341-49.
4. This is evident from any number of historical studies. See Paul Kurt's "Introduction: More Than a Century of Psychical Research," in Paul Kurt, ed., *A Skeptic's Handbook of Parapsychology* (Buffalo, NY: Promethius, 1985), xii-xiv; John Beloff, "Historical Overview," in Benjamin B. Wolman, ed., *Handbook of Parapsychology* (New York: Van Nostran, Reinhold, 1977), 4-7; J. B. Rhine, "A Century of Parapsychology," in Martin Ebon, ed., *The Signet Handbook of Parapsychology* (New York: Signet, 1978), 11.
5. G. H. Pember, *Earth's Earliest Ages* (Grand Rapids, MI: Kregel Publishers, 1975 rpt.), 243.
6. This text and the many issues of the *SCP Journal* (P. O. Box 4308, Berkeley, CA) may be cited in documentation. Concerning the latter, see e.g., Vol. 5, No. 1, "Empowering the Self: A Look at the Human Potential Movement"; Vol. 4, No. 1, "Inner Healing Issue"; Vol. 4, No. 2, "Expanding Horizons: Psychical Research and Parapsychology"; Vol. 3, No. 1, "Eckankar: A Hard Look at a New Religion"; Vol. 2, No. 1, "The Marriage of Science and Religion: Holistic Health Issue"; Vol. 1, No. 2, "UFOs: Is Science Fiction Coming True?"; Vol. 1, No. 1, "Thanatology: Death and Dying," plus Vol. 6, No. 1, *Special Collection Journal* and the many SCP newsletters. Also the *Christian Research Journal* (formerly *Forward* magazine) published by The Christian Research Institute in El Toro, CA.
7. See SCP *Journal,* Vol. 9, No. 1, *Minding the Store: Influences of the New Age in Business* (1989), passim; "Companies Turn to Psychic Advice," *The Daily Californian*, Apr. 23, 1983; L. F. Maire and J. D. LaMothe, *Soviet and Czechoslovakian Parapsychology Research*, Defense Intelligence Agency Report, Sep. 1975, code DST-18105-387-75 and the related report by L. F. Maire, *Controlled Offensive Behavior*. See also the texts by D. Scott Rogo (and others) on Communist research into parapsychology and Roger C. Palms, "Demonology Today," in J. W. Montgomery, ed., *Demon Possession* (Minneapolis, MN: Bethany, 1976), 313-14.
8. Gordon Melton, *New Age Encyclopedia* (Detroit, MI: Gale, 1990), xv, English statistics; Russ Parker, *Battling the Occult* (Downers Grove, IL: InterVarsity, 1990), 18; Patricia Weaver, "Ritual Abuse, Pornography and the Occult," *SCP Newsletter*, Vol. 14, No. 4, 1989, 3.
9. Most of these are mentioned in Os Guinness, *The Dust of Death* (Downers Grove, IL: InterVarsity, 1973), 280-86.
10. Ronald Enroth, "The Occult," in Walter Elwell, ed., *The Evangelical Dictionary of Theology* (Grand Rapids, MI: Baker, 1984), 787-88.
11. John Ankerberg, Craig Branch, and John Weldon, *Thieves of Innocence: A Parents' Handbook for Identifying New Age Religious Beliefs, Psychotherapeutic Techniques and Occult Practices in Public School Curricula* (Eugene, OR: Harvest House, 1993), passim.
12. John Ankerberg and John Weldon, *The Facts on Spirit Guides* (Eugene, OR: Harvest House, 1989); *SCP Journal*, Vol. 7, No. 1, 1987: "Spiritism: The Medium and the Message."

13. John Ankerberg and John Weldon, *Astrology: Do the Heavens Rule Our Destiny?* (Eugene, OR: Harvest House, 1989).
14. John Ankerberg and John Weldon, *Cult Watch* (Eugene, OR: Harvest House, 1991).
15. John Ankerberg and John Weldon, *Can You Trust Your Doctor?* (Dallas, TX: Word, 1991) available from Ankerberg Theological Research Institute, Chattanooga, TN 37411.
16. E.g., John Welwood, ed., *The Meeting of the Ways: Explorations in East/West Psychology* (New York: Schocken Books, 1979); Charles Tart, ed., *Transpersonal Psychologies* (New York: Harper & Row, 1977); and Seymour Boorstein, ed., *Transpersonal Psychotherapy* (Palo Alto, CA: Science and Behavior Books, 1980); Roger N. Walsh, Frances Vaughan, *Beyond Ego: Transpersonal Dimensions in Psychology* (Los Angeles: J. P. Tarcher, 1980); Ken Wilbur, et al., *Transformations of Consciousness: Conventional and Contemplative Perspectives on Development* (Boston, MA: Shambhala, 1986).
17. Martin Ebon, *The Devil's Bride: Exorcism Past and Present* (New York: Harper & Row, 1974), 11.
18. *SCP Newsletter*, Jul.-Aug. 1984, 9, citing *Rolling Stone*, Jun. 25, 1981, 22.
19. E.g., Globe Communications, "Your Hidden Psychic Powers" (New York: Globe Communications, 1987), booklet.
20. Brooks Alexander, "Occult Philosophy and Mystical Experience," in Spiritual Counterfeits Project *Special Collection Journal*, Vol. 6, No. 1 (Berkeley, CA: Spiritual Counterfeits Project, Winter 1984), 14.
21. See the authors' forthcoming encyclopedia on 70 contemporary American sects and cults (Harvest House, 1995).
22. John Ankerberg and John Weldon, *The Facts on Hinduism in America* (Eugene, OR: Harvest House, 1991), and note 21.
23. *SCP Newsletter*, Vol. 5, No. 1, 1.
24. Robert S. Ellwood, Jr., *Religious and Spiritual Groups in Modern America* (Englewood Cliffs, NJ: Prentice Hall, 1973), 12.
25. M. Scott Peck, *The People of the Lie: The Hope for Healing Human Evil* (New York: Simon & Schuster, 1983), 39-40.
26. Robert Burrows, "New Age Movement: Self-Deification in a Secular Culture," *SCP Newsletter*, Vol. 10, No. 5, Winter 1984/85, 4.
27. In Larry Kahaner, *Cults That Kill: Probing the Underworld of Occult Crime* (New York: Warner, 1988), 102.
28. Margot Adler, *Drawing Down the Moon: Witches, Druids, Goddess-Worshippers, and Other Pagans in America Today* (New York: The Viking Press, 1979), 23.

Chapter 4—Evidence for the Devil

1. These polls are widely reported and may be secured from the respective organization. One national prestigious poll revealed that over 40 percent of all American adults claim to have been in contact with someone who has died. Of these, 78 percent claimed they saw, 50 percent heard, and 18 percent claimed to have talked with the dead (Klimo, *Channeling*, 3). The Gallup poll conducted Jun. 14-17, 1990, indicated that belief in the paranormal is "widespread" in society. These beliefs are almost as common among those who are "deeply religious in a traditional sense" as among those who are not, even though these beliefs contradict the beliefs of the more traditional religions. Twenty-five percent of Americans believe in ghosts and astrology; one in five believes in reincarnation, including over 20 percent of those who classify themselves as born-again Christians. Over one in ten Americans beliefs in channeling, and amazingly, only seven percent of Americans denied "believing in any of a list of 18 paranormal experiences," including UFOs, psychic healing, contact with the dead, witchcraft, channeling, etc. Almost 50 percent said they

believe in five or more of these items, and fully 75 percent claimed to have had a personal experience in at least one of the categories. (George H. Gallup, Jr., and Frank Newport, "Belief in Paranormal Phenomena Among Adult Americans," *The Skeptical Inquirer*, Winter 1991, 137-46). See also the report in Andrew Greeley, "Mysticism Goes Mainstream," *American Health*, Jan.-Feb. 1987).

2. In *This Week* magazine, Mar. 2, 1958.

3. J. I. Packer, *God's Words* (Downers Grove, IL: InterVarsity, 1985), 83-84.

4. Brooks Alexander, "The Disappearance of the Devil," *Spiritual Counterfeits Project Newsletter*, Vol. 10, No. 4, Jul./Aug. 1984, 6-7.

5. See the discussion in James Hastings' *Encyclopedia of Religion and Ethics* (New York: Scribner's, n.d.), Vol. 4, 565-636.

6. Sri Chimnoy, *Astrology, the Supernatural and the Beyond* (Jamaica, NY: Agni Press, 1973), 70-72; David Conway, *Magic: An Occult Primer* (New York: Bantam, 1973), 196-99.

7. Conway, *Magic: An Occult Primer*, 196, 198.

8. Sri Chinmoy, *Conversations With the Master* (Jamaica, NY: Agni Press, 1977), 19.

9. Chinmoy, *Astrology*, 94.

10. Cf., Douglas Mahr, letter, in *SCP Newsletter*, Vol. 16, No. 3, Dec. 1991, 3.

11. Doreen Irvine, *Freed From Witchcraft* (Nashville, TN: Nelson, 1973), 138.

12. M. Scott Peck, *People of the Lie* (New York: Simon & Schuster, 1983), 190.

13. Ibid., 196.

14. John W. Montgomery, ed., *Demon Possession* (Minneapolis, MN: Bethany, 1976); W. M. Alexander, *Demonic Possession in the New Testament* (Grand Rapids, MI: Baker, 1980); n.a., *Demon Experiences in Many Lands* (Chicago, IL: Moody, 1960); J. L. Nevious, *Demon Possession* (Grand Rapids, MI: Kregel, 1970); Malachi Martin, *Hostage to the Devil* (New York: Bantam, 1977); Martin Ebon, ed., *Exorcism: Fact Not Fiction* (New York: Signet, 1970); Frank Podmore, *Mediums of the 19th Century*, 2 Vols., (New Hyde Park: University Books, 1973); I. M. Lewis, *Ecstatic Religion— An Anthropological Study of Spirit Possession and Shamanism* (Baltimore, MD: Penguin, 1971); Nicholas Remy, *Demonolatry* (New Hyde Park: University Books, 1975); Nandor Fodor, *Encyclopedia of Psychic Science* (Secaucus, NJ: Citadel, 1974), e.g., 294-95; Leslie A. Shepard, *Encyclopedia of Occultism and Parapsychology* (Detroit, MI: Gale Research Co., 1979), e.g., Vol. 2, 655-64; T. K. Oesterreich, *Possession: Demoniacal and Other Among Primitive Races, In Antiquity, the Middle Ages, and Modern Times* (Secaucus, NJ: Citadel, 1974).

15. John Warwick Montgomery, *Principalities and Powers* (Minneapolis, MN: Bethany, 1975), 146.

16. Erika Bourguignon, ed., *Religion, Altered States of Consciousness and Social Change* (Columbus: Ohio State University Press, 1973), 16-17, Table 2.

17. Martin Ebon, *The Devil's Bride: Exorcism Past and Present* (Harper & Row, 1974), 11.

18. Ibid., p. 14.

19. John S. Mbiti, *African Religions and Philosophy* (New York: Doubleday/Anchor, 1970), 106-07.

20. Rene Pache, *The Inspiration and Authority of Scripture* (Chicago, IL: Moody Press, 1966); Norman L. Geisler, ed., *Inerrancy* (Grand Rapids, MI: Zondervan, 1979); L. Gaussen, *The Divine Inspiration of the Bible* (Grand Rapids, MI: Kregel, rpt. 1971).

21. Denis De Rougemont, *The Devil's Share: An Essay on the Diabolic in Modern Society* (New York: Meridian, 1956), 18.

22. Taken mostly from *The New Schaff Herzog Encyclopedia of Religious Knowledge* (Grand Rapids, MI: Baker, 1977), Vol. 3, 414-15.

23. The following spiritistically inspired books represent only a minute sampling of the numerous books by individual spirits (Seth, Ramtha, Mafu, etc.): *The Seth Material*; *Seth Speaks*; *Ramtha: Voyage to the New World*; *New Teachings for an Awakened*

Humanity; *Voyage to the New World*; the First, Second, etc., *Books of Azrael*; Sullivan, *Arthur Ford Speaks From Beyond*; Houts, *Voices From the Open Door*; Ruth Montgomery, *A World Beyond*; Rosemary Brown, *Unfinished Symphonies*; H. P. Blavatsky, *Isis Unveiled, Vol. 2*; *The Urantia Book*; *Oahspe, A Kosmon Bible*; *A Course in Miracles* (3 Vols.); Levi, *The Aquarian Gospel of Jesus the Christ*; L. M. Arnold, *History of the Origin of All Things*; Phylos, *A Dweller on Two Planets*; Kahlil Gibran, *Jesus the Son of Man*; W. F. Pierce, *The Case of Patience Worth*; Roberts and Woolcock, *Elizabethean Episode*; Juffman and Specht, *Many Wonderful Things*; W. Brandon, *Open the Door*; G. Owen, *The Life Beyond the Veil*; LeBeau, *Beyond Doubt*; Eckert, *Aubrey Messages*; G. Abrahams, *We Come Amongst You*; Taylor Caldwell, *Dialogues with the Devil*.

24. Pat Rodegast, *Emmanuel's Book* (Westin, CT: Friends Press, 1986), 132, 198-201, 227, 232, 205, 161.

25. Ibid., xx, 145, 88, 151, 208, 223, 228.

26. Kathryn Ridall, *Channeling* (New York: Bantam, 1988), 58.

27. C. S. Lewis, *Screwtape Letters* (New York: Macmillan, 1971), vii.

28. John Warwick Montgomery, "Commentary on Hysteria and Demons, Depression and Oppression, Good and Evil" in John Warwick Montgomery, ed., *Demon Possession: A Medical Historical Anthropological and Theological Symposium* (Minneapolis, MN: Bethany, 1976), 232.

29. Martin Ebon, "Psychic Roulette," *Psychic* Magazine, Dec. 1975, 58.

30. J. W. Montgomery, *Principalities and Powers* (Minneapolis, MN: Bethany, 1975), 146.

31. Dave Hunt, *The Cult Explosion* (Eugene, OR: Harvest House, 1980), 15-16.

Chapter 5—Satanism and Witchcraft: The Occult and the West

1. Kahaner, *Cults That Kill*, 112, 120, 126.

2. Maury Terry, *The Ultimate Evil: An Investigation of America's Most Dangerous Satanic Cult* (Garden City, NY: Dolphin/Doubleday, 1987).

3. Ibid., 347.

4. Ibid., picture inserts after p. 346.

5. Citing Peter Haining, *The Anatomy of Witchcraft*, 114-15. This material is on pp. 105-06 of the 1972 Taplinger edition.

6. Ibid., 143.

7. Ibid., 107-08.

8. Arthur Lyons, *The Second Coming: Satanism in America* (New York: Dodd Mead & Co., 1970), 3, 5.

9. Kahaner, *Cults That Kill*, 246.

10. Ibid., 240.

11. In addition to the books cited at the beginning of this chapter, a number of additional texts document the pagan revival and/or the data herein. J. Gordon Melton, *Magic, Witchcraft and Paganism in America: A Bibliography* (1982); *A Sorcery Iceberg in America* (1985)—a private computerized compilation by Caris, a midwestern group listing hundreds of pagan organizations and some 300 periodical reports on paganism; Nigel Davis, *Human Sacrifice in History and Today* (1981); Alastair Scolri, *Murder for Magic: Witchcraft in Africa* (1965); M. P. Dove, *Indian Underworld* (1940); Margo Adler, *Drawing Down the Moon: Witches, Druids, Goddess-Worshippers, and Other Pagans in America Today* (1979); Dr. Sondra O'Neill, *King City: Fathers of Anguish, Sons of Blood: The True Story Behind the Atlanta Murders* (unpublished); Justine Glass, *Witchcraft: the Sixth Sense* (1974); Mircea Eliade, *The Sacred and the Profane* (1959); *The Anatomy of Witchcraft* (1971); Richard Cavendish, *The Black Arts* (1967); Doreen Irvine, *Freed from Witchcraft* (1973); David Conway, *Magic: An Occult Primer* (1973); Kurt Koch, *Between Christ and Satan* (1962); Doreen Valiente, *ABC of Witchcraft* (1973).

12. Adler, *Drawing Down the Moon*, 167.
13. Justine Glass, *Witchcraft: The Sixth Sense* (North Hollywood, CA: Wilshire, 1965), 47-48.
14. Cavendish, *The Black Arts*, 247-48.
15. Ibid., 248-49.
16. Kahaner, *Cults That Kill*, 140-41, 161.
17. Ibid., 17, 103.
18. *Melbourne Observer*, Feb. 17, 1974.
19. Cited in Clifford Wilson and John Weldon, *Psychic Forces*, 12-13.
20. Ibid.
21. *Rolling Stone*, Nov. 22, 1984; cf. *Newsweek*, Jul. 23, 1984.
22. "The Devil Worshippers," ABC News 20/20 transcript, show #521, May 16, 1985, 6-7.
23. Ibid., 8.
24. Ibid., 5, 8,
25. Ibid.
26. Napa *Register*, Mar. 30, 1973.
27. *The San Francisco Chronicle*, May 3, 1973.
28. John Frattarola, *Passport* Magazine, Special Report, 1986, published by Calvary Chapel Church in West Covina, CA, 3.
29. Carl Wickland, *30 Years Among the Dead* (Van Nuys, CA: New Castle Publishing, 1974 rpt.), 116.
30. Alastair Scolri, *Magic For Murder: Witchcraft in Africa* (London: Cassell & Co., 1965), 49.
31. Ibid., 118.
32. Maury Terry, *The Ultimate Evil: An Investigation of America's Most Dangerous Satanic Cult* (Garden City, NY: Dolphin/Doubleday, 1987).
33. Ibid., 511.
34. Ibid., xiii.
35. Ralph Lapp, *The New Priesthood* (1961), 29.
36. Terry, *The Ultimate Evil*, 170.
37. Ibid., 509-11.
38. Ibid., 510.
39. Anton LaVey, *The Satanic Bible* (1972), 11.
40. Publisher's statement.
41. E.g., Kahaner, *Cults That Kill*, 31, 90, 135-37, 190.
42. Ibid., 153.
43. E. J. Moody in Zaretsky and Leone, eds., *Religious Movements in Contemporary America* (Princeton University Press, 1974), 644, 381.
44. Kahaner, *Cults That Kill*, 232-33.
45. Ibid., 87.
46. Craig Hawkins, *Forward* magazine, Fall 1986, 17.
47. Ibid., 21.
48. Ibid., 19, 21-22.
49. See e.g., Department of the Army, *Religious Requirements and Practices: A Handbook for Chaplains*, Washington, D.C., Apr. 1978 (No. 165-13) which alleges that the Church of Satan is compatible with military directives and practices (p. vii-19).
50. Carl A. Raschke, "Satanism and the Devolution of the 'New Religions,'" *SCP Newsletter*, Fall 1985.
51. Ibid., 24.
52. Ibid., 26.
53. Ibid., 27.
54. Ibid., 28; cf., Carl A. Raschke, *The Interruption of Eternity: Modern Gnosticism and the Origins of the New Religious Consciousness* (Chicago, IL: Nelson-Hall, 1980).

55. Given the vast influence of modern astrology, it is relevant that Prof. Moody also observed a frequent need to counter a perceived personal impotence through control of one's fate. Thus, "Those who eventually become Satanists usually have begun with astrology, but have come into contact with other types of magic in the magical subculture of the urban center" (i.e., occult bookstores and supply shops—pp. 362-63 in Zaretsky and Leone, eds., *Religious Movements in Contemporary America*).

56. E. J. Moody, "Magical Therapy: An Anthropological Investigation of Contemporary Satanism," in Zaretsky and Leone, eds., *Religious Movements in Contemporary America*, 358-60.

57. Raschke, "Satanism and the Devolution," 24-25.

58. E.g., John Frattarola, *Passport* Magazine Special Report, 1986, 2, 11.

59. Ibid., 5. See Kahaner, *Cults That Kill*, Chapter 12.

60. Frattarola, *Passport* Magazine Special Report, 7.

61. Ibid.

Chapter 6—Satanism and Witchcraft: The Occult and the East

1. Margo Adler, *Drawing Down the Moon: Witches, Druids, Goddess-Worshippers and Other Pagans in America Today* (New York: Viking Press, 1979), 104-05.

2. Cf., Nigel Davies, *Human Sacrifice in History and Today* (New York: William Morrow, 1981).

3. Mircea Eliade, *Occultism, Witchcraft and Cultural Fashions* (Chicago: University of Chicago Press, 1976), 71.

4. Satindra Roy, "The Witches of Orissa," *The Anthropological Society of Bombay*, Vol. 14, No. 2, 187-88, 194.

5. Ibid., 189-90, 195.

6. Mircea Eliade, *Yoga: Immortality and Freedom* (Princeton, NJ: Princeton University Press, Bollingen, 1973), 263.

7. E.g., David Conway, *Magic: An Occult Primer* (New York: Bantam, 1973), 129-33; Eliade, *Yoga: Immortality and Freedom*, 263-67; Adler, *Drawing Down the Moon*, 107-08.

8. Eliade, *Yoga: Immortality and Freedom*, 202-06, 261, 272, 294-307; Adler, *Drawing Down the Moon*, 10-11, 22, 35-36, 84-86, 107-12.

9. Ibid.

10. R. C. Zaehner, *Our Savage God: The Perverse Use of Eastern Thought* (New York: Sheed and Ward, 1974), 57-58.

11. Ibid., 41.

12. Ibid., 42.

13. Ibid., 42-43.

14. Ibid.

15. Interview, *Rolling Stone*, Jun. 25, 1970.

16. Zaehner, *Our Savage God*, 43.

17. Vincent Bugliosi, *Helter Skelter* (New York: Bantam, 1969), 641.

18. Zaehner, *Our Savage God*, 56.

19. Ibid., 59; cf., Kahaner, *Cults That Kill*, passim.

20. Zaehner, *Our Savage God*, 72-73.

21. Ibid., 63, 65.

22. Ibid., 66-67.

23. Ibid., 60.

24. Ibid., 47.

25. Ibid., 71.

26. Mircea Eliade, *The Sacred and the Profane: The Nature of Religion* (New York: Harcourt Brace Jovanovich, 1959), 104.

27. Davies, *Human Sacrifice in History and Today*, cover jacket.

28. Ibid., 13.
29. Ibid., 15.
30. Ibid., 23.
31. Ibid., 21-22.
32. Ibid., 22.
33. Ibid., 24.
34. See Appendix E.
35. E.g., ibid., 26.
36. Ibid., 27.
37. Ibid., 288-89.
38. Ibid., 289.
39. *Los Angeles Times*, Jun. 15, 1986.
40. Terry, *The Ultimate Evil*, 511-12.

Chapter 7—What Occult Practitioners Say

1. Peck, *People of the Lie*, 104.
2. Cf., Raphael Gasson, *The Challenging Counterfeit* (South Plainfield, NJ: Bridge Publishing, 1966), 48.
3. Ibid.
4. Russ Parker, *Battling the Occult* (Downers Grove, IL: InterVarsity, 1990), 82.
5. Hereward Carrington, *Your Psychic Powers and How to Develop Them* (Van Nuys, CA: Newcastle, 1975 rpt.), 203.
6. Samuel M. Warren, *A Compendium of the Theological Writings of Emanuel Swedenborg* (New York: Swedenborg Foundation, 1977), 618; cf., Slater Brown, *The Heyday of Spiritualism* (New York: Pocket, 1972), 63.
7. J. D. Pearce-Higgins, "Dangers of Automatism," *Spiritual Frontiers*, Autumn 1970, 217.
8. Ibid., 221.
9. Ibid., 223.
10. William G. Gray, "Patterns of Western Magic" in Charles Tart, ed., *Transpersonal Psychologies* (New York: Harper & Row, 1977), 464-66.
11. Martin Ebon, "Psychic Roulette," *Psychic*, Dec. 1975, 56.
12. Ibid., 58.
13. Raymond Van Over, "Vampire and Demon Lover" in Martin Ebon, ed., *The Satan Trap: Dangers of the Occult* (Garden City, NY: Doubleday, 1976), 103.
14. Ibid., 108.
15. Gray, in Tart, *Transpersonal Psychologies*, 466.
16. Kurt Koch, *Occult ABC* (Grand Rapids, MI: Kregel, 1981), 275.
17. Paul Beard, "How to Guard Against Possession" in Ebon, "Psychic Roulette," 187.
18. Ibid., 186.
19. Ibid.
20. Alan Vaughan, "Phantoms Stalked the Room . . ." in Ebon, "Psychic Roulette," 155, 161.
21. Ibid., 162.
22. David Conway, *Magic: An Occult Primer* (New York: Bantam, 1973), 14.
23. Ibid., 180.
24. Ibid.
25. Ibid., 195-98.
26. For documentation on white magic from a Christian perspective see Kurt Koch, *Christian Counseling and Occultism* (Grand Rapids, MI: Kregel, 1972), 145-52; 192-94; and his *Between Christ and Satan* (Grand Rapids, MI: Kregel, n.d.), 65-78; also Merrill Unger, *Demons in the World Today*, Chapter 5.
27. Doreen Irvine, *Freed From Witchcraft* (Nashville, TN: Thomas Nelson, 1973), 102.

28. Koch, *Between Christ and Satan*, 89.
29. W. B. Crow, *A History of Magic, Witchcraft and Occultism* (North Hollywood, CA: Wilshire, 1968), 29.
30. In Fodor, *An Encyclopedia of Psychic Science*, 235.

Chapter 8—What Psychic Counselors Say
1. "News," *Parapsychology Review*, May-Jun. 1980, 11.
2. Eleanor Criswell and Laura Herzog, "Psychic Counseling," *Psychic*, Jan.-Feb. 1977, 46, and D. S. Rogo, "Mental Health Needs and the Psychic Community," *Parapsychology Review*, Mar.-Apr., 1981, 23.
3. L. E. Bartlett, "Second Thoughts," *Human Behavior*, Mar. 1978, 70.
4. Geneane Prevatt and Russ Park, "The Spiritual Emergence Network (SEN)," in Stanislav Grof and Christina Grof, eds., *Spiritual Emergency: When Personal Transformation Becomes a Crisis* (Los Angeles: Jeremy P. Tarcher, 1989), 227-28; Emma Bragdon, *A Source Book for Helping People in Spiritual Emergency* (Los Altos, CA: Emma Bragdon, 1987), passim.
5. Stanislav Grof and Christina Grof, eds., "Spiritual Emergency: Understanding Evolutionary Crisis," in Grof and Grof, *Spiritual Emergency*, 7.
6. Bragdon, *A Source Book*, 7-11.
7. Grof and Grof, "Spiritual Emergency: Understanding Evolutionary Crisis," in Grof and Grof, *Spiritual Emergency*, 13-14.
8. Ibid., 14.
9. Ibid., 15.
10. Ibid., 23.
11. Ibid., 24.
12. Ibid., 15.
13. Bragdon, *A Source Book*, 1.
14. Ibid., 7-11; cf. Grof and Grof, "Spiritual Emergency: Understanding Evolutionary Crisis," 15.
15. Grof and Grof, "Spiritual Emergency: Understanding Evolutionary Crisis," 25.
16. Eleanor Criswell and Laura Herzog, "Psychic Counseling," *Psychic*, Jan.-Feb. 1977, 44.
17. Ibid., 43, 45. A similar approach is endorsed by Freda Morris in "Emotional Reactions to Psychic Experiences," *Psychic*, Nov.-Dec. 1970, 27, 29.
18. Holger Kalweit, "When Insanity Is a Blessing: The Message of Shamanism," in Grof and Grof, "Spiritual Emergency: Understanding Evolutionary Crisis," 81-93; Lee Sennella, "Kundalini: Classical and Clinical," in Grof and Grof, "Spiritual Emergency: Understanding Evolutionary Crisis," 106-15.
19. Freda Morris, "Emotional Reactions to Psychic Experiences," *Psychic*, Nov.-Dec. 1970, 29.
20. In the words of D. Scott Rogo, "Mental Health Needs and the Psychic Community," *Parapsychology Review*, Mar.-Apr. 1981, 20-21.
21. Ibid., 19.
22. Weldon and Wilson, *Occult Shock and Psychic Forces*, Chapters 18, 21-30.
23. Irvine, *Freed From Witchcraft*, 96.
24. Roger Lauer, "A Medium for Mental Health," in Irving I. Zaretsky and Mark P. Leone, *Religious Movements in Contemporary America* (Princeton, NJ: Princeton Univ. Press, 1974), 353-54; cf. John Weldon and Zola Levitt, *Psychic Healing* (Dallas: Zola Levitt Ministries, 1991), 20-22 (for further examples).
25. E. J. Moody in Zaretsky and Leone, *Religious Movements in Contemporary America*, 380-82.
26. Rogo, "Mental Health Needs," 23.

Chapter 9—What Eastern Gurus Say
1. Brooks Alexander, "Book Review: *Riders of the Cosmic Circuit*," in *SCP Journal*, Vol. 7, No. 1, 1987, 39.
2. Bhagwan Shree Rajneesh in Swami Ananda Yarti, *The Sound of Running Water: A Photobiography of Bhagwan Sri Rajneesh and His Work 1974-1978* (Poona, India: Poona Rajneesh Foundation, 1980), 364.
3. Daniel Goleman, "The Buddha on Meditation and States of Consciousness" in Charles Tart, ed., *Transpersonal Psychologies* (New York: Harper Colophon Books, 1977), 218.
4. Swami Muktananda, *Play of Consciousness* (New York: Harper & Row, 1978), xxiii, 155-61.
5. Paramahansa Yogananda, *Autobiography of a Yogi* (Los Angeles: Self-Realization Fellowship, 1972), 16, 55-57, 132, 137, 190, 475-79.
6. Paramahansa Yogananda, "Where Are Our Departed Loved Ones?" in *Self-Realization* Magazine, Spring 1978, 6-7.
7. *Sri Aurobindo and the Mother on Occultism*, compiled by Vijay (Pondicherry, India: Sri Aurobindo Society, 1972), 17.
8. Sri Aurobindo, *A Practical Guide to Integral Yoga*, compiled by Manishai (Pondicherry, India: Sri Aurobindo Ashram, 1973), 273.
9. Chinmoy, *Astrology*, 62.
10. Ibid., 94, and Chinmoy, *Great Masters and Cosmic Gods* (Jamaica, NY: Agni Press, 1977), 8.
11. Meher Baba, *The Path of Love* (New York: Samuel Weiser, 1976), 44, 64, 138; C. D. Deshmukh, *Sparks of the Truth From the Dissertations of Meher Baba* (Crescent Beach, SC: Sheriar, 1973), 45; Meher Baba, *Listen Humanity*, D. E. Stevens, ed. (New York: Harper & Row, 1967), 100.
12. John Weldon, *Eastern Gurus in a Western Milieu: A Critique From the Perspective of Biblical Revelation*, Ph.D. dissertation, Pacific College of Graduate Studies, Melbourne Victoria, Australia, 1988.
13. Swami Muktananda, *Play of Consciousness* (New York: Harper & Row, 1978), 75-81, 84-85, 88-89.
14. Ram Dass, *The Only Dance There Is* (Garden City, NY: Anchor, 1974), 74-75.
15. Ram Dass, *Grist for the Mill* (New York: Bantam, 1979).
16. Serapis Bey, *Dossier on the Ascension*, recorded by Mark L. Prophet (Los Angeles: Summit University Press, 1979), 167.
17. Bubba Free John, *Garbage and the Goddess* (Lower Lake, CA: Dawn Horse Press, 1974), 154.
18. Ibid., 119-20.
19. Ibid., 4.
20. Ibid.
21. Ibid., 20.
22. Ibid., 47-48.
23. Ibid., 48-49.
24. Ibid., 263.
25. Ibid., 71-73.
26. Ibid., 82.
27. Brooke, *Riders of the Cosmic Circuit*, passim.
28. Fuernstein and Miller, *Yoga and Beyond*, p. 8.
29. Moti Lal Pandit, "Yoga As Methods of Liberation," in *Update: A Quarterly Journal on New Religious Movements* (Aarhus, Denmark: The Dialogue Center, Vol. 9, No. 4, Dec. 1985), 41.
30. John Ankerberg and John Weldon, *The Facts on the Occult* and *The Facts on Spirit Guides* (Eugene, OR: Harvest House, 1991).

31. Swami Prabhavananda, *Yoga and Mysticism* (Hollywood, CA: Vedanta Press, 1972), 18-19.
32. Bhagwan Shree Patanjali (translation and commentary by Shree Purohit Swami), *Aphorisms of Yoga* (London: Faber & Faber, 1972), 56-57.
33. E.g., Ernest Wood, *Seven Schools of Yoga: An Introduction* (Wheaton, IL: Theosophical Publishing House, 1973), 77, 79.
34. Chinmoy, *Astrology*, 53-68, 87-89; Chinmoy, *Conversations With the Master*, 9-20, 26-33.
35. Chinmoy, *Great Masters and the Cosmic Gods*, 8.
36. Ulrich-Rieker, *The Yoga of Light*, 9, 134.
37. Krishna, "The True Aim of Yoga," *Psychic* magazine, Jan.-Feb. 1973, 13.
38. Ulrich-Rieker, *The Yoga of Light*, 79.
39. Sri Krishna Prem, *The Yoga of the Bhagavat Gita* (Baltimore: Penguin, 1973), xv.
40. Ibid., 47.
41. Prabhavananda, *Yoga and Mysticism*, 18-19.
42. Ulrich-Rieker, *Yoga*, 30, 79, 96, 111-12.
43. Wood, *Seven Schools*, 14.

Chapter 10—What Theologians Say

1. Kurt Koch, *Occult ABC* (West Germany: Literature Mission Aglasterhausen, Inc., 1980), 282.
2. Kurt Koch, *Occult Bondage and Deliverance* (Grand Rapids, MI: Kregel, 1970), 32.
3. Ibid., 30.
4. Ibid.
5. G. L. Playfair, *The Unknown Power* (New York: Simon & Schuster, 1975), 271.
6. Hans Holzer, *Beyond Medicine* (New York: Ballantine, 1974), 45.
7. J. B. Rhine and Louise E. Rhine, "Automatic Writing and the Ouija Board" (Durham, NC: Foundation for the Research of Man, Spring 1969), Bulletin #12.
8. Ian Stevenson, "Some Comments on Automatic Writing," *ASPR* [American Society of Psychical Research] *Newsletter*, Jan. 1979, Vol. 5, No. 1, 3.
9. Kurt Koch, *Christian Counseling and Occultism* (Grand Rapids, MI: Kregel, 1972), 184-85.
10. Ibid., 188.
11. Koch, *Occult Bondage and Deliverance*, 33-38.
12. Kurt Koch, *Between Christ and Satan* (Grand Rapids, MI: Kregel, 1962), 49-50.
13. Ibid., 102.
14. Ibid., 120.
15. Available from Kregel Publishing, Grand Rapids, MI.
16. Merrill Unger, *Demons in the World Today* (Wheaton, IL: Tyndale, 1972), 50.
17. Merrill Unger, *The Haunting of Bishop Pike* (Wheaton, IL: Tyndale, 1971), 89-90.
18. Unger, *Demons in the World Today*, passim; Unger, *What Demons Can Do to Saints* (Chicago, IL: Moody Press, 1977), passim.
19. John W. Montgomery, *Principalities and Powers* (Minneapolis, MN: Bethany, 1973), 149.
20. E.g., C. Fred Dickason, *Demon Possession and the Christian* (Chicago, IL: Moody, 1987), 191-93, 207-21.
21. Ibid., 221.
22. Clifford Wilson, *The Occult Explosion* (San Diego, CA: Master Books, 1980), 22.
23. In Koch, *Occult Bondage and Deliverance*, 137.

Chapter 11—Suicide, Murder, and Death

1. Koch, *Occult ABC*, 278.
2. Ibid.

3. Irvine, *Freed From Witchcraft*, 121.
4. Unger, *What Demons Can Do to Saints*, 54.
5. Morton Kelsey, *The Christian and the Supernatural* (Minneapolis, MN: Augsburg, 1976), 41.
6. J. D. Pearce-Higgins, "Dangers of Automatism," *Spiritual Frontiers*, Autumn 1970, 216.
7. Hans Bender, "Psychosis in the Seance Room," in Ebon, *The Satan Trap*, 232-36.
8. Ibid.
9. Ernest, *I Talked With Spirits*, 60.
10. E.g., cf. Ramond Van Over, "Vampire and Demon Lover," in Ebon, *The Satan Trap*, 109; Leslie Shepard, *Encyclopedia of Occultism and Parapsychology*, Vol. 2 (Detroit, MI: Yale Research, 1979), 63; Elliot O'Donnell, *The Menace of Spiritualism* (New York: F. A. Stokes Co., 1920), XII, 105-06.
11. Edmond Gruss, *The Ouija Board: Doorway to the Occult* (Chicago, IL: Moody Press, 1975), 86-87. In "The Ouija Board Temptation," in Ebon, *The Satan Trap*, 172, Kent Jordan refers to a similar case; see also Stoker Hunt, *The Ouija: A Most Dangerous Game*; cf., *The Fortean Times*, No. 52, 34; Maury Terry, *The Ultimate Evil*; *The Chicago Tribune*, May 6, 1981; *The Los Angeles Times*, Jun. 20, 1984.
12. Pedro McGreggor, *Jesus of the Spirits* (New York: Stein & Day, 1960), 199.
13. Fodor, *Encyclopedia of Psychic Science*, 266.
14. Ibid., 292.
15. Koch, *Between Christ and Satan*, 81; J. Halifax-Grof, "Hex-Death," *Parapsychology Review*, Sep.-Oct. 1974, 20.
16. Koch, *Between Christ and Satan*, 81.
17. Moody Press, a compilation, *Demon Experiences in Many Lands* (Chicago, IL: Moody Press, 1960), 22.
18. Koch, *Between Christ and Satan*, 79.
19. Ibid., 83-84.
20. John Keel, *Our Haunted Planet* (Greenwich, CT: Fawcett, 1971), 128.
21. Jacques Vallee, *Passport to Magonia* (Chicago, IL: Henry Regnery Co., 1969), 131-32.
22. Jack Roper, *A Sorcery Iceberg in America* (Milwaukee, WI: CARIS, 1985), introduction.
23. Kahaner, *Cults That Kill*, viii.
24. Bob Larson, *Satanism*, 201; Parker, *Battling the Occult*, 16-17; cf. John Weldon and James Bjornstad, *Playing With Fire* (Chicago, IL: Moody, 1984).
25. Parker, *Battling the Occult*, 16-17.
26. Ibid., 17.
27. Ibid., 35-36.
28. *The Washington Post*, Mar. 30, 1984.
29. *Christianity Today*, Dec. 5, 1978, 38; Hunt, *Cult Explosion*, 157; *The Los Angeles Times*, Nov. 24, 1978.
30. Dave Hunt, *The Cult Explosion*, 221.
31. *The Los Angeles Times*, Jan. 19, 1981.
32. Fodor, *Encyclopedia of Psychic Science*, 237.
33. Gasson, *The Challenging Counterfeit*, 87.
34. Brennan, *Astral Doorways*, 9.
35. Unger, *Biblical Demonology*, 95.

Chapter 12—Psychiatric Illness and Related Problems

1. Koch, *Occult ABC*, 272, 274.
2. In Kahaner, *Cults That Kill*, 59; cf., Georgio Alberti, "Psychopathology and Parapsychology—Some Possible Contacts," *Parapsychology Review*, May-Jun. 1973, 11;

cf. Fodor, *Encyclopedia of Psychic Science*, 234-35; the cited writings of Kurt Koch, and Doreen Irvine (*Freed From Witchcraft*), spiritists converted to Christian faith (e.g., Gasson), and the studies on Satanism cited in Chapter 5 document the psychological disturbances.

3. Koch, *Occult Bondage*, 31.
4. Koch, *Demonology, Past and Present*, 41-42.
5. D. Scott Rogo, "Mental Health Needs and the Psychic Community," *Parapsychology Review*, Mar.-Apr. 1981, 20.
6. Ibid.
7. John Dart, "Peril in Occult Demonic Encounters Cited," *Los Angeles Times*, Dec. 30, 1977.
8. Ibid.
9. A. M. Ludwig, "Altered States of Consciousness," in Charles Tart, ed., *Altered States of Consciousness* (Garden City, NY: Anchor, 1972), 16.
10. Elsa First, "Visions, Voyages and New Interpretations of Madness," in John White, ed., *Frontiers of Consciousness* (New York: Avon, 1975), 65.
11. Wanda Parrott, "Inside the Psychic Jungle," in Ebon, *The Satan Trap*, 67.
12. Irvine, *Freed From Witchcraft*, 95.
13. Cited by Martin Ebon in *Fate* Magazine, Feb. 1971, 104; cf., Albert W. Potts, Jr., "ESP or Madness," *Spiritual Frontiers*, Summer 1972, 143-44.
14. R. Ashby, "The Guru Syndrome," in Ebon, *The Satan Trap*, 39-40.
15. Raymond Van Over, "Vampire and Demon Lover," in Ebon, *The Satan Trap*, 110.
16. Anita Muhl, *Automatic Writing: An Approach to the Subconscious* (New York: Helix, 1963), 42.
17. Ibid., 45.
18. Ibid., 48.
19. Ibid., 51-52, 87, 163.
20. Ibid., 170.
21. Seymour Boorstein, ed., *Transpersonal Psychotherapy* (Palo Alto, CA: Science and Behavior Books, 1980); Charles Tart, ed., *Transpersonal Psychologies* (New York: Harper Colophon, 1977); cf., Robert Monroe, *Far Journeys*, 22-25; Roger N. Walsh and Frances Vaughan, *Beyond Ego: Transpersonal Dimensions in Psychology* (Los Angeles: J. P. Tarcher, 1980).

Chapter 13—Sexual Immorality and Other Personal and Social Consequences

1. Unger, *Demons in the World Today*, 28, cf. 72.
2. Channel 7 Eyewitness News, KABC-TV, Feb. 1986.
3. John Symonds and Kenneth Grant, *The Confessions of Aleister Crowley: An Autobiography* (New York: Bantam, 1971), 517, opposite picture.
4. Bhagwan Shree Rajneesh, *I Am the Gate: The Meaning of Initiation and Discipleship* (New York: Parenial, 1978), 16.
5. Bhagwan Shree Rajneesh, *The Book of the Secrets: Discourses on "Vigyana Bhairava Tanra"* (New York: Harper Colophon, 1977), Vol. 1, 22, 36-37.
6. Rajneesh, *Book of Secrets I*, 399, cf. Rajneesh, *The Mustard Seed: Discourses on the Sayings of Jesus Taken From the Gospel According to Thomas* (New York: Harper & Row, 1975), 69.
7. Letter to the editor, *Radix* magazine, Nov.-Dec. 1976, 2.
8. William Rodamar, "The Secret Life of Swami Muktananda," in *Co-Evolution Quarterly*, Winter 1983, 110.
9. Swami Muktananda, *Siddha Meditation: Commentaries on the Shiva Sutras and Other Sacred Texts* (Oakland, CA: Siddha Yoga Dham of America Foundation, 1975), 34; Swami Muktananda, *Mukteshwari*, Part 2 (Ganeshpuri, India: Shree Gurudev Ashram, 1973), 29.

10. Personal conversation with devotee.
11. Sita Wiener, *Swami Stachidananda* (San Francisco: Straight Arrow Books, 1970), 156.
12. Personal conversation with devotee.
13. Paramahansa Yogananda, *Man's Eternal Quest* (Los Angeles: Self-Realization Fellowship, 1975), 332.
14. Bhagwan Shree Rajneesh in Swami Anand Yarti, *The Sound of Running Water: A Photobiography of Bhagwan Shree Rajneesh and His Work 1974-1978* (Poona, India: Poona Rajneesh Foundation, 1980), 382.
15. Bhagwan Shree Rajneesh, *The Rajneesh Bible*, Vol. 1 (Rajneeshpuram, OR: Rajneesh Foundation International, 1985), 368.
16. Bhagwan Shree Rajneesh, "I Am the Messiah Here and Now," in *Sannyas*, Sept.-Oct. 1978, 34.
17. Bhagwan Shree Rajneesh in Yarti, *Sound*, 153.
18. Swami Adbhutananda, "Brahman and Maya," in Christopher Isherwood, ed., *Vedanta for the Western World* (New York: Viking, 1968), 160.
19. Swami Nikhilananda, *Vivekananda, the Yogas and Other Works* (New York: Ramakrishna-Vivekananda Center, 1953), 512.
20. Rajneesh in Ma Satya Bharti, *Drunk on the Divine: An Account of Life in the Ashram of Bhagwan Shree Rajneesh* (New York: Grove Press, 1981), 35.
21. Da Free John, *Garbage and the Goddess*, 32-33.
22. Sri Krishna Prem, *The Yoga of the Bhagavad Gita* (Baltimore, MD: Penguin, 1973), 53; Arthur Avalon (Sir John Woodroffe), *The Serpent Power: The Secrets of Tantric and Shaktic Yoga* (New York: Dover, 1974), 190.
23. *Fate* Magazine, Feb. 1971, 103.
24. Wanda Sue Parrott, "Inside the Psychic Jungle," in Ebon, *The Satan Trap*, 73.
25. William Rodamor, "The Secret Life of Swami Muktananda," *Coevolution Quarterly*, No. 40, Winter 1983.
26. Ibid., 110.
27. Editorial, "Perils of the Path" Issue, *Yoga Journal*, Jul.-Aug. 1985, 3.
28. Jack Kornfield, "Sex Lives of the Gurus," *Yoga Journal*, Jul.-Aug. 1985, 28.
29. Ibid., 27.
30. Ibid., 27-28.
31. Ibid., 28.
32. Brooks Alexander, "Book Review: *Riders of the Cosmic Circuit*," *SCP Journal*, Vol. 7. No. 1, 1987, 39.
33. *The San Francisco Chronicle*, Apr. 3-4, 1985.
34. *Kaushitaki Upanishad*, 3.1-2.
35. Maharishi Mahesh Yogi, *On the Bhagavad Gita: A New Translation and Commentary*, Chapters 1-6 (Baltimore, MD: Penguin, 1974), 76.
36. See Vincent Bugliosi, *Helter Skelter* (New York: Bantam, 1969), 624 and "Charles Manson: Portrait in Terror," Feb. 16, 1976, Channel 7, KABC-TV Los Angeles, 11:30 P.M., interview with Bugliosi.
37. Bugliosi, *Helter Skelter*, 327, 330.
38. Ibid., 129.
39. Stanislav and Christina Grof, "Spiritual Emergency: Understanding Evolutionary Crisis," in Stanislav and Christina Grof, *Spiritual Emergency: When a Personal Transformation Becomes a Crisis* (Los Angeles: J. P. Tarcher, 1989), 21.
40. Ernest, *I Talked With Spirits*, 38.
41. Emma Harding, *Modern American Spiritualism* (New Hyde Park, NY: University Books, 1970), 208.
42. Nandor Fodor, *The Haunted Mind: The Psychoanalyst Looks at the Supernatural* (New York: Signet, 1968), 184.

43. Keel, *Our Haunted Planet*, 160.
44. M. Lamar Keene as told to Allen Spraggett in *The Psychic Mafia* (New York: St. Martin's, 1976), 133.
45. Ibid., 140.
46. Interview in Harold Sherman, *Your Power to Heal* (Greenwich, CT: Fawcett, 1973), 154-55.
47. Ibid.
48. Carolee Collins, "Reincarnation as Alibi" in Ebon, *The Satan Trap*, 140.
49. Ibid., 135-36.
50. Raymond Van Over, "Vampire and Demon Lover" in Ebon, *The Satan Trap*, 107.
51. Thanks to Edmond Gruss for this article.
52. John Weldon, *Psychic Healing* (Dallas: Zola Levitt Ministries, 1991), 20-21; cf. *Human Behavior*, Sep. 1977, pp. 18-27. *The Los Angeles Times*, Oct. 15, 1979, and several other newspapers carried an exposé of the purported sexual activity. See also Frances Adney, "Hope and Reincarnation: Elizabeth Kubler Ross and Life After Death" *SCP Newsletter*, Aug.-Sep. 1982.
53. Fodor, *An Encyclopedia of Psychic Science*, 234; cf. Crow, *A History of Magic, Witchcraft and Occultism*, 248-49; Vallee, *Passport to Magonia*, 116-29; Unger, *Demons in the World Today*, 32.
54. Doreen Valiente, *An ABC of Witchcraft Past and Present* (New York: St. Martins, 1973), 200-01.
55. Vallee, *Passport to Magonia*, 117 (cf. 116-29).
56. According to the Arts and Entertainment Network Investigative Reports series "Sins of the Fathers" (Jan. 1993), 400-500 Catholic priests have been charged with pedophilia and sources cited on the program estimated 25 to 50 percent of priests were homosexually inclined. See the book *Lead Us Not Into Temptation* by Jason Berry (New York: Doubleday, 1992).
57. Keel, *Our Haunted Planet*, 161; Hans Holzer, "The Strangest Case of All" (Chapter 8), *The UFO Nauts*. A number of cases have been listed in the British journal, *Flying Saucer Review*.
58. Koch, *Christian Counseling and Occultism*, 162-63.
59. Ibid., 164.
60. Unger, *Demons in the World Today*, 32.
61. Fodor, *The Haunted Mind*, 180. Many people today are skeptical of the very idea of the incubus/succubus under the assumption that spirits cannot assume tangible form. But the history of the occult shows this to be false. In addition, there are many incubus/succubus experiences associated with poltergeist phenomena. Robert Curran's book *The Haunted: One Family's Nightmare* recounts a contemporary example of an incident with a succubus (a devil that rapes a man). In this case, Jack Smurl of West Pittston, Pennsylvania, who had moved with his family into a house inhabited by a poltergeist, was attacked by a succubus. Smurl described the succubus as a woman "around 65 or 70" with "serpentine-snake-like scales" who paralyzed him in some way, had sexual intercourse with him, and left him covered with a pungent, sticky fluid. The demonic nature of the poltergeist was seen not only in its stench, but also in its destructive ability, its desire to harm people, its aversion to Christian items, and also in its sexual activity.
62. Unger, *Demons in the World Today*, 99, citing Brad Steiger, *Sex and Satanism* (New York: Ace, 1969).
63. Irvine, *Freed From Witchcraft*, 90-91, 96.
64. Cited in M. Gaddis, "Teachers of Delusion" in Ebon, *The Satan Trap*, 57.
65. R. J. Rushdoony in "Symposium on Satanism," *Journal of Christian Reconstruction*, Vol. 1, No. 2, Winter 1974, 190-91.
66. Freda Morris, "Emotional Reactions to Psychic Experiences," *Psychic*, Vol. 2, No. 5, 26-30.

67. Robert Monroe, *Journeys Out of the Body* (Garden City, NY: Anchor, 1971), 120; cf., Robert Monroe, *Far Journeys* (Garden City, NY: Dolphin, 1985).
68. Ibid., 127.
69. Ibid., 204.
70. Yogi, *On the Bhagavad Gita*, 157; cf., 212; Maharishi Mahesh Yogi, *Transcendental Meditation* (New York: Signet, 1968), 183; cf. 224-25.
71. R. C. Zaehner, *Zen Drugs and Mysticism* (New York: Vintage, 1974), 162.
72. Bob Brier, "The Consolidated Athletic Commission," in Ebon, *The Satan Trap*, 134.

Chapter 14—Hereditary Coherence and Other Forms of Transference

1. Marian Nester, "Dear ASPR," *The Christian Parapsychologist*, March 1980, 191.
2. Ibid, 191-95.
3. For examples, see Fay E. Levine, *The Strange World of the Hare Krishnas* (Greenwich, CT: Fawcett, Gold Medal, 1974), 151-52; Earlyne Chaney, *The Masters and Astara: The Great Work of the Penetralia*, Book One, (Upland, CA: Astara, Inc., 1976), 37.
4. Koch, *Christian Counseling and Occultism*, 117-18.
5. Ibid., 131-35.
6. Parker, *Battling the Occult*, 86, 98-99.
7. Fodor, *Encyclopedia of Psychic Science*, 233.
8. The editors of *Psychic* magazine, *Psychics: In Depth Interviews* (New York: Harper & Row, 1972), 16, 35, 47, 68, 79, 113, 104.
9. Ibid., 1, 31, 47-49, 81, 96.
10. Martin Ebon, *Demon Children* (New York: Signet, 1978), 2, 6, 10, 74 with, 25, 60, 91-92, 108-09; cf., Samuel H. Young, *Psychic Children* (Garden City, NY: Doubleday, 1977).
11. Fodor, *Encyclopedia of Psychic Science*, 234.
12. Koch, *Christian Counseling and Occultism*, 138-39.
13. Parker, *Battling the Occult*, 98.
14. Tal Brooke, *Riders of the Cosmic Circuit* (Berkeley, CA: Spiritual Counterfeits Project, 1991).
15. John Weldon and Zola Levitt, *Psychic Healing* (Chicago, IL: Moody Press, 1984).
16. Samuel Sandweiss, *The Holy Man and the Psychiatrist* (San Diego, CA: Birth Day Publishing, 1975), 220, 222.
17. Michaelsen, *The Beautiful Side of Evil*, 88, cf. 13.
18. Rudi (Swami Rudrananda), *Spiritual Cannibalism* (Woodstock, NY: Overlook, 1978), 20.
19. Ibid., 103.
20. Ibid., 13.
21. Personal correspondence, May 28, 1981.
22. Fodor, *Encyclopedia of Psychic Science*, 236-37.
23. Koch, *Demonology Past and Present*, 62.
24. Karagulla, *Breakthrough to Creativity*, 95.
25. Martin Ebon, "Jung's First Medium," *Psychic*, May-Jun. 1976, 43.
26. Fodor, *Encyclopedia of Psychic Science*, 238.
27. Koch, *Christian Counseling and Occultism*, 41.
28. Unger, *Demons in the World Today*, 81-82.
29. Koch, *Occult Bondage and Deliverance*, 138-39.
30. Hereward Carrington, *Your Psychic Powers and How to Develop Them* (Van Nuys, CA: New Castle, 1975), 67-68.
31. *Psychic* magazine, Nov.-Dec., 1970, 28-29.
32. N. Kasturi, *Sathyam-Shiram-Sundaram (Part II): The Life of Bhagwan Sri Sathya Sri Baba* (Brindavan, Whitefield, Bangalore, India: Sri Sath Sai Publication and Education Foundation, 1973), 78-83.

Chapter 15—Physical Harm, Disease, and Torture by the Spirits
1. The editors of *Psychic* magazine, *Psychics*, 16-17; cf. Arthur Ford's autobiography, *Unknown But Known: My Adventure Into the Meditative Dimension* (New York: Harper & Row, 1968); cf. Unger, *The Haunting of Bishop Pike* for a detailed account, and Keene, *The Psychic Mafia*, who provides examples, 142; also R. K. McAll, "Taste and See" in Montgomery, *Demon Possession*, 274.
2. Susy Smith, "ESP and Drugs" in Ebon, *The Satan Trap*, 122.
3. Joseph Millard, *Edgar Cayce: Man of Miracles* (Greenwich, CT: Fawcett Gold Medal, 1967), 98, 104-08, 115-16, 198-201.
4. Mary Lutyens, *Krishnamurti: The Years of Awakening* (New York: Avon, 1976).
5. Carrington, *Your Psychic Powers and How to Develop Them*, 62.
6. Fodor, *Encyclopedia of Psychic Science*, 235.
7. Henry Gris and William Dick, *The New Soviet Psychic Discoveries* (Englewood Cliffs, NJ: Prentice-Hall, 1978), 28-29, 31.
8. Lutyens, *Krishnamurti*, 178-93.
9. Gris and Dick, *New Soviet Psychic Discoveries*, 34-35.
10. Fodor, *Encyclopedia of Psychic Science*, 234.
11. Ibid., 85, 219; cf., Arthur Conan Doyle, *The History of Spiritualism* (New York: Arno, 1975), Vol. 1, 278.
12. Fodor, *The Haunted Mind*, 183.
13. Fodor, *Encyclopedia of Psychic Science*, 84-85.
14. Gasson, *The Challenging Counterfeit*, 130.
15. Aleister Crowley, *Magic in Theory and Practice* (New York: Castel, n.d.), 152-53; J. Symonds and K. Grant, *The Confessions of Aleister Crowley* (New York: Bantam, 1971), 575-76.
16. Symonds and Grant, ibid., 165, citing Dennis Wheatley, *The Devil and All His Works* (New York: American Heritage Press, 1971).
17. Fodor, *Encyclopedia of Psychic Science*, 237.
18. Whitley Strieber, *Transformation: The Breakthrough* (New York, William Morrow, 1988), 44-45.
19. J. M. Rodwell, trans., The Koran (New York: Dutton, 1977), 64; cf., 5, 8, and W. Miller, *A Christian Response to Islam* (Nutley, NJ: Presbyterian Reform, 1977), 19-20.
20. Thomas Sugrue, *There Is a River* (New York: Dell, 1970), 210.
21. Andrija Puharich, *Uri* (New York: Bantam), 173, 188-89.
22. Penny Torres in *Holistic Life* Magazine, Summer 1985, 30; cf., Laeh Garfield, *Companions in Spirit: A Guide to Working With Your Spirit Helpers* (Berkeley, CA: Celestial Arts, 1984), 92-93.
23. John Symonds and Kenneth Grant, eds., *The Confessions of Aleister Crowley: An Autobiography* (New York: Bantam, 1971), 1-18.
24. Michaelsen, *The Beautiful Side of Evil*, 123.
25. Ibid., 134-35.
26. Holger Kalweit, "When Insanity Is a Blessing: The Message of Shamanism," in Grof and Grof, *Spiritual Emergence*, 81.
27. Ibid., 83.
28. Lee Sannella, "Kundalini: Classical and Clinical," in Grof and Grof, *Spiritual Emergence*, 106.
29. Kalweit, "When Insanity Is a Blessing," 95-96.
30. Joseph Millard, *Edgar Cayce: Mystery Man of Miracles* (Greenwich, CT: Fawcett, 1967), 52, 64, passim; cf., Thomas Sugrue, *There Is a River: The Story of Edgar Cayce* (New York: Dell, 1977), 210, 220-21.
31. Kalweit, "When Insanity Is a Blessing," 91.
32. Fodor, *Encyclopedia of Psychic Science*, 235.

33. Koch, *Occult ABC*, 238.
34. Ibid., 278.
35. Norma Bowles and Fran Hynds, *Psi-Search* (San Francisco, CA: Harper & Row, 1978), 89.
36. D. Scott Rogo, *Parapsychology: A Century of Inquiry* (New York: Dell, 1976), 66.
37. J. G. Bennett, *Gurdjieff: Making a New World* (New York: Harper & Row, 1973), 160; John G. Fuller, *Arigo: Surgeon of the Rusty Knife* (New York: Pocket, 1975), 237; William Branham, *Footprints in the Sands of Time: The Autobiography of William Marion Branham* (Jeffersonville, IN: Spoken Word, 1976), 705.
38. Lutyens, *Krishnamurti*, 302.
39. Da Free John, *The Enlightenment of the Whole Body* (Middletown, CA: Dawn Horse Press, 1978), 14.
40. Lutyens, *Krishnamurti*, 308.
41. John Weldon and Zola Levitt, *The Transcendental Explosion* (Eugene, OR: Harvest House, 1975), Chapter 5, pp. 121, 156, 161, 163 for documentation.
42. Swami Bhakita Vishita, *Genuine Mediumship* (n.p.p.: Yoga Publication Society, n.d.), 262, rpt. 1919 ed.
43. Vincent Gaddis, *Mysterious Fires and Lights* (New York: Van Rees Press, 1967), Chapters 12, 14, 15; John Mitchell and Robert J. M. Rickard, *Phenomena: A Book of Wonders* (New York: Pantheon, 1977), 34-35.
44. Gary North, *None Dare Call It Witchcraft* (New Rochelle, NY: Arlington House, 1976), 7-8.
45. M. Gaddis in Ebon, *The Satan Trap*, 122, 208.
46. Carrington, *Your Psychic Powers*, 200-01.
47. Fodor, *Encyclopedia of Psychic Science*, 265-66.

Chapter 16—Fraud

1. Fodor, *Encyclopedia of Psychic Science*, 148.
2. Ibid., 149.
3. Weldon and Levitt, *Psychic Healing*, Chapters 6-7.
4. Ibid.
5. *New York Times*, Mar. 6, 1970.
6. Kent Jordan, "The Ouija Board Temptation," in Ebon, *The Satan Trap*, 173-74.
7. Margaret Gaddis, "Teachers of Delusion," in Ebon, *The Satan Trap*, 61.
8. Fodor, *Encyclopedia of Psychic Science*, 274.
9. Ibid.
10. Carrington, *Your Psychic Powers*, 292.
11. Fodor, *Encyclopedia of Psychic Science*, 148.
12. Danny Korem and Paul Meier, *The Fakers* (Grand Rapids, MI: Baker, 1980); Danny Korem, *Powers: Testing the Psychic and Supernatural* (Downers Grove, IL: InterVarsity, 1988).
13. Korem, *Powers*, 168.
14. Keene, *The Psychic Mafia*, 150.
15. Ibid., 16.
16. Ibid., 71.
17. Gasson, *The Challenging Counterfeit*, 131-32.
18. Keene, *The Psychic Mafia*, 147-48.
19. Ibid., 141-42.
20. Ibid., 153.
21. Ibid., 156.
22. Ibid., 156-57.
23. Ibid., 159.

Chapter 17—Spiritual Deception, Destruction, and Deliverance
1. Jane Roberts, *The Seth Material* (New York: Bantam, 1976), 6.
2. Sally Hammond, *We Are All Healers* (New York: Harper & Row, 1973), 149.
3. Guy Playfair, *The Unknown Power* (New York: Simon & Schuster, 1975), 166.
4. David Conway, *Magic: An Occult Primer* (New York: Bantam, 1973), 22.
5. Robert A. Monroe, *Journeys Out of the Body* (Garden City, NY: Anchor, 1973), 22.
6. Ibid., 262.
7. Wanda Parrott, "Inside the Psychic Jungle," in Ebon, *The Satan Trap*, 80-81.
8. Cited in Edmond C. Gruss, *The Ouija Board* (Chicago, IL: Moody, 1975), 80-81.
9. Ibid., 79-80.
10. Koch, *Occult Bondage and Deliverance*, 133-90.
11. Ibid., 87-88.
12. Ibid., 90.
13. Ibid., 92.
14. Ibid., 93.
15. Ibid., 94.
16. Ibid., 126.
17. Ibid., 98.
18. Ibid., 99.
19. Ibid.
20. Ibid., 100.
21. Ibid., 100-01.
22. Ibid., 101.
23. Ibid., 102.
24. Irvine, *Freed From Witchcraft*, passim.
25. Koch, *Demonology Past and Present*, 106.
26. Ibid., 105.
27. Ibid.
28. Ibid., 119.
29. Ibid., 120.
30. Ibid., 124.
31. Ibid., 128.

Appendix A—Biblical Warnings Against Occult Involvement
1. Brooks Alexander, "What Is Spiritism . . . and Why Are They Saying Those Awful Things About It?" (Berkeley, CA: Spiritual Counterfeits Project, 1986), 3.

Appendix B—The Teachings of the Spirits
1. Jon Klimo, *Channeling: Investigations on Receiving Information From Paranormal Sources* (Los Angeles: Tarcher, 1987), 151, 173.
2. Jane Roberts, *The Seth Material* (New York: Bantam, 1976), 270.
3. Robert E. Leichtman and Carl Japikse, *The Life of the Spirit* (Columbus, OH: Ariel, 1987), Vol. 1, 137-38, 146-53.
4. White Eagle Publishing Trust, *Wisdom From White Eagle* (Liss, Hampshire, England: 1978), 26.
5. Leichtman and Japikse, *The Life of the Spirit*, Vol. 1, 83-84.
6. Ibid., 138, 141.
7. Ibid., 149.
8. Ibid., 184.
9. E.g., ibid., 83-87.
10. Ibid., Vol. 2, 43.
11. Ibid., 41-42, 67-69.
12. Colin Wilson, *The Occult: A History* (New York: Vintage, 1973), 523.

13. Leichtman and Japikse, *The Life of the Spirit*, Vol. 1, 67.
14. The Christ, *New Teachings For an Awakened Humanity* (Santa Clara, CA: S.E.E. Publishing, 1987), 2, 21, 35, 51, 53, 62, 72, 82, 92-5, 139, 188.

Appendix C—Occult Criminality
1. Patricia Weaver, "Ritual Abuse, Pornography and the Occult," *SCP Newletter*, Vol. 14, No. 4, 1989, 3.
2. Ibid.

Appendix D—Magical Implements
1. Koch, *Between Christ and Satan*, 89; cf. Chapter 4.
2. G. W. Peters, "Demonism on the Mission Fields" in Montgomery, *Demon Possession*, 199-201.
3. Koch, *Christian Counseling in Occultism*, 161.

Appendix G—Where Do We Find a Scorecard?
1. Gasson, *The Challenging Counterfeit*, Chapter 10.
2. Fodor, *Encyclopedia of Psychic Science*, 132-33.
3. Satprem, *Sri Aurobindo or the Adventure of Consciousness* (New York: Harper & Row, 1974), 199; cf., 197, 201.
4. Conway, *Magic: An Occult Primer*, 196.
5. Monroe, *Journeys Out of the Body*, 138-39.
6. Michaelsen, *The Beautiful Side of Evil*, 77.
7. Ibid.
8. Roberts, *The Seth Material*, 194-95.
9. Michaelsen, *The Beautiful Side of Evil*, 102.
10. John Ankerberg and John Weldon, *Everything You Ever Wanted to Know About Mormonism* (Eugene, OR: Harvest House, 1992).
11. Ibid., passim.
12. Paramahansa Yogananda in *Self Realization* magazine, Summer 1976, 8-9.
13. Arthur Ford, *The Life Beyond Death* (New York: G. P. Putnam, 1971), 147; Yogananda's disciples have also exerted their influence, e.g., Swami Kriyananda founded The Yoga Fellowship; Roy Eugene Davis, The Center for Spiritual Awareness.
14. Gasson, *The Challenging Counterfeit*, 123-25.
15. Michaelsen, *The Beautiful Side of Evil*, 148.
16. Gasson, *The Challenging Counterfeit*, 83.
17. Ibid., 29.
18. Ernest, *I Talked With Spirits*, 59-60.
19. Irvine, *Freed From Witchcraft*, 94-95.
20. Ibid., 95.
21. Ibid., 133-34.
22. Ibid., 54-55.
23. Ibid., 101-02.

Appendix H—Demonization of Christians: Pros and Cons
1. John Weldon, *Eternal Security*, ms.
2. C. Fred Dickason, *Demon Possession and the Christian* (Chicago, IL: Moody, 1987), 37.
3. Thomas Ice, "Demon Possession and the New Clinical Deliverance," *Biblical Perspectives*, May/Jun. 1992, 3.
4. Dickason, *Demon Possession and the Christian*, 185.
5. Ibid., 94.
6. Ibid., 95.

7. Ibid., 99.
8. Ibid., Chapters 8-11.
9. Irvine, *Freed From Witchcraft*, 7, 112-38.
10. Mark I. Bubeck, *The Adversary* (Chicago, IL: Moody, 1975), 144-45.
11. Summarized in William P. Wilson, "Hysteria and Demons, Depression and Oppression, Good and Evil" in J. W. Montgomery, *Demon Possession*, 224.
12. Koch, *Demonology Past and Present*, 85.
13. Parker, *Battling the Occult*, 71.
14. Ibid., 72.
15. Bubeck, *The Adversary*, 140-44,
16. Parker, *Battling the Occult*, 82.
17. Ibid., 86.
18. Ibid., 144.
19. Ibid., 119.
20. Gary Collins, "Psychological Observations on Demonism," in Montgomery, *Demon Possession*, 246.
21. Dickason, *Demon Possession and the Christian*, 278.
22. Parker, *Battling the Occult*, 148.

Index

Other Books by
John Ankerberg and
John Weldon

The Facts on ... Series:

Astrology
Creation vs. Evolution
Faith Movement, the
False Teaching in the Church
Hinduism in America
Holistic Health
Islam
Jehovah's Witnesses, the
Jesus the Messiah
Life After Death

Masonic Lodge, the
Mind Sciences, the
Mormon Church, the
New Age Movement, the
Occult, the
Rock Music
Roman Catholicism
Sex Education
Spirit Guides
UFO's and Other Supernatural
   Phenomena

CULT WATCH

Cult Watch provides historical backgrounds and vital facts on the major beliefs of modern religious movements and looks closely at the reasons people become entrapped in them. Drawing from years of research and interaction with representatives of each movement, the authors offer penetrating analysis of how each religious system clearly contrasts with the essential doctrines of biblical Christianity.

EVERYTHING YOU EVER WANTED TO KNOW ABOUT MORMONISM

Like no book before it, this definitive work covers every aspect of the history, beliefs, and practices of the largest, wealthiest, and most influential sect in America, comprehensively tracing its early schemes and modern deceptions in nearly 300 detailed and information-packed pages.

THIEVES OF INNOCENCE

by *John Ankerberg, John Weldon*, and *Craig Branch*

Thieves of Innocence is a provocative, no-holds-barred exposé of the growing occult/New Age influence invading America's schools. This book provides the documentation, direction, and encouragement parents need to investigate ungodly forces at work in the lives of their children.

Dear Reader:

We would appreciate hearing from you regarding this Harvest House nonfiction book. It will enable us to continue to give you the best in Christian publishing.

1. What most influenced you to purchase *The Coming Darkness*?
   - ☐ Author
   - ☐ Subject matter
   - ☐ Backcover copy
   - ☐ Recommendations
   - ☐ Cover/Title
   - ☐ _____

2. Where did you purchase this book?
   - ☐ Christian bookstore
   - ☐ General bookstore
   - ☐ Department store
   - ☐ Grocery store
   - ☐ Other

3. Your overall rating of this book:
   - ☐ Excellent ☐ Very good ☐ Good ☐ Fair ☐ Poor

4. How likely would you be to purchase other books by this author?
   - ☐ Very likely
   - ☐ Somewhat likely
   - ☐ Not very likely
   - ☐ Not at all

5. What types of books most interest you?
   (check all that apply)
   - ☐ Women's Books
   - ☐ Marriage Books
   - ☐ Current Issues
   - ☐ Self Help/Psychology
   - ☐ Bible Studies
   - ☐ Fiction
   - ☐ Biographies
   - ☐ Children's Books
   - ☐ Youth Books
   - ☐ Other _____

6. Please check the box next to your age group.
   - ☐ Under 18
   - ☐ 18-24
   - ☐ 25-34
   - ☐ 35-44
   - ☐ 45-54
   - ☐ 55 and over

Mail to: Editorial Director
Harvest House Publishers
1075 Arrowsmith
Eugene, OR 97402

Name _____

Address _____

City _____ State _____ Zip _____

**Thank you for helping us to help you
in future publications!**